Juan Luis Segundo
And First-World Ethics

THE
BIBLE
FOR
ETHICS

Anthony J. Tambasco

UNIVERSITY
PRESS OF
AMERICA

Copyright © 1981 by
University Press of America, Inc.™
P.O. Box 19101, Washington, D.C. 20036

All rights reserved

Printed in the United States of America

ISBN: 0-8191-1557-6 (Perfect)
0-8191-1556-8 (Cloth)

81-10425
Library of Congress Number: ~~80-6253~~

for

JOAN

ACKNOWLEDGEMENTS

The author wishes first of all to express thanks to Rev. Gerald Persha, M.M., for making available almost all of the Spanish bibliography of Juan Luis Segundo, some of which would have been impossible to obtain otherwise. The author is also grateful to Rev. Charles Curran of Catholic University of America for his consultation on parts of the manuscript. Special thanks is offered particularly to Professors Roger Shinn and J. Louis Martyn of Union Theological Seminary for their extremely helpful guidance and encouragement all along the course of this writing. Finally, among the many who supported this undertaking in different ways, the author is grateful especially to the Pastore family who provided a quiet place for study as this manuscript was being researched.

Acknowledgement is made to the following authors and publishers for permission to use material under their copyright:

To the Crossroad Publishing Company for permission to use "Capitalism-Socialism: A Theological Crux" by Juan Luis Segundo. From Concilium, vol. 96, copyright (c) 1974 by Herder and Herder, Inc., and Stichting Concilium.

To Orbis Books for permission to use Grace and the Human Condition by Juan Luis Segundo, copyright (c) 1973; Our Idea of God by Juan Luis Segundo, copyright (c) 1974; The Liberation of Theology by Juan Luis Segundo, copyright (c) 1976, all by Orbis Books.

To the author Charles E. Curran for permission to use excerpts from his book, Catholic Moral Theology in Dialogue, copyright (c) 1972 by Fides Publishers, Inc.

TABLE OF CONTENTS

PREFACE

This study has grown out of two interests, partly from previous studies and partly from more recent teaching and travel experiences. Up until several years ago the focal point of my studying and of my teaching was the New Testament. This continues to be a central concern for me, and remains, in fact, an important part of my teaching. However, I have also undertaken more recently the study of Christian ethics. My desire has been to gain a competence in this field, while not abandoning my previous field of interest. For this reason I have been curious about the relationship of the Bible to Christian ethics.

This relationship is a subject that is not without importance in our time. The renewal within the Roman Catholic Church since Vatican II has stimulated a return to the use of the Scriptures as foundation for all theology. Catholic moral theology is just beginning to explore the ramifications of a return to Scripture for its own discipline. Protestant theology in general is continuing its focus on the use of Scripture, but is asking more often how the Bible is normative. There is more and more recognition of the historical conditionedness of the Christian faith, the relativity of any of its theological formulations, and the presuppositions brought by theologians to any of their studies. This means that, while theologians are citing Scripture for their arguments, they are often using it in different ways and with different kinds of authority.

This use applies equally to ethical concerns and to other areas of theology, and so, even within Protestant circles, there are the hermeneutical questions of the relationship of the Bible to Christian ethics. This study grew, then, out of an interest in Scripture and the desire to incorporate this previous study into more current undertakings in Christian ethics.

Recent teaching and travel experiences, however, have developed another interest as well. I am indebted to the Maryknoll Missioners for some years involved with the preparation of missionaries and for exposure to third-world problems. This has led me to curiosity about Latin American liberation theology. As a final outcome, this recent interest has provided the way into the topic I propose to study in this book. As a way of studying liberation theology, I have decided to analyze the writings of Juan Luis Segundo. Not only is he one of the more prominent and prolific theologians of Latin America. He is also the one who pays conscious attention to methodology and tries to apply it to the whole range of theology. He more readily provides the material for the specific aspects of liberation theology that I propose to study. While he is only one Latin American theologian his writing covers the entire range of liberation theology and is representative of the many.

My aim is not only to study Segundo, but to do so as a way into my other interest in the Scriptures. I will limit my analysis of Segundo to certain perspectives in his writings. I will investigate his use of Scripture for his ethical concerns of liberation. More specifically, the study will be outlined around Segundo's hermeneutic circle, his attempt to show how the Bible can be normative for Christian theology and ethics.

In this way, the study will meet my two recent interests. By studying Juan Luis Segundo, it will explore an example of liberation theology. By studying his use of Scripture, it will make a contribution towards the question even in the first world, How is the Bible related to Christian ethics?

x

CHAPTER I

HERMENEUTICAL MODELS OF THE USE OF

SCRIPTURE FOR CHRISTIAN ETHICS

Juan Luis Segundo is one of the central figures among the Latin American liberation theologians. Like his fellow scholars, he maintains that liberation theology is not simply a subdivision of theology, as, for example, one section of social ethics dealing with justice. Rather, it is an entire way of doing theology. Segundo has, as a matter of fact, written a five-volume work that is a brief compendium of all the major areas of theology.[1] In any case, part of the claim of liberation theology--part of its way of doing theology--is its offer of a new hermeneutics for reading the Bible. This new method of interpretation is described by Segundo as his hermeneutic circle.[2]

The steps within that circle will be described in the next chapter, and will, in fact, form the basis for the next three chapters. However, in order to appreciate Segundo's contribution to the hermeneutical questions of the relationship of the Bible to theology--and especially ethics--we must first of all establish a context of hermeneutics in general. The purpose of this chapter, therefore, will be to survey the area of hermeneutics in order to arrive at three models for the use of Scripture for Christian ethics.

In view of our purposes, this chapter will not be a detailed study of hermeneutics, but simply an overview of three particular authors who represent three different approaches to the use of the Bible for Christian ethics. The hope is to establish, not only a context for Segundo's hermeneutical approach, but also to introduce models with which we can compare Segundo's.

1

After we have studied Segundo's hermeneutic circle, we will return in the final chapter of this book to the models we are about to establish in this chapter.

In constructing models for the use of Scripture in Christian ethics, many different kinds of questions could be asked, and hermeneutical models arranged according to the answers given to these questions.[3] Our study will revolve around two questions that we can address to Scripture--questions that are suggested by a survey article of Allen Verhey.[4] Both these questions will be approached from the point of view of the light they shed on how norms of conduct are or are not derived from the Bible. First, in seeking how the Bible can be normative for Christian action, we will ask what one understands when one understands Scripture. More specifically, when we ask what one understands, we are asking questions about the wholeness of Scripture, its basic message, its perspective which may take different embodiment in different historical situations, but which remains the fundamental proclamation. Our assumption and starting point regarding what one understands is that the wholeness of Scripture includes an eschatological message. While it may not be the only underlying perspective through all the Bible, the eschatological teaching as a fundamental proclamation of Scripture seems taken as an established fact.[5] Thus, in asking what one understands when one understands Scripture, we will be asking how various authors interpret the eschatological teaching in these writings. This, in turn, will give us varied hermeneutical models for using the Bible for ethics.[6]

Closely related to this will be our second question concerning the relation of the Bible to other sources of moral wisdom. More specifically, we will not consider all other sources, e.g., Tradition, the Church, koinonia, etc., but will study the relation of the Bible to natural law or to moral reasoning or, as David Tracy words it

2

for a broader ecumenical perspective, we will see the correlation of Christian texts with common human experience.[7] Once again, depending on how one views the link of Bible and human insight, varied hermeneutical models will emerge for the use of Scripture for Christian ethics. We have now to see some prominent authors and their views of how much we derive from the Scriptures in terms of eschatology and how much the Scriptures also need human experience to arrive at ethical norms. These prominent authors will illustrate our models of hermeneutics for the use of the Bible for Christian ethics.[8]

Deliberative Model

Roman Catholic moral theology has always had a strong confidence in human experience for deriving ethical teaching. This has often led to a minimal use of Scripture for a large part of ethics. While biblical data were used in the past to support and elucidate considerations of the theological virtues or the sacrament of penance or the call to conversion, etc., little biblical material entered into the formulation of ethical norms. Often, when the Bible was cited, it was more as a proof-text to verify a point being analyzed from the perspective of human experience. This was especially characteristic of the manuals that were prominent up until Vatican II.[9] At present there is the move toward greater consideration of the Bible for all facets of Christian ethics, but Roman Catholics continue to affirm a strong role for human experience. Scripture is seen as supporting that role.

Tracing the roots of Roman Catholic ethical tradition will shed light on this particular model that we wish to consider. It will prepare the way for a study of Charles E. Curran as representative of this model today. Most of the contemporary Roman Catholic ethics are a revision or a restructuring of the moral

3

reasoning of St. Thomas Aquinas. Aquinas built his system around Aristotelian ethics, especially as this filtered through Stoicism.[10]

Aristotle made the move from idealism to realism by moving the norm of morality from Plato's world of ideas to the material world which was constituted by form. Form was said to be that constituent element in a created being which established it as that kind of being. It was the formal cause of material being. Ethically, formal cause also determined final cause, the end toward which the being tended and which was its completion and perfection. According to Aristotle, all beings tended of their nature toward their end; they conformed to their formal cause and arrived at their final cause. However, humanity had a unique nature, one characterized by free will consequent upon powers of reason. It arrived at its final goal or destiny only by examining with its reason its formal cause, and by choosing those goods which would enable it to reach its final cause in accord with its form.

The Stoics took this worldview of Aristotle and put it into a framework of law and ethical obligation that then became the focus of Aquinas' Christian ethics. The Stoics saw all of creation governed by a universal law of reason. They called this logos. It moved everything toward its predetermined end. Humanity participated in logos by use of its reason, and it was to move in its life in harmony with the destiny already determined by logos.

For the Stoics it was never clear whether logos was a personal or impersonal force, and the movement of all creation was much more of a cyclic history than a linear one. Aquinas adapted this vision to his Christian faith and produced his ethical teaching of natural law and the centrality of human reason, determining for humanity what is its good and what thereby should

4

become its moral choices. What the Stoics saw as (impersonal) logos, Aquinas saw as eternal law or divine providence of God moving all of creation toward perfection in accordance with a divine plan of salvation. Like the Stoics, Aquinas saw humanity as participating in the universal law by reason, but now this was seen as natural law, and was defined as the rational creature's participation in the eternal law.[11]

We can see how Aquinas' ethical methodology can be described as deliberative.[12] It not only shows confidence in human reason, but also establishes autonomous human philosophy as means of judgment for Christian ethics. Reason is not only the servant of revelation, further clarifying norms that are given in revelation. Rather, reason is the vehicle of formulating ethical norms independently of revelation. It may be that sometimes in the given situation, humanity does not determine moral norms correctly from reason, and needs the help of revelation, but this does not deny the intrinsic ability of reason to form moral judgments.

There is a basic optimism in human nature and human experience. "St. Thomas Aquinas understands . . . that man possesses an innate tendency through which, without instruction and outside help, he can recognize whatever fundamental demand is made of him for his own self-realization."[13] From natural law humanity can formulate abstract, universal, objective norms of morality.

This basic approach of Aquinas represents very well H. R. Niebuhr's "Christ-above-culture" model in explaining the relationship of the Christian message to human experience.[14] Thomas Aquinas speaks of the relationship of Christ to culture as a "both-and" relationship, although Christ is seen as far above culture. The world, culture, and reason are seen as stable, even if transitory, and this order of nature forms a unity with the order of revelation, the world of

5

the supernatural. Humanity can move from one into the other by recognizing the gift of God as completing, elevating, and perfecting what is already discerned through human reason, even if only partially discerned.

Grace builds on nature and respects nature, even if it is above it. Whether humanity contemplates with reason its last end, or the meaning of virtue, or the nature of law, it will discover that the ultimate truth of all these realities is not within range of sheer human possibility, but is the gift of God in Christ. Humanity's ultimate end is the happiness of possessing God; its virtue is not just its natural ability, but the possibility of infused supernatural virtue; its law is all a share in the eternal law, or the divine law given in revelation.

Basically, there is a synthesis between nature and supernature, and a hierarchy of truths. The leap from one to the other is ultimately the gift of faith, but reason is the starting point. Christ is above culture, but there is harmony between them, and confidence that culture and reason begin the insight that culminates above in Christ.

With this background in view, we can see this model as it is presented by a contemporary ethicist, Charles E. Curran. Like most of his contemporaries in the Roman Catholic tradition, he has modified Thomistic methodology, but one can still see within him the basic deliberative model. For Curran, there is still confidence in reason and a harmony between the Bible and reason, or human experience.

James Gustafson has pointed out a trait among Roman Catholic ethicists that applies equally to Curran as to the others:

On the Roman Catholic side, as we have noted, there has been a growing criticism

of the "non-historical" character of traditional natural law theory, of the impersonal
character of the theory as it was formulated
in the manuals of moral theology (the view
of individuals was "physicalist" rather than
"personalist"), and of the absence of a
decisive role of a biblically based theology
in moral thought. The third, the biblical
concern, is a matter deferred.[15]

In our following analysis we will present the
main points about natural law theory which continue to show Curran's approach to be a deliberative model. We will then analyze what he does
say about Scripture to show its relationship to,
and harmony with human experience.

First of all, Curran himself admits that
he follows in the hermeneutical model of St.
Thomas, a deliberative motif joining reason to
Scripture (and revelation). He says:

The future development of Catholic moral
theology can well profit from some of the
traditional emphases--the ability of human
reason to arrive at good ethical decisions,
a basic goodness in man which despite
sinfulness remains in some continuity, as
well as some discontinuity, with grace and
redemption. Likewise the traditional
Catholic emphasis on the structure of man
and human experience can be of help if
interpreted in a way to appreciate the web
of relationships in which man finds himself so that he cannot be defined primarily
in terms of an unrestricted freedom which
does not take into account the relationships which both limit and perfect him.[16]

As the last sentence of this quotation
indicates, Curran accepts natural law and reason,
but he wishes to adapt the traditional Thomistic
notions into more personalistic categories. This
suggestion comes clearly in a treatment of
natural law which compares Thomas to Ulpian, a

7

lawyer of the third century. While Thomas tended toward a more idealistic view of natural law, seeing humanity as different from nature and creation below it, he tended toward a more naturalistic view in his sexual morality, a view of natural law that eventually prevailed in the tradition. In this naturalistic view humanity's nature is identified with physical and biological processes.

Thomas came to this definition in some passages under the influence of Ulpian. Whereas Aristotle distinguished iustum naturale (natural law) and iustum legale (positive human law), Ulpian proposed a threefold division. Thomas reconciled them by subdividing Aristotle's iustum naturale into two of Ulpian's categories. He defined the ius naturale of Ulpian as that which humanity has in common with the animals, and ius gentium as that which is unique to humanity. The third Ulpian category of ius civile he equated with Aristotle's iustum legale. In this view of things, natural law came to be defined biologically and physically, as that which humanity has in common with the animals. It lost some of its distinctively human qualities which appeared in other parts of Aquinas. Curran seeks to restore this personalistic context to the natural law theory.[17]

This recognition that Thomas varied in his definitions of natural law led Curran also to claim that there is no hard-and-fast philosophical system that must be part of the Roman Catholic or Thomistic methodology. Not even Thomas can be said to rely strictly on the Stoic approach. In one article, Curran shows how Thomas took at least four different definitions of natural law from Cicero, Ulpian, Isidore of Seville, and Gratian.[18] This leads to Curran's contention that natural law is itself historically conditioned. While it is helpful to reason for determining norms of morality, it cannot be seen anymore as absolute and universal on every question. There is "always the danger

of identifying a particular order or structure as
the immutable order of God when in reality it was
only an historically and culturally conditioned
attempt to respond as well as possible to the
needs of a particular period and very often mani-
fested the desires of the dominant power group in
the society."[19]

Curran shows how natural law is historically conditioned by comparing the classicist
worldview to that of a more historically conscious
worldview of man and woman.[20] The classicist
worldview stresses the static, immutable, eternal,
and unchanging. It tends to be abstract, a
priori, and deductive. When it speaks of any
development at all, it presumes that truth always
remains the same, but that its mode of expression
changes in different settings. It concentrates
on an essentialist view of being, i.e., on its
substance or nature in itself apart from relationship. Nature is conceived as a given, and as
part of a well-ordered hierarchy of being, and
humanity conforms to creation around it.

The more contemporary worldview, on the
other hand, the view embraced by Curran himself,
emphasizes the dynamic, the changing, the
developing, the evolving. Its methodology is
more concrete, a posteriori, and inductive.
Development is conceived as a genuine growth in
apprehending the truth. Truth may remain the
same, but not as we perceive it. We cannot
attain truth pure and simple, but are always in
approach to full truth.

Thus, it is not only our mode of expression of truth that varies, but our apprehending
of truth itself. The historically conscious
worldview has a more existentialist approach to
being, seeing it more in terms of relationship
than substance. Nature is in process, and
humanity creates and shapes reality around it.
In all of this we can see a continued appreciation of human experience, and a deliberative
model on the part of Curran, but not in the rigid

9

categories of past Roman Catholic tradition.

Another way in which Curran shows his confidence in human experience is by his assertions
concerning a specifically Christian ethic. He
strongly opposes such a distinction, and maintains that what a Christian knows from an
explicitly Christian dimension can also be known
by all others in some other way. He approaches
this view from the de facto historical situation,
not being overly concerned even with the
abstract, transcendental metaphysical basis for
denying a specificity to Christian ethics.[21] He
maintains that humanity in its actual, historical
reality is humanity created, fallen, and redeemed.
That means that God's saving grace is offered to
all in some fashion. The human and the Christian
coincide.

This coincidence does not render Christianity unnecessary, for it can give a specific
thematic elaboration to the common material content of ethics. However, for the elaboration of
the material content and for the elaboration of
norms of ethics, reason and other non-biblical
sources function greatly, since they are in
harmony with the Bible.

Curran expresses this same thought in
another fashion by adopting the Thomistic views
of nature and grace, but by tightening their
relationship more closely.[22] Rather than the
seeming two-level reality which ran the risk of
separating nature from grace, Curran defines
nature as itself in the de facto reality of our
creation as already transformed by the supernatural gift of God. Reason is already--at
least implicitly--infused with revelation. However, within the economy of redemption, reason
has its autonomy. Scripture will be helpful
sometimes in pointing to the same norms derived
from reason, might encourage reason that is
weakened by sin, or might clarify some norms.
But by and large, reason will be able to
function--keeping in mind the historical

conditionedness we mentioned above--and Scripture will function primarily to thematize in an
explicitly Christian dimension the ethical conclusions of human reason. Curran says:

> This approach, if properly understood and
> utilized, would differ from the older Catholic
> approach that talked about the gospel and
> reason or the evangelical law and the natural
> law. Human experience does not just corre-
> spond to the sphere of the natural which all
> men can arrive at by the use of their reason
> unaided by grace. Such dichotomy must be
> avoided. Human experience in the world today
> includes elements which belong to the order
> of incarnation, redemption and resurrection
> destiny as well as elements relating to crea-
> tion and sinfulness. . . . Human experience
> thus can include at least implicitly what
> the gospel contains by way of ethical con-
> clusions, and proximate attitudes, disposi-
> tions and values.[23]

Having shown up to this point how important human experience is for Curran in the hermeneutical question of the use of the Bible for
Christian ethics, let us now turn to what he says
explicitly about Scripture, as a way of rein-
forcing our conclusions about his deliberative
model. First of all, Scripture is seen as historically conditioned in itself. This leads
Curran to be skeptical about the ultimate use of
Scripture for moral norms. He prefers to use
Scripture for character formation and for general
attitudes and dispositions rather than for
ethical norms.[24]

Curran elaborates this function of character formation by showing how the Bible stresses
virtue, especially those virtues enabling more
creativity in humanity.[25] However, he is also
quick to point out with H. R. Niebuhr that "no
human virtue can adequately explain the ethical
teaching of Jesus."[26] This leads him to sum up
Christian character in terms of one single

11

fundamental attitude of interiority or radical conversion and trust.[27] Finally, he considers the most important contribution of the Bible to character formation to be the offering of a basic stance or horizon which underlies all moral choices. Stance is logically prior to every other question in ethics and is the basic field of vision. Curran offers a fivefold stance of creation, incarnation, sin, redemption, and resurrection.[28] In all of this treatment, he believes that there is a harmony between Scripture and human experience, but they are not identical in their explication of ethics.

In deliberating how Scripture is more immediately connected with norms, Curran proposes that it offers a model of response morality, or relationality: "In my understanding of Christian ethics the primary model should be that of responsibility and relationality, but there remains a need for some teleological and deontological considerations even though they are of secondary importance."[29] Nevertheless, even this does not bring the Scriptures any closer to specifying how humanity is to respond to God, for Curran leaves that to reason to decipher: "The responsibility motif does not call for an abandonment of reason and an embracing of disorder, but rather such an approach realistically recognizes that there is no order in the sense of a detailed plan already existing, but responsible men must work together to forge ahead in a never-ending struggle for peace and justice."[30] Curran does recognize, in that same paragraph, that even reason is inadequate as a total solution, but he remains obviously within the deliberative model for his use of Scripture for ethics.

At best Curran derives general norms from the Bible:

My own solution is based on the realization that good moral discourse should carefully distinguish between the general and

12

the particular, with the realization that the competency of Christian ethics and of the church teaching [based on Scripture] can include all truly human decisions, but in different ways. In the area of the more general the church [with Scripture] can speak with a high degree of certitude. Above all the church should concentrate on this aspect of its teaching mission by entering into the area of what John Coleman Bennett has described as "middle axioms"--somewhere between vague generalities and specific statements on particular issues.[31]

Human experience and its creative ingenuity in the situation will have to work out the rest.

Sometimes authors will advocate using the Bible parabolically or narratively in order to apply it normatively to present action. Again Curran rejects this approach. "There exists little or nothing in terms of rational criteria or even debatable criteria for discerning how precisely the Bible functions as a parable for normatively directing Christian ethics today."[32] We can see then, from these few places where Curran does explicitly treat of Scripture, that he has great confidence in reason for elaborating moral norms, and less confidence in Scripture for the same use. His confidence in reason is not unqualified, but he sees the deliberative model as the best.

Up to this point we have been considering one of the two major questions that we announced at the introduction of this chapter, namely, the relationship of the Bible to human experience as a hermeneutical principle for the use of Scripture in Christian ethics. We have now to consider briefly the second question, the understanding that Curran has of biblical eschatology, how he construes its import and translates it for today. As we examine this point, we will readily notice what we mentioned also in the introduction, that the two points are closely connected.

If we examined the relevance of eschatology for the deliberative model as formulated
in the traditional Thomistic line of thinking,
we could say that eschatology would most
prominently be an affirmation of an other-
worldly reality in discontinuity with this world.
There is not a transforming power of the
eschaton on the natural state of humanity in the
present. In the terminology of H. R. Niebuhr,
we have a "Christ-above-culture" model and Christ
is not seen as transforming culture.

Curran's drawing together of nature and
grace gives keener definition to the eschatological elements of the deliberative model and
allows for more continuity than the traditional
Thomistic model. Humanity's final end should be
in some ways the outcome of a basic goodness in
it which reaches full fruition. "The individual
person now shares in the redemptive activity of
God and in death the final transformation will
take place so that there is continuity between
this present existence and his future existence
as well as an aspect of discontinuity."[33]

Nevertheless, Curran does not shift all
the emphasis to the side of continuity, as is the
tendency of the worldly model of liberal theology,
as we shall see in our second typology. As our
quotation in the above paragraph indicates,
Curran holds for some eschatological discontinuity
with this world. "Christian eschatology would not
necessarily see the future as just an extrapola-
tion from the present, but the 'in-breaking'
future calls for some discontinuity between the
present and the future even in this world."[34]
Hence, Curran adopts Niebuhr's model of "Christ-
transforming-culture," so that while there is
still an autonomy to human experience, there must
also be a discontinuity brought by the eschaton,
even in the present. This is the deliberative
model that we will adopt as our hermeneutical
example of the use of Scripture for ethics. As
Curran himself summarizes:

14

Contemporary theological concerns express great interest in the future and see the human vocation in terms of taking responsibility for building the new heaven and the new earth. There is a decided emphasis on the continuity between this world and the next. . . . A proper Christian understanding of eschatology, in my judgment, must include three different aspects--the teleological, the prophetic and the apocalyptic. In the past theology overstressed the apocalyptic and consequently saw little or no continuity between this world and the next. The prophetic and teleological aspects of eschatology . . . accentuate man's vocation to cooperate in building the new heaven and the new earth. A balanced eschatological outlook will embrace these three different aspects.[35]

It is interesting to see how Curran interrelates his confidence in human experience with his discontinuous eschatology. The eschatology relativizes all ethical thinking. Reason may derive norms of morality. However, to make all norms absolute, even granted the validity of natural law, will tone down and weaken the radical, dynamic demands of Jesus in the gospels. It may very well be that one is more secure with material and absolute norms, but that very security has one settle for less than Jesus demands. Put another way, one never abandons reason, but one challenges it to search to revise and improve its ethical conclusions.[36]

By a strange paradox, the strict eschatological teaching of Jesus, with its discontinuity with the present, may even push the Christian to rely more on reason in some tentative way. It may be that in our present reality we cannot meet all the demands of Jesus' eschatological ethic. "On the other side of the paradox, there are times when the universal norms in Catholic theology do not sufficiently take into consideration the

15

reluctant but necessary possibility of not fully accomplishing the moral demands of Jesus."[37] Reason may have to find accommodation to the eschatology of Scripture.

We are now ready to sum up this first hermeneutical model that we will eventually compare with Juan Luis Segundo concerning the relationship of the Bible to Christian ethics. What we can describe in Charles Curran as the deliberative model is characterized above all by its strong affirmation of human experience for the derivation of moral norms. By modification of the "Christ-above-culture" pattern of his traditions, he presents a "Christ-transforming-culture" model. Reason still has autonomy, although it cannot be separated from grace and the Scriptures. There is a unity but not identity.

Again modifying the traditions, natural law is seen as more personalist and more historical, and so is less absolute and universal in final application. Scripture will be needed to qualify and complement reason, but does not replace it. Especially as Curran describes this methodology, the prime place is given to reason for deriving ethical norms, for while reason and Scripture are in harmony, they do not say the identically same things. Scripture gives attitudes, dispositions, general norms, and a response morality; reason spells it all out in norms in some qualified way.

The other characteristic which we have considered for this model is its use of eschatology for ethical norms. Curran modifies the other-worldly and discontinuous traits of traditional Thomism to arrive at a model that maintains both continuity and discontinuity. Nature and supernature must be seen as one concrete mode of existence, affecting each other intimately, so that this-world reality begins to manifest the eschaton. Nevertheless, the other-worldly and future dimension of the eschaton must also relativize this-world reality. Reason has its role, but it is relative.

Ultimately, then, the deliberate model as we describe it gives strong emphasis to human experience, supported by and giving specificity to the biblical data. At the same time, the tension between a continuous and discontinuous eschatology ultimately has the Bible challenging reason to revision in the light of an in-breaking kingdom of God.

Worldly Model

In examining Charles Curran, we focused on what can be described at least generally as a current Catholic approach to ethics. Reason and natural law predominate, and Scripture, if it is considered at all, has not a central, direct role for moral norms. The following models will come more out of various Protestant traditions, and James Gustafson has helpful insight in describing a general trait of all such hermeneutical models:

The liberal Christian social-gospel writers, fundamentalist writers, and those called "neo-orthodox" all grounded their ethics basically in Scripture. Just as the theory of a natural moral law set the boundaries within which debates took place in Catholic moral theology, so it is not unfair to claim that the debates within Protestant ethics took place within the boundaries of Scripture.38

There is, of course, a great deal of variety as to how Scripture functions for ethics, but the priority is given to Scripture in different ways, even for determining moral norms of action. As we examine this second model and the third as well, we will try to highlight their different hermeneutic in this regard. At least from this start we see their first major difference from the model we have first considered.

17

This second model, which we describe as worldly, captures two realities, again interrelated. It does not disparage the use of reason or human experience, though it relates these to Scripture in a different way from that of the deliberative model as we defined it. Secondly, it views eschatology predominantly from the perspective of this-world reality. The proponents of this hermeneutical model for the use of Scripture in Christian ethics belong primarily to the school of liberal theology.

There may seem some objection to considering this model for our own day, since the author whom we will see has been superseded by other schools of thought. However, several reasons present themselves for seeing this model as important for our own time. First of all, any model of our own day must render account of human experience and must take seriously this-world reality. Even if it does not take all the conclusions of the liberal model, it must nevertheless incorporate many of its salient insights. David Tracy observes, "With the relative strengths and limitations of liberalism, orthodoxy, neoorthodoxy, and radical theologies in mind, the revisionist theologian is committed to continuing the critical task of the classical liberals and modernists in a genuinely post-liberal situation."[39]

A second reason for looking at this model is advanced by Richard Hiers:

> Liberalism has survived into the twentieth century, both among churchmen of liberal or humanistic persuasion in various Protestant denominations--Unitarian and Quaker, notably, but by no means exclusively-- and also among various Protestant theologians. . . .
> There have recently been several signs of a return, if not exactly to liberal theology, at least to many of the problems that were of concern to Protestant liberalism: the renewed

18

"quest of the historical Jesus"; a revival of interest in ethics, accompanied, in many instances by a turn away from or even against dogma.[40]

Finally, we may point out that the focus of our main study, Juan Luis Segundo, will bring us into many of the areas of interest of liberal theology, especially social ethics.

We turn now to more detailed study of this worldly model, and to the two questions which we will address to each model, namely, its view of the relationship between Scripture and reason or human experience, and its eschatological view. We have mentioned that it does not disdain the use of human experience, but links it to Scripture differently from the general Catholic approach as shown in Charles Curran.

More precisely, the theologians of this hermeneutical model give the priority to Scripture, but find that Scripture gives the material of a good humanistic or a good rational ethic. It is not even simply a question of Scripture pointing to reason, but Scripture itself details the material for reason. Whereas we could say for Curran that Scripture simply supported reason, but that it was silent on details, we can say for the worldly model that Scripture spells out a great deal which reason can then support. For Curran, Scripture and reason were in harmony. For the liberal theologians, Scripture and reason are in many details identical.

The historical context of liberal theology helps to explain its view.[41] On the one hand, liberal theology was shaken by Kant's critical epistemology. For Kant, knowledge--which results from the interaction of our sense perceptions with a priori forms of perception and categories of understanding--is possible only of perceived phenomena. Metaphysical knowledge is impossible. Kant's critical philosophy led to the rejection of metaphysics, of natural theology, and of any claim for the knowledge of God. It led also to the rejection of all ethical doctrines of natural law derived from metaphysical principles. Thus it differs from traditional Catholic morality with its metaphysical presuppositions that never accepted the Kantian philosophy.

On the other hand, liberal theology is keenly attuned to human experience, the study of history, and the general cultural milieu. Its main intention is to make Christianity speak to its own times. One of the great fathers of liberal theology, F. D. E. Schleiermacher, asked people to find religion by looking to their deepest human experiences. This religion was a deep mystical experience, a "feeling" in which God is not deduced, but is given as part of this consciousness. Another of the fathers of liberal theology, Albrecht Ritschl, built upon Kant's emphasis on moral experience, relating it to the Lutheran theological heritage.

Liberal theology thus came to emphasize human experience, human worth, human personality, and its many ethical implications. It also came to emphasize (with the Enlightenment) the possibilities of human action to correct the evils of society and to improve the world. We will now consider one outstanding liberal theologian, Walter Rauschenbusch, to see how he begins from Scripture and supports it by reason or human experience, especially to present an anthropology that will be the basis for ethical norms.

Like most of the liberal theologians of his time, Rauschenbusch developed his links between the Bible and human experience within a very optimistic evaluation of human possibilities. This optimism, of course, must not be overstated. Perhaps more than most of his contemporaries in that school of thought, Rauschenbusch had a keen sense of evil in the world, and devoted chapters to that topic.[42] He also realized that the idea of progress was flawed by the facts of many failures in civilization. He explicitly wrote:

20

"History laughs at the optimistic illusion that 'nothing can stand in the way of human progress.'"[43] Nevertheless, he ardently believed that the evil could be overcome in this world and that Christianity could provide the ingredients for the development of the human race in a forward direction.

In both his appreciation of the powers of evil and his optimism over human possibilities Rauschenbusch saw the interplay of biblical teaching and human experience. On one occasion he wrote:

We need a combination between the faith of Jesus in the need and the possibility of the kingdom of God, and the modern comprehension of the organic development of human society. Jesus was not a mere social reformer. Religion was the heart of his life, and all that he said on social relations was said from the religious point of view. He has been called the first socialist. He was more; he was the first real man, the inaugurator of a new humanity. But as such he bore within him the germs of a new social and political order.[44]

For Rauschenbusch, Scripture was the starting point for theology, but it embraced what was of high value in the political, sociological, and cultural milieu of the time. "The gospel, to have full power over an age, must be the highest expression of the moral and religious truths held by that age."[45] He says in one section of his writings that the force of religion can best be applied to social renewal by sending its spiritual power along the existing and natural relations of people, to direct them to truer ends and govern them by higher motives.[46] But the relations are already there.

As Scripture is elaborated in this fashion we see themes in Rauschenbusch that are similar to those found in other liberal theologians. We

21

will treat three themes: the kingdom of God, the conception of God, and the nature of Christian love. In all of these Rauschenbusch shows his strong evangelical roots and insists on the biblical data as central to his teaching. No doubt it is this insistence which clearly separates him from sheer humanism or the secular idea of progress so prevalent in his day. Nevertheless, there is a clear interplay between the biblical data and human experience as it was interpreted at that time. As a distinctive contribution Rauschenbusch drew from his themes much more of a social concern rather than an individualistic perspective so prevalent among liberal theologians. In any case the Bible was seen as describing what could also be developed from human experience, often speaking in quite concrete and specific ways.

For instance, our author insists that one of the themes that needs to be made central again is that of the kingdom of God. His view of the kingdom, however, has deep social overtones, moving well beyond the individual characteristics that were given the kingdom by liberal theology: "Seek ye first the Kingdom of God and God's righteousness, and the salvation of your souls will be added to you. Our personality is of divine and eternal value, but . . . must get its interpretation from the supreme fact of social solidarity."[47]

Moreover, the social overtones are always consistent with human reason and humanity's highest aspirations. Humanity is seen as developing cultural and communitarian consciousness, so that reason deals more and more with this as the destiny of the human race. Scripture and what it offers to theology must be consonant with this communitarian vision of reason: "Unless theology has a solidaristic vision higher and fuller than any other, it cannot maintain the spiritual leadership of mankind, but will be outdistanced."[48] As Scripture gives us these social themes consonant with reason and human nature, it also points to concrete ethical propositions:

> Suppose that we had successfully demo-
> cratized our government, made our laws just,
> and socialized our industries. We should
> still have with us a great body of people
> who have been crippled by war or industry,
> exhausted by child labor, drained of vitality
> in their mothers' wombs, unbalanced by alco-
> holism, or made neurotic by drug habits and
> sexual excesses.[49]

The kingdom of God was certainly not seen by
Rauschenbusch as an unrealizable utopia, but
rather as a concrete program of socialization, or
social action.

The social gospel also developed its own
conception of God. The stress moved especially
to the social dimension of humanity, and once
again found concrete applications of the Scriptures:

> When we learn from the gospels, for instance,
> that God is on the side of the poor, and that
> he proposes to view anything done or not done
> to them as having been done or not done to
> him, such a revelation of solidarity and
> humanity comes with a regenerating shock to
> our selfish minds. . . .
> Wherever we encounter such a strain of
> social feeling in our conception of God, it
> is almost sure to run straight back either
> to Jesus or the prophets.[50]

Rauschenbusch then continues to describe
human suffering as a means of human solidarity,
making humanity aware of the plight of the oppressed classes, and promoting in the long run
their alienation. The concept of God should
ultimately lead to racial unity.

One final category we will consider aims
at the essence of Christianity. It is the
derivation of the love commandment from the

23

Scriptures. Rauschenbusch interprets this in rational and humanistic terms both socially and concretely. In a chapter of his booklet, <u>Dare We Be Christians?</u> he devotes the contents to a study of chapter 13 of First Corinthians.[51] He begins with consideration of the family as an early expression of human love and then comes to the conclusion that love always connects us with a group. It produces enduring loyalties and makes us willing to sacrifice for the common good. It is, in other words, social.

Love is the society-making force. All human progress demands an increase in love. Ultimately, this means concrete decisions, as for example, in business, where cooperation is still wanting, where violence predominates, and where people use other people instead of enhancing their dignity. Rauschenbusch even writes an entire paraphrase of Paul's hymn of love, applying it directly to modern business. In another work he makes a similar point by linking love to the kingdom of God, and then showing how the Scriptures mean ultimately social, concrete ethical norms:

Since love is the supreme law of Christ, the Kingdom of God implies a progressive reign of love in human affairs. We can see its advance wherever the free will of love supersedes the use of force and legal coercion as a regulative of the social order. This involves the redemption of society from political autocracies and economic oligarchies; the substitution of redemptive for vindictive penology; the abolition of constraint through hunger as part of the industrial system; and the abolition of war as the supreme expression of hate and the completest cessation of freedom.[52]

Thus Rauschenbusch in all his major theses begins with the Scriptures as his assumption and suggests interpretations that spell out the basic human needs of man and woman, especially in a

24

social context. He suggests interpretations that can ultimately be drawn from the sociological, political, and economic philosophy of his day. Scripture is one with human experience.

Having viewed the relationship of Scripture to human experience in the worldly model, let us now consider the second major question that we are asking each model, namely, its understanding of eschatology. In general in this model its eschatology is predominantly this-worldly. In effect it does not stress the future dimensions that transcend this life, and so, its efforts are directed primarily to the perfection of human possibilities even now in this world.

Walter Rauschenbusch diminishes the eschatological significance of Jesus' preaching. He cites the observations of Adolf Harnack, saying that the earliest of the gospel documents, the Q source, contains the least of the eschatological teachings. Thus, these materials would be later accretions, not in keeping with the authentic preaching of Jesus himself.[53] He also uses other arguments to diminish the eschatological significance of the gospel message, and to focus it on this world.

One of the arguments Rauschenbusch uses against eschatology is reminiscent of an argument to be used later by Bultmann, i.e., that the eschatological message must be demythologized: "Our traditional eschatology never was a purely Christian product, growing organically from Christian soil and expressing Christian convictions. . . . Like all eschatologies it expresses ideas about the universe, but these cosmic conceptions are prescientific."[54]

Along the same lines of thought, he urges that we distinguish some important points regarding eschatology. First of all, we must distinguish Old Testament mythical ideas from its ethical and religious insights regarding an oppressed people. Then we must also distinguish

25

prophetic eschatology from apocalypticism, so
that we do not take all fundamentalistically.
On the basis of this we sift out what is properly
New Testament and Christian, as opposed to what
the New Testament simply takes over from the Old.
Finally, we must recognize that there is no uniformity in eschatological teaching, and that some
of its aspects may be more pertinent than others.[54]

Sometimes Rauschenbusch tries to interpret
the eschatological teaching immediately into
social categories of this world, and in that way
give it his basic perspective without denying it
at all. He says that the central section of
Christian eschatology is based on Jewish and
Greek eschatology. The Jewish view really comes
out of the fight of God and his people for the
freedom of the common people. The Greek part
deals with the future of the individual and
tells of his immortality. It was an escape
theology, the only recourse open to those who had
no other way to freedom in their society. In
either case, "eschatology has all along been
influenced by social causes, while keeping on its
own conservative path of tradition."[56] His suggestion is that we continue to vivify some
aspects of eschatology, modify others, and eliminate others still, all on the basis of present
social causes.

Rauschenbusch also thinks that Jesus himself intended only the humanistic, reasonable
aspects of his message to be of permanent value.
"He was shaking off catastrophic ideas and sub-
stituting developmental ideas."[57]

From a positive point of view, Rauschenbusch makes some constructive proposals regarding
the eschatological teaching of Jesus.[58] He
believes the future aspects of the teaching should
be translated into the future development of the
race; it should also remind one that God has the
initiative, although it is all within the concept
of development, growth, and progress in history.
This can be translated in terms of the operation

26

of present spiritual forces affecting an historic development that has no final consummation. Finally, "we need a restoration of the millennial hope. . . . The duration of a thousand years is a guess and immaterial. . . . But the ideal of a social life in which the law of Christ shall prevail, . . . and a glorious blossoming of human life, is a Christian ideal."[59]

Rauschenbusch sums up the eschatological teaching of liberal theology, showing that it has some difficulty explaining away the future otherworldly dimensions, but stressing that the most important aspects are the realization of God's reign now. He says that many of his explanations of eschatology are indeed fanciful, but one fact remains sure: "All true joys on earth come from partial realizations of the Kingdom of God; the joy that awaits us will consist in living within the full realization of the Kingdom. Our labour for the Kingdom here will be our preparation for our participation hereafter."[60] This world is the focus of attention for ethics.

As we sum up our second hermeneutical model for the use of Scripture in Christian ethics, we can do so in terms of H. R. Niebuhr's "Christ-of-culture" description. This worldly model, as we have termed it, is one that is very optimistic toward the world, toward the sciences, toward politics, and toward culture in general. As Niebuhr words it, "They feel no great tension between church and world, the social laws and the Gospel, the workings of divine grace and human effort, the ethics of salvation and the ethics of social conservation or progress."[61]

The attempt is made by these authors to draw from the Scriptures an abiding and universal ethical teaching, consonant with reason, even if there are misgivings about building this teaching on a metaphysical basis. They will distinguish within Scripture the abiding and the transient or accidental, but will find in Scripture itself the material that reason works with and that can be

supported by reason or human experience in some
way. The difference between this model and the
deliberative model that we described earlier is
in the extent that Scripture is the starting
point. Whereas for the deliberative model Scripture might support reason and the burden is upon
reason to come to norms of action, for the
worldly model reason supports Scripture and the
burden is upon Scripture to arrive at norms.
The difference is put succinctly when, for
example, Charles Curran faults Walter Rauschenbusch for drawing too many conclusions regarding
social ethics from the Bible.[62]

The second major aspect of the worldly
model, which distinguishes it even more from the
deliberative model, is its deemphasis of the
eschatological message of the Bible. While it
may acknowledge that Jesus did preach an other-
worldly future kingdom, it does not consider
this important as the gospel focal point. The
worldly model will generally either explain away
the eschatology or will interpret it in terms of
this-world reality. The future dimensions of the
kingdom will be the perfection of what has
already begun now. The important point is the
present and the perfection of human possibilities here and now. Thus, whereas the deliberative model acknowledges this world but qualifies
it by the critical in-breaking of a transforming
eschaton, the worldly model accepts this world in
a more optimistic way. The eschaton brings little
radical transformation or criticism to the
present. It simply completes it, thus affirming
and emphasizing all that we do in this-world
reality.

Scriptural-Deontological Model

We move now to a third approach to the use
of Scripture for Christian ethics. In contrast
to the deliberative model, which gives relative
autonomy to reason beyond Scripture, and to the
worldly model, which has Scripture enunciate what

reason could conclude, the particular deontological model that we are presenting stresses
the superiority of Scripture to any other source
of ethical norms. Paul Ramsey is representative
for this model as we define it.

We should also make clear that this model
does not always follow deontology as such--as
for instance in a Kantian perspective--but
emphasizes reading Scripture deontologically.
In this view norms are not based on value judgments derived from the inherent properties of
being, but are viewed as expressions of commitment or decision on command from some source
outside of the being. Thus, Scripture does not
relate in one way or another things pertaining
to human reason. Rather, it offers commands
based on a human dignity transcendent to and
different from human reason as such. Likewise,
the norms are not derived from considerations of
the end or goal of being to be accomplished, but
are based on features of rightness or necessity
built into the action or rule indicated by Scripture. These are to be kept regardless of consequences.

James Gustafson describes the methodology
of Paul Ramsey and summarizes the scriptural-
deontological model we are presenting:

> The authorization of Ramsey's view of love
> "in-principled" in covenant-partnership is
> primarily "revelational," though he also
> appeals to common human experience. It is
> not natural law in the classic Roman Catholic
> sense. Although Ramsey has adopted,
> developed, and even refined certain moral
> principles and procedures that have their
> historic home in natural law tradition, in
> my judgment he does not have a theory of
> natural law but engrafts his principles into
> his own biblical theological model.[63]

The importance of Scripture in Ramsey's
ethics is highlighted by the treatment he gives

to the question of a unique Christian ethics. Here again we find a difference from the two preceding models, for Ramsey claims to find much more specificity in Christian ethics, and even tries to spell out more explicitly what he finds to be unique. To begin with, he reproaches any morality that begins with the empirical and works back to Christ. Relevancy should come after Christ is accepted, not as a wedding of the modern mind to Jesus, or as a simple baptism of current opinion. If one starts with the present mind, then Jesus is used simply to confirm what has already been decided, and ultimately he is not needed at all.

Just how Scripture is normative, what it gives specifically to ethics, and how nature is a secondary source of ethical norms can be seen more clearly by now dealing with those texts of Ramsey that treat of the Bible directly. He seems to build his biblical ethics around three main themes similar to Rauschenbusch, but Ramsey certainly develops them differently. The three biblical themes are: (1) God's righteousness and love; (2) the reign of this righteousness in the kingdom of God; (3) the covenant relationship which provides the context of God's righteousness and humanity's response of obedient love. He writes: "Never imagine you have rightly grasped a biblical ethical idea until you have succeeded in reducing it to a simple corollary of one or the other of these notions."[64]

The theme of covenant seems the pivotal one, and illustrates Ramsey's approach of reading Scripture deontologically. In his view the covenant expressed by Scripture introduces humanity into a relationship in which its ethical obligation is to respond to God's love by keeping God's commands. Thus, human nature is not the basis of ethical action, but rather the basis derives wholly from divine action.

When Rauschenbusch talked about the relationship of covenant, it was mainly to support basic natural experience of human worth and dignity. Scripture and reason said the same thing. For Ramsey, on the other hand, the covenant relationship brings something to humanity that is not inherent in its own human experience apart from God. Scripture actually affirms something that only it can uniquely affirm: "We are driven to regard all truly human worth as derivative, not inherent. Christian interpretations of man's dignity affirm something about man in relation to God, not just something about man per se."[65]

The deontological qualities of Scripture are spelled out specifically in terms of character formation. Ramsey asserts that the Bible corrects the classical Greek treatment of the virtues that derives even from Augustine and Aquinas. He thereby makes a specifically Christian presentation unique to the Bible itself. The classical approach builds on human nature or experience. Ramsey believes that the major concern must be Christ as presented in the Scriptures. He alone can be the standard of all virtues. Aristotle's ethic of the "mean" is not the same as Jesus' ethic of the "extreme."[66] This same point is made in Ramsey's critique of Paul Lehmann regarding what is ultimately the "human" which God is making and keeping. According to Ramsey, Lehmann relies on a secular view of wholeness to interpret what is mature humanity, whereas the measure should be the stature of the fullness of Christ.[67]

The specifically Christian element which the Bible gives to ethics shows itself not only in virtue, however, but also in norms for action. Sometimes the specifically Christian aspects of virtue will lead to specifically Christian decisions regarding action. For example, when human nature is seen according to the light of Christ, there is a combination of increasing humility and a real sense of sinfulness, even while there is increasing achievement.

This can be seen in comparing the biblical view of humanity to the scientist's own view of ethics. The view of science

is a limiting view; and the limits arise from the fact that the ethics is a fruit of intending the world as a scientist, and expressly from intending the world as a man among men (much less from intending the world as a Christian or as a Jew). This accounts for the fact that when geneticists begin to describe those human qualities to be selected and bred into the race of men, they write remarkably as if they were describing the attributes of mind and character that would make a good geneticist, or at least a good community of scientists. Acknowledging that these are notable humanistic values, still there are other modes of being human.[68]

Thus, the love of the biblical covenant is deontological in form, and makes deontological demands even in actions. This will show itself, for instance, in canons of loyalty in medicine, whereby the physician will recognize a bond established between himself and his patient that will demand truth-telling and respect beyond just seeking cures.[69] It will prohibit some forms of genetic experiments in which the results do not respect the dignity of the fetus or zygote. In other words, Scripture can make demands which may not be derived from simple calculations of reason or human experience.

To this point we have been considering especially Ramsey's use of the covenant theme in the Bible to show the specificity of Christian ethics and to show its deontology. This theme, as we mentioned above, is also spelled out in terms of God's righteousness and the kingdom of God. We will see the latter term when we consider Ramsey's eschatology. For now we can examine the theme of the righteousness of God, and again see how Ramsey interprets it as unique in Scripture and far above reason or human experience.

It makes its own demands as well.

Ramsey says, to begin with, that justice and love should not be contrasted, and that righteousness should be seen always as permeated with hesed or steadfast love, showing God's impartial concern for each of his chosen people. Moreover, there is a unique quality to this love in that it is always other-directed and non-preferential. God has nothing in mind other than the welfare of the object of his love. Moreover, the people whom he loves are equally the just and the poor, the orphans, and the widows; his preference is equally for the Israelite and for the alien in the land. Ultimately, the righteousness of God is summed up in Jesus, whose love was self-emptying, and embraced all men including the sinner.[70]

Not only is the concept of righteousness and the command of love unique in Scripture; it is also deontological in nature. Ramsey is strong to remove the teleological dimensions of Christian love, and to make it a matter of obedience, based on God's own righteousness. It is to give good, not to seek good. A good deed claimed is not a Christian deed.

This places a different perspective on love of self, again showing biblical ethics to be different from and superior to reason. In fact, at first glance one would conclude that Ramsey's view of non-preferential love eliminates love of self. Actually, it includes self-love, but only in one context, love of neighbor. For Ramsey, the problem of ethics has been in loving neighbor for the sake of self. One should, in reality, love neighbor for the neighbor's sake. However, once one is past self-regarding love to neighbor-regarding love, then care of self may enter in. One does all one can for self insofar as that will foster one's love of neighbor. Self-love is simply another form of neighbor-love performed first on self.[71]

The fact that Ramsey stresses the Bible over reason, and sees it as giving commands, leads to the question of whether he asks from Scripture a code morality or not. Ramsey himself claims to be consistent in his thought, but it seems clear that he has shifted perspectives from his earlier book, Basic Christian Ethics, to his more recent writings. The obvious difference in titles from "An Ethic without Rules" in the earlier work to an entire book called Deeds and Rules in Christian Ethics illustrates the shift.

In his earlier writing Ramsey states: "In place of rules of conduct . . . comes . . . not merely the self-regulation of free, autonomous individuals but the self-regulation of persons unconditionally bound to their neighbors by obedient 'faith working through love.'"[72] He stresses that what love teaches cannot be identified for all time and all circumstances and all places with any particular activity or prohibition. Thus, the biblical contribution is unique and is deontological, but is not a moral code.

Nevertheless, in more recent works Ramsey is preoccupied with checking situation ethics and relativism and spells out morality in more specific norms of conduct. He says that biblical agape can lead to general rules of practice, for there is no reason to assume that agape in its freedom cannot bind itself unreservedly and not change.[73] He comes to the same conclusion from a consideration of love from God's point of view. God's freedom should not have the limitation that God cannot act generally and bind himself to steadfastness and consistency of action.[74] Thus, the Bible in its deontological use may approach more closely to a moral code.

Ramsey may not be consistent, then, in his own use of the scriptural-deontological model. In any case, his model remains basically a deontological one. He always begins from biblical

agape, whether to transcend rules or, later on in
his writing, to offer rules. In the end result,
his books show two possibilities of using Scripture deontologically, and Ramsey does remain
consistent as an example of the ethical model we
are presenting in this section.

There seems another shift of emphasis in
Ramsey's model, although again he stays within
the general framework of a scriptural-
deontological model. When one examines especially the books that are devoted to specific
ethical issues, one sees Ramsey making more and
more use of natural reasoning as well as biblical
teaching. In _Fabricated Man_, a summary of his
basic approach to genetic experimentation highlights appeal to human nature: "One who intends
the world as a Christian will know man's dignity
consists not only in thought or in his freedom,
and he will find more elements in the nature of
man which are deserving of respect and should be
withheld from human handling."[75] Application of
this is made over and over again in the book.

Likewise, in _Patient as Person_ Ramsey
carries out arguments based on the sacredness of
humanity in the biological, as well as in the
sociological and political order. We have
already mentioned how some of this sacredness is
based on biblical covenant fidelity. However,
he also argues that this sacredness seems to
exist in its own right as well. The question of
consent is discussed a number of times and is
based on a view of a person which must never see
him or her as a means only, but as an end also.[76]

While Ramsey believes he is consistent in
his method, keeping Scripture superior and natural
law secondary, Charles Curran does not think he
is.[77] Curran voices the opinion of many ethicists
regarding Ramsey's shift of emphasis. Ramsey says
in _Deeds and Rules_ that his first book, _Basic
Christian Ethics_, stressed what was primary, and
that his _Nine Modern Moralists_ and later writing
developed natural law as a secondary source.

Curran concedes that Ramsey did make the distinction of primary and secondary sources already in his first book, but he also believes that there is more discontinuity between the books than Ramsey would admit. "Aspects of the theory proposed in Basic Christian Ethics do not allow a place for natural law and justice. . . . nowhere in Basic Christian Ethics does Ramsey give sufficient development to the role of creation in Christian theological ethics."[78]

In any case, even granting that Ramsey gives more importance to natural law than he admits, his concept of natural law is different from Roman Catholic perspectives and from the models that we developed previously. Curran himself makes observations that distinguish his model from Ramsey's. He points out that two aspects of natural law must be considered in the traditional Roman Catholic viewpoint. The first is a theological consideration which examines whether or not there is a natural order in distinction from a supernatural one. The second consideration is of a philosophical dimension asking if the natural order is of an ontological or simply a gnoseological level. While Ramsey acknowledges an order of nature that can be distinguished from the supernatural, he does not admit the ontological grounding of this nature. Hence, his natural law is not the same as what we considered in the previous two models of Christian ethics.[79]

In the long run, then, Ramsey bases his arguments for universal, concrete norms on the biblical notions, especially agape, as we noted. He does not build ultimately on natural law. Thus, one may question how much he should bring in natural law and reasoning, and one may criticize his consistency, but Ramsey remains deontological in his use of the Bible for ethics. He advocates the superiority of Scripture to any other source of ethical norms, and in this way is distinct from the two models previously presented.

As a final analysis of this scriptural-deontological model we have now to consider its eschatological perspective. We see once again that it is consistent with its perspective on the link of Scripture to reason and human experience. Ramsey's basic approach to eschatology may be characterized as other-worldly and in discontinuity with this-world reality. In the same way that there is ambiguity as to how much Ramsey actually uses natural law, so there is ambiguity as to how much he would allow for continuity and affirmation of this-world reality. It does seem, however, that he puts the stress on discontinuity and in his own evaluation of eschatology challenges this-world reality.

Much of the teaching is summed up in the biblical theme of the kingdom of God, as Ramsey analyzes it. He sees little continuity between this world and the eschaton in his view of the biblical concept. Nor does he see gradual growth in this world as part of the kingdom, as would liberal theologians. The only aspect of gradualness that he accepts is for the proclamation of the reality, not for the fact itself. The kingdom was a bursting in of God's reign, and left humanity with only a choice of whether it will be blessed or cursed. Our author points out that many have seen the ethic from this kingdom as being interim or for the future, and he thinks it should be both. However, he also believes that the future dimensions must impinge in some way on the present and should be spelled out in concrete reality with firm and definite content. "Interpreters speak of an esoteric 'intuition' of God's 'absolute demands' moment by moment, without giving these demands much content, or else they verge on transforming the ethics of Jesus into an 'eternal idea' more appropriate to the ahistorical Greek temper."[80]

Ramsey believes that the eschatological preaching of the kingdom must be translated into non-eschatological concerns:

The ethical teachings of Jesus may be true and
he may have said what he did because of firm
conviction of God's approaching completion of
his reign among men. What Jesus said, and said
only under the stimulus of his eschatological
expectation, should be weighed for its own
merit or demerit alone and not by reference to
psychological, historical and cultural conditions out of which his teaching arose. . . .
Indeed, precisely from the utter removal of
all other considerations, Jesus' ethic gained
an absolute validity transcending limitation
to this or that place or time or civilization.[81]

Actually, when he says the eschatological preaching must be translated into non-eschatological
concerns, he is not saying that it should lose
its eschatological significance. As one can
gather from the quotation, the time-conditioned
ways in which the eschaton was conceived have to
be eliminated. It is a question of terminology
more than content itself. But the eschaton is
certainly not collapsed into regard simply for
this world. It has its effects in offering
critique and in challenging this world, in showing discontinuity.

When the eschatological preaching of the
kingdom is translated into non-eschatological
vocabulary, is made concrete for this-world
reality, it leads to non-preferential love and
to deontology in applying that love:

In the face of the inbreaking kingdom, moral
decision was stripped of all prudential
considerations, all calculations of what is
right in terms of consequences which in this
present age normally follow certain lines of
action. . . . Preferential loves, even those
justifiable in normal times, were supplanted
by entirely non-preferential regard for whom-
ever happened to be standing by. . . . All
that mattered was perfect obedience.[82]

Thus, non-preferential love and obedient love derive from apocalyptic teaching, but can be translated into universal norms valid today. Apocalyptic says that Christian ethics derive from no particular historical situation and transcend any teleological consideration.

Ramsey believes that the theme of the kingdom can ultimately be joined to that of the righteousness of God, thus showing the relationship between the eschatological perspective of Ramsey, and his view of the superiority of Scripture over reason:

Apocalypticism served as a burning-glass to bring biblical ethics to pin-point focus and intensity. The biblical idea of the righteousness of God was the crater from which, when stirred into renewed action by apocalypticism, burst forth the flame of the eternal religion of love. . . . It was apocalypticism within the context of biblical faith in God's saving love which produced Jesus' decisive statement of divine righteousness as the measure and meaning of human obligation.[83]

The righteousness of God in the Bible offers unique content to Christian ethics and norms. Biblical eschatology offers this same content as critique and challenge to this world and to any other way of doing ethics.

Ramsey talks again about his eschatological viewpoint in considerations of the Sermon on the Mount. He believes the sermon gives norms for action as well as attitudes, but that it must be transposed out of its apocalyptic setting. The crux for transposing and translating the text is to see how an ethic which specifies what a person should do in relation to a single neighbor can be applied in a world where there is always more than one neighbor, and where there is a whole cluster of claims and responsibilities.

The teaching of Jesus describes not only what a person should be disposed to do, but what he or she should actually do. In a more complex, settled society, where neighbor-claims are many, there is a tendency to want to lapse into self-concern. We need to be challenged by the eschaton and the eschatological preaching of Jesus to acquire an attitude of other-directed love. We need to be transformed by the Sermon on the Mount.[84]

Finally, the other-worldly, discontinuous aspects of the eschaton, impinging on this-world reality and challenging it, are seen in a comparison that Ramsey makes with scientific apocalypticism. Both the scientist and the Christian are convinced that humanity moves to a world beyond this present reality, i.e., to a new kind of creation. However, the ultimate interpretation of all the action is significantly different. The scientist is optimistic in this-worldly terms, which ultimately make him pessimistic. The Christian with a biblical eschatology is optimistic with a faith in other-worldly realities. The scientist has the sense of having need to succeed, while the Christian is aware that he does not have to succeed at all. He has only to do the Lord's will.

This aspect of eschatology might also challenge worldly decisions, so that the Christian might make other decisions than the scientist. He may recognize that some genetic experiments, for example, are never to be performed, whereas the scientist may be impelled by his eschatology to do whatever he is able to do. The Christian's view of the end-time gives him more a sense of humility and dependence than the scientist's sense of unbounded freedom and self-creation. Eschatology challenges and offers critique to this world and humanity's decisions in it.[85]

We are now ready to sum up our considerations of the deontological use of Scripture as a model for ethics. First of all, it is characterized by a strong emphasis on Scripture over reason or human experience. Unlike the deliberative and worldly models, the scriptural deontological model not only proposes to support or explicate what can also be based on reason, but claims also to offer anthropology and ethical norms that are beyond reason. Reason would be of use, but always in a secondary way. There are some points that are unique to Scripture and that render it central to ethical thought.

In this model we see also a difference from the other two in another aspect. Whereas the other two models can be described as basically teleological, this model does not build its ethical norms out of goals or consequences. Once again, the commands come out of Scripture, and cannot be derived from reasoning on ends or consequences. As we saw for Ramsey, there may be dispute as to how specific the norms may become, but the basic pattern is the same for authors in this model.

Finally, the eschatology of this scriptural-deontological model is characterized by a sense of discontinuity, more than that of continuity. While it may not fit perfectly into any category, it seems to fit most easily into H. R. Niebuhr's category of "Christ-and-culture-in-paradox."

The dualist Christians differ considerably from the synthesists in their understanding of both the extent and the thoroughness of human depravity. . . .
. . . In all the synthesist's defences of rational elements in culture the dualist sees this fatal flaw, that reason in human affairs is never separable from its egoistic, godless, perversion. . . . Hence the dualist joins the radical Christian in pronouncing the whole world of human culture to be godless and sick unto death. But there is a

difference between them: the dualist knows
that he belongs to that culture and cannot
get out of it, that God indeed sustains him
in it; for if God in his grace did not sus-
tain the world in its sin it would not exist
for a moment.[86]

Summary

There are, of course, many other models
that could be outlined in this study. For the
two questions that we are addressing, however,
these three set the polarities, while not being
extreme viewpoints in the authors we have chosen.
With regard to the question of the relationship
of the Bible to human experience, we have a model
that gives priority to reason for deriving
ethical norms, a model that has Bible and reason
say the same things, and a model that gives
priority to the Bible for deriving ethical norms.

With regard to the interpretation of biblical eschatology for ethics, we have a model
that stresses continuity with this world, one
that stresses discontinuity, and one that sees
healthy tension between both continuity and discontinuity. With this as our context now, we
are ready to approach Juan Luis Segundo, to see
what use he makes of Scripture for Christian
ethics, especially with regard to the two questions we are posing to each model of hermeneutics.

CHAPTER I

NOTES

[1]Juan Luis Segundo, A Theology for
Artisans of a New Humanity, trans. John Drury,
vol. 1: The Community Called Church; vol. 2:
Grace and the Human Condition; vol. 3: Our Idea
of God; vol. 4: The Sacraments Today; vol. 5:
Evolution and Guilt; 5 vols. (Maryknoll, N.Y.:
Orbis Books, 1973-74).

[2]See especially Juan Luis Segundo, The
Liberation of Theology, trans. John Drury
(Maryknoll, N.Y.: Orbis Books, 1976), p. 9.

[3]One could do, for instance, a logical
analysis of Scripture, and ask if it is intui-
tional language, or emotive, or prescriptive,
etc., as in G. J. Warnock, Contemporary Moral
Philosophy (London: Macmillan & Co., 1967).
In the same vein one could ask if Scripture
offers ethical teaching in the form of concepts
or as narrative or in images, as David Kelsey
has asked about the content of Scripture for
theology in general. See The Uses of Scripture
in Recent Theology (Philadelphia: Fortress
Press, 1975). One could ask about the relationship of Scripture to Tradition, as did
James Gustafson, The Church as Moral Decision-
Maker (Philadelphia: Pilgrim, 1970); Paul
Ramsey, Who Speaks for the Church? (Nashville:
Abingdon, 1967); Roland Murphy and Carl Peter,
"The Role of the Bible in Roman Catholic
Theology," Interpretation 25 (January 1971):
78-94. Finally, one could examine the link of
the Old Testament to the New Testament, as in
James D. Smart, The Interpretation of Scripture
(Philadelphia: Westminster, 1971), pp. 65-133.

[4]We are concerned with questions 3 and 4
in Verhey's summary in "The Use of Scripture in
Ethics," Religious Studies Review 4 (January
1978): 29-30: "This survey of studies that

describe and explain the diversity in the use of
scripture suggests that we may profitably analyze
recent recommendations with respect to their
answers to the following questions. (1) What are
these writings [i.e., the relationship of the
Bible to the Word of God as such]? (2) What
question is appropriate to them [i.e., whether
the level should be moral, ethical, or post-
ethical, and the type of question should deal
with the good, the right, or the moral agent]?
(3) What does one understand when one understands
them? (4) What is the relation of biblical
materials to other sources of moral wisdom?"
Although our study will concentrate on questions
three and four, the first two questions will be
treated as they clarify or are clarified by
these other two. For example, the relationship
of the Bible to the Word of God is linked to the
question of using sources other than the Bible.
Also, question two, as it relates to looking to
the Bible for the moral agent, can clarify
question four about what to seek from the Bible
and what to seek elsewhere.

⁵"One of the most significant events in
modern Protestant theology was the discovery of
the dominance of eschatology in the teaching of
Jesus. . . .

A further consequence of the new emphasis
on eschatology was the need to revise its place
in dogmatic theology. Traditionally, eschatology was written as the last chapter in dog-
matics, without explicit connection with what
went before. It served more as an appendix to
theology. Now it was seen that all theology
must be penetrated by eschatology, for eschatology deals not only with 'the last things' in
the order of chronology but also with 'the
ultimate things' in an existential sense."
William Hordern, gen. ed., New Directions in
Theology Today, 7 vols. (Philadelphia: Westminster, 1966), vol. 2: History and Hermeneutics, by Carl Braaten, pp. 160-61.

⁶There are still varied hermeneutical
models, applying the eschatological teaching

44

differently, because the eschatology is described differently by different authors: "While there is general agreement among scholars that eschatology cannot be a bloodless chapter tacked on to a theological system, a sort of speculative gazing into the future, there is lacking a consensus on several crucial points: (1) on the nature and development of eschatological thinking in the New Testament and (2) on how to translate the meaning of eschatology into categories somewhat congenial to the modern temper." Ibid.

[7] David Tracy, Blessed Rage for Order (New York: Seabury, 1975), pp. 43-56.

[8] Roger Mehl, Catholic Ethics and Protestant Ethics (Philadelphia: Westminster, 1971), p. 45, correlates well the two questions we are asking the Scriptures. We are searching for some aspects of anthropology and for a vision of history: "We will not find ready-made models of action in the Bible. But we may hope to find there a vision of man and of his destiny, a meaning and a finality to history which are precisely the elements that our present society is incapable of considering. This twofold search for an anthropology and for a vision of history (which naturally implies an eschatology) is no doubt the common objective of present-day Catholic and Protestant ethics."

[9] Henry Davis, S.J., Moral and Pastoral Theology, 4 vols., 6th ed. (New York: Sheed and Ward, 1949).

[10] Heinrick A. Rommen, The Natural Law: A Study in Legal and Social History and Philosophy, trans. Thomas R. Hanley (St. Louis: B. Herder Book Co., 1947), pp. 3-57.

[11] Etienne H. Gilson, The Christian Philosophy of St. Thomas Aquinas, trans. L. K. Shook, C.S.B. (New York: Random House, 1956), p. 266.

[12] Edward LeRoy Long, Jr., A Survey of Christian Ethics (New York: Oxford University Press, 1967), pp. 45-52.

[13]Franz Böckle, Law and Conscience, trans. M. James Donnelly (New York: Sheed and Ward, 1966), p. 81.

[14]H. Richard Niebuhr, Christ and Culture (New York: Harper and Row, Harper Torchbooks, 1951), pp. 128-41.

[15]James M. Gustafson, Protestant and Roman Catholic Ethics (Chicago: University of Chicago Press, 1978), p. 80. (Italics mine.)

[16]Charles E. Curran, New Perspectives in Moral Theology (Notre Dame: Fides, 1974), p. 44.

[17]This is a discovery popular with Curran, and also strategic. He repeats his treatment of Ulpian in several places: Absolutes in Moral Theology? (Washington: Corpus Books, 1968), pp. 115-20; Christian Morality Today (Notre Dame: Fides, 1966), pp. 80-82; A New Look at Christian Morality (Notre Dame: Fides, 1968), pp. 79-80; "Absolute Norms in Moral Theology," in Norm and Context in Christian Ethics, eds. Gene Outka and Paul Ramsey (New York: Charles Scribner's Sons, 1968), pp. 142-44; Themes in Fundamental Moral Theology (Notre Dame: University of Notre Dame Press, 1977), pp. 35-40.

[18]Curran, "Absolute Norms," pp. 143-44.

[19]Charles E. Curran, Catholic Moral Theology in Dialogue (Notre Dame: Fides, 1972), p. 121.

[20]Curran, Absolutes?, pp. 120-45.

[21]See, for example, J. Fuchs, who says man has transcendental openness in his very humanity. Christianity enunciates this in Christian terms, but every man experiences it, at least pre-reflexively, in his knowledge of truth and in his moral choices. See Charles E. Curran, Ongoing Revision (Notre Dame: Fides, 1975), pp. 18-29.

[22]This also alters the model, in Niebuhr's terms, from "Christ-above-culture" to "Christ-

transforming-culture." See Curran, New Perspectives, p. 30.

[23]Curran, Dialogue, pp. 21-22.

[24]Curran, "Absolute Norms," pp. 152-53.

[25]Curran, Dialogue, pp. 33-34.

[26]Curran, New Look, pp. 4-5.

[27]Ibid., p. 47.

[28]Curran, New Perspectives, pp. 47-86.

[29]Curran, Dialogue, p. 32.

[30]Ibid., p. 177.

[31]Charles E. Curran, Politics, Medicine
and Christian Ethics (Philadelphia: Fortress
Press, 1973), p. 54.

[32]Curran, Dialogue, p. 52.

[33]Ibid., p. 18.

[34]Ibid., p. 79.

[35]Ibid., p. 101.

[36]Curran, New Look, pp. 49-53.

[37]Ibid., p. 16.

[38]Gustafson, Protestant and Catholic
Ethics, p. 21.

[39]Tracy, p. 32.

[40]Richard H. Hiers, Jesus and Ethics
(Philadelphia: Westminster, 1968), pp. 11-12.

[41]Langdon Gilkey, Naming the Whirlwind:
The Renewal of God-Language (Indianapolis:
Bobbs-Merrill Co., 1969), pp. 73-80.

[42]See his chapters on the fall, sin,
super-personal evil, and the kingdom of evil in
A Theology for the Social Gospel (New York:
Abingdon, 1945), pp. 31-94.

[43]Walter Rauschenbusch, Christianity and
the Social Crisis (New York: Macmillan Co., 1920),
p. 279.

[44] Ibid., p. 91.

[45] Ibid., p. 339.

[46] Ibid., pp. 344-48.

[47] Walter Rauschenbusch, Christianizing the Social Order (New York: Macmillan Co., 1921), p. 465.

[48] Rauschenbusch, A Theology, p. 142.

[49] Rauschenbusch, Social Order, p. 466.

[50] Rauschenbusch, A Theology, pp. 168-69.

[51] Walter Rauschenbusch, Dare We Be Christians? (Philadelphia: Pilgrim, 1914).

[52] Rauschenbusch, A Theology, pp. 142-43.

[53] Ibid., p. 219.

[54] Ibid., p. 209.

[55] Ibid., pp. 215-18.

[56] Ibid., p. 215.

[57] Ibid., p. 220.

[58] Ibid., pp. 223-27.

[59] Ibid., p. 224.

[60] Ibid., pp. 238-39.

[61] Niebuhr, p. 83.

[62] Curran, New Perspectives, p. 136.

[63] Gustafson, Protestant and Catholic Ethics, p. 151.

[64] Paul Ramsey, Basic Christian Ethics (New York: Charles Scribner's Sons, 1950), p. 2.

[65] Ibid., p. 277.

[66] Ibid., pp. 194-95.

[67] Paul Ramsey, Deeds and Rules in Christian Ethics (New York: Charles Scribner's Sons, 1967), pp. 65-66.

[68] Paul Ramsey, Fabricated Man (New Haven:

Yale Press, 1970), p. 22.

[69]Paul Ramsey, The Patient as Person (New Haven: Yale Press, 1972), p. xii.

[70]Ramsey, Basic Ethics, pp. 3-24.

[71]Ibid., pp. 153-66.

[72]Ibid., p. 78.

[73]Ramsey, Deeds, pp. 21-48.

[74]Ibid., p. 58.

[75]Ramsey, Fabricated Man, p. 31.

[76]Cf. pp. xiii, xiv, 11, 35, 190, 195.

[77]Curran, Ongoing Revision, pp. 238-45.

[78]Ibid., pp. 244-45.

[79]Ibid., pp. 245-50. This observation also accounts for why Gustafson said that Ramsey does not have a theory of natural law. See page 29 of this chapter.

[80]Ramsey, Basic Ethics, p. 31.

[81]Ibid., p. 41.

[82]Ibid., p. 39.

[83]Ibid., pp. 44-45.

[84]Ibid., pp. 42-45.

[85]Ramsey, Fabricated Man, pp. 25-32.

[86]Niebuhr, pp. 152-56.

CHAPTER II

SEGUNDO'S SOCIAL ANALYSIS

In the first chapter we have considered the two major questions that we are addressing to the use of the Bible for Christian ethics, namely, the relationship of the Bible to other sources of human morality, especially to human experience, and the understanding of the eschatological motif in the Scriptures. We have also presented three viewpoints that represent the spectrum of opinions concerning these questions. What we have seen in chapter one is to prepare the way for the central subject of our study, the specific contribution of Juan Luis Segundo to these questions.

As we indicated at the beginning of chapter one, Segundo offers a new hermeneutic for interpreting the Bible for all theology. We will try to apply what he says to the specific area of morality. Sometimes this will entail taking his points regarding theology in general, and applying them as his indirect viewpoint regarding morality more specifically. At other times we will be able to draw from statements he makes directly about the use of the Bible for morality. In both cases our starting point will be the hermeneutical principles offered explicitly by Segundo.

If we look to The Liberation of Theology, we find there the most detailed and explicit statement by Segundo of his hermeneutical approach to the Scriptures. We will begin our study here. In fact, if we see what Segundo says in his key statements on biblical interpretation, we also see why we chose the two particular questions that we did regarding the use of the Bible for Christian ethics. Our author maintains that for all of our reading of the Bible there is a hermeneutic circle. "Here

is a preliminary definition of the hermeneutic
circle: it is the continuing change in our
interpretation of the Bible which is dictated by
the continuing changes in our present-day
reality, both individual and societal."[1]

Segundo posits two preconditions for this
hermeneutic circle. We can, as a matter of fact,
call them not only the preconditions, but the
major ingredients of his biblical hermeneutics.
The first of these preconditions and ingredients
would be a deep, enriching analysis of our real
life situation and the suspicions it would awaken
about previous judgments concerning life. "The
first precondition is that the questions rising
out of the present be rich enough, general
enough, and basic enough to force us to change
our customary conceptions of life, death, knowledge, society, politics, and the world in
general."[2]

The second precondition (and major ingredient) of Segundo's biblical hermeneutics is
the willingness and the ingenuity to constantly
reinterpret the Scriptures in the light of the
present life situation. "If theology somehow
assumes that it can respond to the new questions
without changing its customary interpretation of
the Scriptures, . . . if our interpretation of
Scripture does not change along with the problems, then the latter will go unanswered; or
worse, they will receive old, conservative,
unserviceable answers."[3] This observation says
that theology is an ongoing discovery in history. Whereas the first precondition says that
history must influence what theology treats, the
second precondition affirms that theology must
speak to the real events of history.

A closer look at these two ingredients and
how Segundo elaborates them, shows his approach
to the two major questions we are addressing on
the use of the Bible for Christian ethics. In
the first ingredient of hermeneutics, Segundo
says that life situation must influence theology

and its interpretation of the Bible. In other words, he brings in human experience as a necessary element in interplay with the Bible for all theology, and therefore, for morality as part of theology.

In the second ingredient of his hermeneutics, he says that theology and the Bible must yield teaching that speaks in some way to the present situation as perceived in one's personal and communal historical experience. This can result in a number of theological doctrines, but one especially that is developed by Segundo, and one which has more immediate relevance for morality, is the eschatological interpretation of the Scriptures. In other words, the two major ingredients of biblical hermeneutics for Segundo ultimately speak to the two questions we are asking for the hermeneutical links of the Bible to Christian ethics.

As our author develops these two preconditions for his hermeneutic circle, he evolves to four final elements for that circle:

These two preconditions mean that there must in turn be four decisive factors in our circle. Firstly there is our way of experiencing reality, which leads us to ideological suspicion. Secondly there is the application of our ideological suspicion to the whole ideological superstructure in general and to theology in particular. Thirdly there comes a new way of experiencing theological reality that leads us to exegetical suspicion, that is, to the suspicion that the prevailing interpretation of the Bible has not taken important pieces of data into account. Fourthly we have our new hermeneutic, that is, our new way of interpreting the fountainhead of our faith (i.e., Scripture) with the new elements at our disposal.[4]

We can use these four factors as the basis for our more detailed study of Segundo's hermeneutics, addressing ourselves to the relationship of the Bible to other sources of morality in human experience, and to the eschatological interpretation of the Bible for morality.

The three chapters of our study which deal with an analysis of Segundo himself will be outlined around the four factors. This chapter will deal with the first and second elements which, in turn, elaborate the first precondition for Segundo's hermeneutic circle. We will see the two factors as combined, since they really are inseparable in spite of being distinguishable. We will consider what Segundo sees as the reality around him, and will find this to be especially the situation of poverty and oppression. We will see that for Segundo the heart of the first step of his hermeneutic circle is a commitment to the poor.

At the same time, however, this commitment to the poor must be submitted to categories of analysis which can give it shape and efficacy, and also enable one to speak to the sciences and to challenge the entire ideological superstructure. We will see that for Segundo the best categories of analysis are supplied by the social sciences, which then offer insights which challenge the accepted ways of looking at reality and effect change especially for the oppressed. That is the second step of the hermeneutic circle.

In effect, then, the categories of analysis already define in some way the experience of reality. The first factor of the hermeneutic circle is already carried out in the light of the second factor. We will see that for Segundo commitment to the poor is best expressed and carried out in terms of social analysis and sociology. Thus, the human experience which Segundo thinks should be joined to the Bible as a source of morality is primarily conceived in sociological terms.

We do well to remember, however, that
Segundo's starting point is not academic, but
from a concrete commitment to the poor and oppressed. Such commitment reduces his concern
for tight academic categories, increases the
chances of inconsistency in his theoretical
presentations, and offers the probability of
exaggerations of one side of the hermeneutical
picture. As we struggle to study in a scholarly
way his methodology for the use of the Bible for
ethics, we can expect to find unanswered questions. That will require that we supply answers
on the basis of what he does offer, that we
further suggest points that he does not cover,
and that we criticize some of this method precisely because it does not adequately deal with
some questions.

After dealing with the human experience
of poverty and the way it challenges our views
of reality through social analysis, we will then
treat in chapter three the movement from the
second to the third step of the hermeneutic
circle. That is, social analysis will challenge
theological concepts and force new ways of conceiving the theology. In this chapter we will
look especially at the eschatological interpretations in theology and at other themes
related to this, especially as they bear on
morality. Finally, in chapter four, we will
treat the movement from step three to step four
of the circle. We will see specific biblical
passages emphasized by Segundo, and see how he
brings social analysis and theological concepts
into relation with the Scriptures.

This treatment of Segundo will enable us
to move to our final two chapters. In chapter
five we will offer critique of Segundo's hermeneutics. We will judge if the method is valid
in terms of Segundo's ability to use the method
and to use it consistently. We will also judge
in relation to other, and especially our own,
hermeneutical perspectives, observations, and
suggestions. With all of this we will then have

the material to compare with the authors we treated in chapter one. This will comprise our final chapter, to see how the Bible may be used for Christian ethics.

Need for Social Services

We now consider Segundo's social analysis of reality. One of the statements made by our author regarding the theological endeavor and biblical interpretation puts all of our study into an ecumenical context. He says that Catholicism as well as Protestantism has need of the "protestant principle."[5] Tillich stressed this point, and it has been taken over by Segundo. He says that one must protest against the absolute claims made for anything that is actually relative. Catholicism has tended to absolutize many structures, and has carried out many inquisitions in the name of absolutes. The need for Catholicism to recognize its own relativities has moved the Church away from a Protestant-Catholic opposition to a common Christian task of balancing absolutes with the relative.

This need for the "protestant principle" is explicitly linked by Segundo to ethical considerations. "Without minimizing the dogmatic points that are not agreed upon and that still persist, the ethical decisions which define the behavior of Christians, above all on the social level, not only allow but demand a common reflection."[6] This relativizing of moral theology and biblical interpretation begins with commitment to the poor which, when brought to the level of disciplined reflection, introduces social analysis. Segundo posits his principle that the sociological interpretation of life experience prepares the way for new theological and exegetical interpretations. Social analysis shows the relativity of many structures, and this reflects onto the theology related to these structures.

56

The basis for beginning with social
analysis, while it may seem novel, is actually
just the working out of arguments parallel to
some that have been common in biblical hermeneutics for a long time. One line of reasoning
derives from similarities with the thought of
Rudolph Bultmann. Building on the philosophy of
Heidegger, this exegete said that any accurate
understanding of the Scriptures requires a
prior existential preparation, so that one knows
the concerns of one's self-creation and also
knows what to ask of the Scriptures for these
concerns. Segundo's contention is that personalist philosophy is not the only thing that
prepares for the authentic reading of Scripture,
but that social analysis is also necessary.

He writes:

> Readers understand that if political
> engagement . . . is going to illuminate not
> only our profane praxis, but our very under-
> standing of the gospel message, we are here
> before a level as radical or more radical
> than that of Bultmann. Bultmann requires an
> existential preunderstanding of man by man
> in order that the message of God can be
> directed to him. It is an authenticity whose
> criterion is prior to the very revelation,
> since without it (without this existential
> authenticity) the Christian message would
> remain mute, foreign to man.[7]

Segundo will be cautious about the nature
of this social analysis. He will not maintain
that it must be one particular system of social
or political thought, as we shall see, but he
will insist on some system of social analysis in
the concrete. It is the same line of argument
as for the position of Bultmann. Bultmann's
critics ask why all Scripture reading must presuppose the philosophy of Heidegger, although
there is great agreement that preunderstanding
does precede exegesis.

Another line of argumentation revolves around the relationship of theology to the sciences ancillary to it. Segundo argues that theology, for all its attempts to be an autonomous science, can scarcely be independent of the other sciences. It draws on them for its interpretation of life. The problem is that theology up to now has not been impartial as to which sciences it will use for its own thought. "Theology does not assert its independence from the past or from the sciences which help it to understand the past. . . . On the other hand theology does implicitly or explicitly assert its independence from the sciences that deal with the present."[8]

Segundo contends that theology has always made good use of philosophy, and in more recent times, of history, anthropology, and psychology. Biblical exegesis in modern times has made extensive use of literary analysis, semantics, historical criticism, archaeology, and other related sciences. It is still a rare case, however, in which sociology, political science, or other forms of social analysis have been central to theological and exegetical study.

It is the contention of liberation theologians, including Segundo, that these latter social sciences must be important for their work. Theology does not work in an historical vacuum totally immune from present-day struggles and ideas. It does not simply analyze the past and then apply it to the present. The liberation theologian believes that the present very much affects theology, especially the social and political present. "His suspicion is that anything and everything involving ideas, including theology, is intimately bound up with the existing social situation in at least an unconscious way."[9]

Our author finds indirect confirmation of the need to begin more thoroughly with social analysis for (moral) theology in the evolution of

58

papal teaching in modern times. He points out that there has always been a social doctrine within the Church, i.e., a concern for social morality. However, for the greater part of the history of the Church this social doctrine has remained purely moral, and not political in its concrete expression. The given social order was usually accepted as the starting point. Christianity was at best non-conformist, but did not offer any challenges toward changing the given political order.

Even in modern times, with the social teaching from Leo XIII at the beginning of capitalism, there was concern to correct abuses, but not to offer concrete social analysis or direct political theories. "The Church's social teaching was not an ideology; it was a moral force--a nonconformist one perhaps, but only a moral one--over against the existing fact of capitalism."[10] The social doctrine broke with capitalism only to try to avoid its defects.

With the social teaching of John XXIII, however, there is a shift in the methodology. The world is seen as of such construction that politics are inherent in any social analysis. The social doctrine of the Church has to involve political doctrine to be truly effective. Whereas many social questions in the past could be left to the private domain (patron-worker relationships), now these same questions are related to the structures of an entire society.

In the past the political functions could be handled by the Church through a division of roles: the Church handling them from its spiritual authority, and the State from its temporal authority. Now this treatment of society seems insufficient. The Church often challenges the State. There is often polarization of political systems. The application of the very Christian moral principles may entail political and concrete social analysis in order to be truly Christian and moral.

As we delve more deeply in this chapter into the social analysis which Segundo offers as precondition to biblical interpretation, we will be centering on the social analysis of the Latin American scene, the place of commitment for Segundo. His desire is to move away from dependency on European and North American influence. Thus, our author finds indirect confirmation of the need to begin with thorough social analysis for (moral) theology and biblical exegesis in the evolution of the ecclesial documents proper to Latin America itself. This complements what he drew out of Church documents in general.

Segundo points out that in a certain sense Latin America did not take part in Vatican II. The council was prepared by Europeans, planned according to European structures and needs, while trying to be universal in scope. In effect, even the problems broached were not Latin American problems. Moreover, applying the council decisions was difficult because the laity in the Latin American church were of a different mentality from the laity in the first world. He describes the situation at that time as follows: "In Latin America the Church which had still to realize this change was qualitatively poor, that is, clerical although lacking clergy, without support from a laity which was instead more insecure than creative, with the initial lack of evangelization in depth."[12]

When the effects of Vatican II did begin to take root in Latin America, they had different dimensions and directions from the Church elsewhere. This came mostly from the fact of a rapid and urgent social consciousness which developed in these countries. This political conscientization led to strong social analysis and political theory as part of the social doctrine of the Church. Like the Church at large, though in a more radical way, the Latin American Church could not see its moral teaching as simply non-conformist to a political order accepted as given. Ecclesial documents began to suggest that

even the political and social structures were
optional, and that perhaps true Christian social
doctrine demanded the choosing of new options.

This trend in ecclesial social doctrine
began with the Latin American episcopal conference held at Medellín, Colombia, in 1969.[13]
It was a time of fresh beginnings, enthusiasm,
and freedom. One could discuss political options, the need for humanization, the role of
the Church in history. The documents began
always from the concrete reality of injustice,
and offered a theology that brought concrete
solutions. There was little moralism.

At the same time, Medellín was also
ambiguous and just a start. The sense of
urgency did not always allow time to relate
the social analysis to the biblical literature.
Texts of the Bible were misused or not used at
all. The political analysis was still simplistic in some ways. Since that time there has
been much work done to try to correlate more
sophisticated social analysis with more exact
biblical exegesis. This is the work of theologians like Segundo, and this is what we will
continue to analyze in what follows. For now,
we do see, however, that Segundo can draw from
the basic thrust of Latin American Church documents a further confirmation of his first precondition for the hermeneutic circle. Social
analysis creates ideological suspicion of previous theology and exegesis, and demands new
ways of conceiving these activities.

With this section of our chapter we have
the first exposition of a methodology for the
use of the Bible for Christian ethics. It
certainly has its value, but it already engen-
ders questions. To what extent can social
analysis be the starting point for exegesis and
ethics? Is it always the start? Where is
revelation if social analysis sets the terms of
the message? Is it in the gospel or in the
social analysis? How does one guard against

sheer relativism? Is this an area where Segundo exaggerates a point because of his commitment? Further study of this aspect of his method will shed some light in the rest of this chapter, and study of subsequent aspects of his method in following chapters will also help. We will have to come back to the questions in our critique in chapter five.

Role of Marxism

Moving more deeply now into the specifics of Segundo's social analysis and political theory, we find it including, as an important though relative element, Marxist sociology. Segundo is an eminent spokesman for the whole movement of liberation theology, which builds on this approach. He is not wedded to Marxism, however, and does use other theory. However, since Marxism sparks such controversy in Christian circles, we will look at this element particularly. Before examining the details of Marxist influence on Segundo, we will look at the justification which he offers for using Marxism, as well as the qualifications that he makes on it which show that he is not committed to Marxism as such.

First of all, our author is insistent that he wants to consider this methodology as an approach to the whole of theology, not just one portion of it. He believes that the only way to do theology authentically is to pose the socio-political questions to it as part of the fundamental methodology. "It is theology seen not from one of the various possible standpoints, but from the one standpoint indicated by Christian sources as the authentic, privileged one for the understanding of divine revelation in Jesus Christ."[14]

Precisely because this social analysis is for the whole of theology, Segundo rejects the reasons that may have been offered by classical theology for considering the socio-political questions. One of those reasons was that such questions were part of the moral theology that needed study. Segundo rejects this because it maintains the now-disparaged separation of moral theology from dogmatic theology. He wants the social analysis to be the foundation of the whole of dogmatic or systematic theology and through that, perhaps, to have its moral conclusions. The implications of Marxism must be more extensive than they are in first world theology.

In the same way, he rejects the second reason offered by classical theology for consideration of the socio-political questions, namely, that socialism must be treated as a violation of natural law and its recognition of the right of private property. This is simply one aspect of the first reason, and is rejected by Segundo for the same reason that it does not place Marxist social analysis as part of the basic methodology, but only as a particular point of moral analysis. Segundo is, indeed, quite strong about the centrality of his social analysis: "Neither the abysmal separation between a dogmatic theology and a moral theology, nor the notion of 'natural law,' nor especially its application to the defence of the private possession of such means by some people, and only some, appear to me to be principles of enough substance to merit particular attention."[15]

While he rejects the reasons offered by classical theology for posing socio-political questions to theology, our author does offer some reasons of his own. One such reason would be the example offered by the teaching authority of the Church in its recent statements of social doctrine. As we indicated above, these documents saw the need of social analysis. We can now elaborate that this social analysis moves toward socialism.

Leo XIII showed one side of the attitude toward socialism, the initial attitude of total rejection. However, the condemnation of socialism was based on two reasons, which would eventually be refuted. The first was the association of Marxism automatically with atheism. The other was the oversimplification of Marxism, which had not yet been worked out in practice, and was condemned in some theoretic fashion.

John XXIII showed the other end of the spectrum of attitudes toward socialism, moving the social doctrine in its direction. His major emphasis is that one must consider, not a theoretic socialism, but a concrete, lived socialism facing concrete problems of humanity today. From John, Segundo concludes:

. . . Despite the anti-religious venom socialism has displayed and its constant denial of religious freedom, the Church must objectively and neutrally examine what possibilities this existing socialism, as lived by men today, holds for the Christian way of life.
Because of our peculiar social conditions, it may be that we Latin Americans are obligated more than anyone else to see if certain facets of socialism are not, after all, compatible with Catholic social teachings.[16]

The result of such examination of socialism is now, according to Segundo, the beginning of some Marxist analysis in Catholic social teaching. John XXIII, for example, continued to maintain the right of private property, but absorbed into it some socialist concepts. He said the right of ownership applied not only to the consumer goods, but also to the means of production. However, the basis of the right is that the good is indispensable for the human condition, and that therefore the right is not for a few, but for all. Likewise, the means of production cannot be divided up indefinitely and need to be shared in community. In that case, "private" ownership does not mean "with exclusive title to dispose of in an arbitrary way," but rather the ability to apply one's creative responsibility to the good possessed. In other words, the right of private property incorporates more and more the ideas of Marxist or socialist analysis.[17]

In another section of his writings Segundo further elaborates how Marxism can be separated from its atheistic tenets, so that its sociological insights can be used by theology. In fact, this section is an illustration of the hermeneutic circle itself, and does in miniature with Marx what we are doing in large scale in this entire study. Segundo's contention is that Marx's atheism or antagonism toward religion is really a breaking of the hermeneutic circle, and is an inconsistency in Marx.

Marx begins his hermeneutics with a genuine commitment to life experience and with an analysis of that experience in sociological terms. For example, he is convinced that every existing society is the history of class struggle, and that every attempt to change the world must think within that struggle, especially on the side of the proletariat. With this theory of historical materialism he brought his hermeneutical process to the second step, i.e., to the sociological challenge to other accepted views of present life.

At this point Marx should have made the third step of the hermeneutic circle. His sociological theory should have challenged theology to renew its concepts. Instead, Marx rejection religion as ahistorical and useless for the changing of the world. He thus terminated the hermeneutic circle.

Now, according to Segundo, "instead of 'abolition,' one would expect Marx to have talked about 'changing' religion so that it might accentuate and eventually correct the situation being protested against."[18] With this statement, our author shows how Marxism can be separated from its atheism, and can even be made more consistent, at least in terms of the hermeneutics that we are considering. At the same time we have seen an example of how Segundo believes social analysis can be the starting point for all of theology and biblical exegesis. After we have finished these general points regarding Marxism in Segundo, we will outline the principal data of social analysis that he finds helpful in Marx for his own theology and exegesis.

Before we do move to these details, however, we must note that our author makes some qualifications of his use of Marxist analysis, and we must keep these in mind throughout our study. For one thing, he insists that socialism as he uses it is not the particular socialism as practiced, for instance, in the Soviet Socialist Republic. Nor, for that matter, is capitalism exclusively that practiced in the United States. By the same token, his social analysis is not pure abstraction. Its starting point must be concrete reality. Thus, we have the paradox that Segundo's analysis must draw from capitalism and socialism as they exist in the world, but his ultimate models try to surpass any concretely existing instances of these models. He tries to sum up the paradox in this way:

. . . By "socialism" we do not mean a complete, long-term social project, endowed with a particular ideology or philosophy. . . . It may be objected--why not give a more detailed account of the socialist model? . . . There is one very simple reason for not doing this--we cannot foresee or control the universe of the future. The only real, possible option remaining to us is within our own countries as they are.[19]

Another qualification that Segundo makes is that Marxism is not the only determining factor in theological elaboration. Moreover, its

66

use, even in what it offers of merit, is not absolute. It just seems the best at this time, at least for part of the picture of theology. Regarding its not being exclusive, Segundo says in criticism of many Marxist sociologists, that they have not accepted the relative autonomy of the superstructural levels in their methodology. That is, many present-day Marxists fail to realize that Marx and Engels "referred to the economic element as ultimately the determining factor, but not as the only determining factor on the superstructure."[20]

Marxism can certainly criticize theology and its own hidden ideologies, but its economic and political theories cannot replace theology. In fact, according to Segundo, it is precisely when Marxism tries to become a faith rather than a science that it loses its efficacy. By this he means that Marxism does not have all the elements to construct a total image of humanity and the universe. It needs theology for this. By the same token, theology would not speak to actual life and practice if it were not challenged by Marxist sociology. Within those limits, Marxism is important to Segundo's hermeneutics, at least until another sociology comes along that impresses him more.

Observations from Marxist and Other Sociology

Having established Segundo's principle that social analysis is a precondition for theological and biblical hermeneutics, and having also established that this social analysis can incorporate Marxism, we can now study what, in the concrete, Segundo derives from Marxist and other sociology. In other words, we will elaborate in more detail the first two steps of the hermeneutic circle as our author carries it out in his own writings.

Liberation theology has maintained that its very essence is doing theology from a commitment to the poor and oppressed, especially in Latin America. Segundo is certainly of that mind, and so his first steps, his commitment and his social analysis, are centered on the situation of the poor of Latin America. A good starting point for that analysis is what our author has to say about the evolution of the term "development" as it has been used for Latin America.

His first statement in that matter is a strong confrontation, which lays the groundwork for his final conclusion that the problem of development is ultimately caused by the first world powers. Segundo says the word "underdeveloped" is not an exact term, but is broad enough to describe the situation of Latin American countries. However, "it is not helpful to change the expression to 'developing countries,' though it might have more emotional appeal. Our sensibilities are one thing; the truth quite another."[21]

By tracing the evolution of the word "underdeveloped," we can see how it tells of the poverty of Latin America, while at the same time showing that it does not imply that they are able to move out of that poverty within the present structures. The word came into usage in the nineteenth century as a term of comparison. It started by showing how the Spanish and Portugese colonies in the new world were better developed than the English ones. The term was kept in that usage through the time of the Alliance for Progress program in the early sixties of this century. As a point of comparison it implied that the conditions of underdevelopment could be reversed. It was simply a question of finding the causes and changing the reasons for this lack of development.[22]

However, as the Alliance for Progress got underway, it was discovered that the fact that some countries started earlier toward development was not a secondary or irrelevant point. It actually blocked the development of others. Thus, "underdevelopment" was no longer taken as a term of comparison, but as the description of a static situation. It expressed the impossibility of changing in the present structures. The vicious circle of poverty became the new image: consumption demands production which demands work which demands more consumption. One does not become richer a little at a time. The rich become richer and the poor become poorer. Thus, the Alliance for Progress turned to placating immediate needs.

This whole view of underdevelopment made it natural that the term should reach a third stage in its evolution, the stage of its present meaning, at least in Marxist analysis. Segundo cites an economist to sum up this present connotation of the word:

. . . It is erroneous, therefore, to envision underdevelopment as an independent fact from economic development. Underdevelopment and development are the two faces of the same coin. . . . The dominant country has to acquire cheap raw materials and place its manufactured goods at a maximum price; the dominated country must produce at low cost and be in a position to acquire the greatest possible volume of manufactured goods.[23]

This recognition of the vicious circle of poverty and of the condition of oppression becomes for Segundo the basis of his social analysis from a Marxist perspective. It is the outcome of his commitment to the poor; it challenges theology and biblical exegesis.

These basic observations of Segundo lead him to a further conclusion that ultimately social analysis must touch on the political structures themselves, and that theology and exegesis will be challenged by the decisions that must be made in terms of these political structures. He spells out this political theory in terms of the Latin American scene.[24]

At first sight, Segundo observes, Latin countries seem to be those places where politics is reduced to a minimum. There are few parties and few elections. In reality, however, politics is even more important than elsewhere, and there is a hidden form of political life behind what is the suppression of the classical forms of political life. Moreover, this political function does not depend on the length of time a government is in office. It depends, rather, on how it conceives that office.

Segundo gives a definition of that office: "The political function is the ultimate deciding function for the common good of a global society, above all for the goods and interests of its different sectors."[25] The political function is to be the final instance of the common good. This comes, not by having its own techniques, science and laws, but by scrutinizing and synthesizing the techniques, science, and laws of the other sectors of society, e.g., the economic, the cultural, and the religious sectors. The political sector is to order the needs of these other sectors. This political function is truly helpful, and is stable in the measure in which the other sectors have their own development and their own autonomy without disturbing the common good.

As a matter of fact in Latin America, however, the political function, which should be secondary, is exaggerated. This is due to the vicious circle of poverty and the condition of oppression of these so-called underdeveloped countries. It is the result of a whole society not being suitable for the market, since they are always in the position of supplying cheap raw materials and buying expensive manufactured goods.

This fact of not being able to compete in the marketplace leads an underdeveloped economic sector to rely on the political sector for its survival. Thus, the economic sector needs protection from foreign competition. Since its capital is not able to be guaranteed economically, the political sector enters to guarantee it politically. That leads to particular interests, to the sustaining of only some of the economy, and to the formation of an oligarchy that alienates the masses.

Moreover, the artificial fabrication of the economy influences the very products marketed. These tend to be luxury items that can be fixed in prices outside the law of supply and demand. It leads to a vicious circle of needing politics to maintain the stability of prices. Internal balance of the society is never attained. The economic sector atrophies and the political sector of the society grows out of all proportion.

With this kind of situation, which is the prevalent situation for all of Latin America, social analysis must include consideration of ways to affect the political structures. This, in turn, will have its bearing on theology and exegesis, as we shall see. As far as Segundo is concerned, the options are not restricted to only one political theory, at least with all things being equal. He even analyzes, as the two approaches to helping sectors develop themselves, the liberal and the socialist approach. He also calls them the system of decentralizing and the system of centralizing, the continuation of structures in a legal evolution, and the breaking of structures through revolution.

Nevertheless, Segundo seems also of the mind that all things are not equal in Latin America and that good social analysis will lead to a choice of the socialist political theory. He finds that there is such polarization of political options in Latin America that the choices are not that vast. One either opts for change that means in effect a socialist option, or one maintains the present situation, even if only by silence:

> In effect, before the problematic of the poor
> countries-rich countries there do not exist
> many options. There do not exist even
> three. . . .
> . . . That the word "left" covers in this
> context indecision and controversy over strate-
> gy, and tactics that are different and even
> opposed in order to rise to power, is clear
> for what remains. However, that its funda-
> mental content is a preference in order to
> jump effectively out of the capitalist orbit,
> paying the necessary price for this, . . .
> that, I believe, has nothing to ignore or
> place in doubt.[26]

In continuing our study of Segundo's use
of sociology as precondition for the hermeneutic
circle, we now touch upon what is without doubt
the most important of all the categories he
employs. It is a conclusion of his analysis of
Latin American society from the perspective of a
commitment to the poor. It is a keen observation on how a dominant society keeps a suppressed
society in control, and how a marginated society
develops social mechanisms. Segundo develops the
concepts of masses and minorities.

The concept of masses, or mass-man, is an
ambiguous one, and has had a number of meanings.
For some it simply means people. For others it
implies the exploited or the proletariat. For
still others the word denotes the terrible
results of a culture in which the human person
is destroyed by the institutions. Segundo
rejects each of these meanings and opts for a
definition that is phenomenological. "For the
present [Lenin] attributes one, fundamental
[trait]: mass spontaneity 'moves in the path of
least resistance'."[27]

In this matter Segundo relies on Marxist
sociology that derives principally from Lenin,
who in turn modified the theory of Marx.[28] Marx

72

had a vision of the development of socialism that was both economic and humanistic. In terms of economic laws he foresaw that capitalism in the developed countries of England and Germany would come to such concentration of capital in fewer and fewer hands that there would be general pauperization. This would lead to the uprising of the poor and power passing into their hands. The humanistic Marx also foresaw that this passing of power would be in two stages, an intermediate or socialist stage, and a definitive or communist stage. In the intermediate stage the old machinery and division of work would have to continue, while rejecting the old ideologies. The State would continue to function.

Marx's foresight turned out to be less than accurate, since the middle class arose in England and Germany, and the socialist revolution unfolded in the most backward country of Europe, the Soviet Union. Lenin developed Marx in order to allow for this historical phenomenon. In doing so he developed the concept of the masses. This group, he said, was incapable of a revolution. It was the majority of a society, and it followed the law of least resistance. In terms of time and space, the masses chose the simplest and the most immediate course of action. In this way, Lenin could account for the role of the State as being a permanent function, since it was the mechanism of mass-man. At the same time he could account for the existence of the party, which would serve as a minority group always counteracting the inertia of the masses of the society and always feeding the revolution.

Segundo does not adopt the class distinctions that the Marxist view embraces, and does not define the masses in terms of the proletariat. Mass-man can pertain to every social class. The key ingredient is that one tends to absolutize and to mechanize. One acts out of a routine and tends to want to remove options from life. The law of inertia is much to the fore. Mass-man tends to "massify" his or her actions.

73

We might also note that this concept of masses is not taken by Segundo in a pejorative sense. It is an inbuilt trait of every society, and even an aspect of every person. "The absolutization, mechanization, and routinization of behavior patterns is the psycho-sociological precondition for individual security in social life and for the social consensus that permits a socio-political system to continue in operation."[29] The problem is not one of eliminating mass-tendency, but of balancing mass-tendency with the movement of the minorities (who bear all the traits opposite to the masses).

In summary, the characteristics with which we define mass-man or, if you want, massive conduct, are the following:
i) . . . the greater part of the activities are realized by following the line of least resistance, . . . the most mechanized, the simplest and the most immediate solutions. . . .
ii) Without excluding the possibility that a person might be totally "massified," the most normal experience would be that men save their energies "massively" on many levels of existence in order to obtain richer and more effective synthesis in a larger scale on a determined level: conjugal love, the family, politics, profession. . . . The mass is not constituted by one group of men and the minority by others. . . .
iii) . . . the social sciences can, to a certain point, establish laws with high probability, even in what concerns human attitudes that are free in principle. . . . If such were not based on the quantitative mass, sociology would have no sense.
iv) . . . the minority cannot progress by itself alone, but only by elevating the behavior of the masses in such a way as to provide the generalized base of energy by which the minority can realize a richer and more effective synthesis.[30]

74

This central concept of masses and minorities is illustrated by Segundo in several social analyses of the Latin American scene. We will look at how he shows the interplay of rapid urbanization with the mass communications media and social consciousness, and how the mass-tendency is interwoven throughout this analysis.[31] His first point in this regard is that the state of underdevelopment in Latin America has forced the poor to seek work in the cities. Thus, one of the most significant phenomena in this part of the world is rapid urbanization. Even so, the urbanization in this third world area is different from other countries, for it is not a movement upward socially. There is still a gap between the rich and the poor. Even worse, there is now added the alienation of the poor, who are uprooted from their culture and society and thrown into a new and very strange environment.

The urbanization creates complex and even dangerous problems in terms of the masses. They come from a society of traditions, sanctions, plausible world views and unified ways of living, and they enter the urban complex in a rapid period of time. This leads to insecurity, especially since they enter a highly competitive world, with a plurality of values.

To help control the problems of alienation of the masses, communications media play a vital function. Segundo points out the insights of Marshall McLuhan: "When the needs of the division of labor necessitated the explosion of a uniform culture, the 'galaxy' of Gutenberg appeared as a marvelously opportune coincidence; . . . when societies could survive only when interconnected, . . . communications media like those we are discussing suddenly appeared as if by magic."[32]

Elaborating on this insight, our author shows how the urban civilization is a complex network of interrelationships, which is really a system in unstable equilibrium. The entire city must be made all over again each day, with the interaction of specialized and interconnected activities. The members of society now are members of a consumer society. They depend on each other for their very existence. Moreover, what gets to be important is that the services are rendered, not the reasons behind the services, nor the human values promoted or denigrated. "Urban socialization is based on the most important questions being allotted the least important time."[33]

The most important ingredient of urbanization is mechanization and automation, and this is the role of the communications media. "Making man in his urban society more like a cybernetic instrument, that is what the network of communications media is doing already. . . . we now have to control attitudes not by a legislative fiat but by a concealment of its always debatable purposes."[34] It is as if modern society must create a second nature, to perform with acquired instincts what original nature performed in the past, and to perform them with regularity and accuracy. Ultimately, we are talking about a restructuring and a recreating of the masses.

Theoretically this massification could be a normal and positive social process. It could leave leisure time for the reflection upon and development of basic human values. However, as a matter of fact, such is not the case. All revolves around consumer uniformity, to guarantee the creation and consumption of products that ensure survival and that can be exchanged for satisfaction of further needs. There is no longer a sharing of human values, nor a scale of values, as in traditional society. As Segundo puts it, "It makes no difference whatsoever what human beings think or feel about the universe; indeed it makes no difference whether they feel anything deeply at all."[35] To overcome his feelings of insecurity and alienation, mass-man just gives up or relativizes the basic values of traditional society and takes what the media offer for consumer values.

Especially in Latin America the process of
urbanization is further complicated by the vicious
circle of poverty. Segundo points out that in
the capitalist system the media have created
artificial needs far beyond what society really
needs to survive. Even worse, the creation of
these needs has had adverse effects on the marginated peoples, effects which social consciousness is bringing to the surface.

It must not be forgotten that the communications media are transported from one culture to
another. In addition, as Segundo says, "the communications media are in McLuhan's own words, 'a
classroom without walls,' where the majority of
people in the underdeveloped countries learn to
live."[36] He makes three observations regarding
the impact of the media from the first world on
the third world.

First of all, many of the needs that are
created are not really so in a global vision of
humanity, of which two-thirds is hungry.
Secondly, the attractions of these needs and
the arguments which make them appealing transcend
national borders. Thirdly, these enticements are
means to keep some people developed by keeping
others underdeveloped. The media call the masses
to participate in the consumer society from which
they are actually excluded. "There is perhaps
no more alienating function than that of
interiorizing in the slave the reflexes of his
slavery."[37]

Conscientization is a process growing more
and more in Latin America as part of this social
analysis. It uncovers group interests and propa-
ganda. It creates a minority which can balance
the mass-tendency and eventually influence it.[38]
This minority no longer simply assumes that whatever can be translated into increased consumption
is good. It no longer sees values in the abstract, but in terms of the group that has

personal interest in propagating the values.   It
passes judgment on these values, and it also
takes steps to attain the values by changing
structures.   Conscientization:

> is rightly applied to any form of social
> mobilization that seeks to inculcate a more
> realistic and critical awareness of the real
> interests, particularly group interests, at
> work in society under the trappings of
> propaganda, paternalism, and promises that
> seek to maintain society as it is for the
> most part and to allow only insignificant
> minor social changes insofar as the total
> populace is concerned.[39]

Segundo offers other insights of social
analysis, and makes further applications of
Marxist sociology to the Latin American scene.
What we have just considered, however, gives his
central thinking and enables us to continue to
make his hermeneutic circle.   Especially with
his concept of the masses and minorities, in the
background of the other points of social analysis that we have mentioned, he has the material
which should create ideological suspicion and
should challenge the previous ways of conceiving
theology and biblical exegesis.   This will
affect the ways he believes the Bible should
contribute to Christian ethics, for it shows how
he conceives the relationship of Scripture to
human experience.

Social Analysis and Ecclesiology

Before we move to the third step of the
hermeneutic circle and before we consider how
theology can renew itself in face of the life
situation described by social analysis, we have
one final aspect of the social analysis itself to
examine.   This aspect can fittingly be called a
sociology of religion, for it takes the Marxist
social analysis and introduces it, so to speak,
within the very confines of theology.   It is an

examination of the social and political principles hidden within theology itself that must
eventually challenge theology to recognize and
respond to this fact. Segundo addresses this
social analysis especially to ecclesiology and
through that to moral theology. We will now see
his social analysis of the Church and its pastoral action in Latin America.

A good starting point for this social
analysis is what Segundo says about the role of
theologians and the role of bishops in Latin
America. The social status of the theologian
sheds light on how his theology is conceived and
on how it is related to his society. A number
of facts indicate that Latin American theology
is conceived as mostly a copy of European
theology, and that it is not in any way creative.

For one thing, Latin American theologians
have to emigrate for their higher education, and
go mostly to Europe. Their studies in Europe
entail the solution of problems related to
another culture, and the pleasing of theological
masters of another cultural interest. These
same theologians return home and continue the
study of these same foreign problems. Moreover,
they have to do it in even more handicapped ways,
namely, without libraries, books, or other
valuable primary sources of research.[40]

Bishops in Latin America are named according to their competence in canon law, which does
not speak to the creative aspects of pastoral
action, but rather to the maintaining of institutions. Moreover, the interrelationship between
the bishops and the theologians is also outside
of the framework of Latin American needs.
Whereas theology should often be a charismatic
challenge to the episcopacy, instead it is used
to spell out canon law and institutional needs.
This same kind of theology is perpetuated in
seminary training, which therefore does not train
men well for the real needs of Latin America.[41]

When one looks to the external help given
to the Church in Latin America, one sees also the
perpetuation of the problems of theology and the
episcopacy there. The help is usually given in
the form of personnel and institutions. The
fact that, after four centuries, Latin America
still has to rely on foreign clergy says there
is not enough communication with the real world
on the part of the Church. Even the other help
beyond clergy tends to create, expand, and sus-
tain institutions, often beyond their real
usefulness to the area.[42] In summation, the
formulas behind theology, episcopacy, and
external help to Latin America come from the
past. They presuppose a Christianity that is
part of the culture, a true Christendom
inherited from Europe, which is to speak to the
majority of the society. All of this builds on
a religion of the masses, which Segundo considers inadequate for the times.

Our author details this analysis by a
thorough study of Christendom's decline and the
reasons for it. This social analysis, built on
that of his analysis of masses and minorities,
is the central insight of most of Segundo's
writing. As a prelude to theology, it lays the
groundwork for ecclesiology as his most central
theological topic.

Segundo's main contention is that Christendom not only failed as a matter of fact or
historical circumstance. It failed on principle
as well. Christendom was the exception rather
than the rule. It was a civilization in which
the culture was Christianity and therefore, the
social institutions supported and maintained
Christianity. Nevertheless, even within this
Christian culture it is one thing to say that
there were massive conversions to Christianity,
and another to say that people freely chose
Christianity in terms of their own personal
convictions.

The very origins of Christendom reveal that the movement came through the conversion of a people around the conversion of its leader, Constantine. Christendom was a sociological phenomenon encouraged by the authorities and supported by the social institutions. Institutions are not, a priori, a deformation of the Christian message, and they can genuinely facilitate Christianity. Nevertheless, more often than not, the masses are bound to the institutions rather than to the Christianity. It is in the nature of the masses to do this: "Habit on one side, convenience on the other--this is exactly the essence and the role of a social institution: to create a second nature which facilitates choice on the level of the masses; to put inertia itself at the service of the common good."[43]

Sociologists now point out that this Christian culture has broken apart. Progress results in upheaval in society, and upheaval results in dechristianization. Most of the elements of social analysis that we considered before now enter the scene and topple Christendom. Urbanization moves people out of their closed society, where tradition has primacy and where Christianity is the primary element in that tradition.

Segundo points out that the laity in Latin America are like children growing up quickly. In the rural areas, the child and parent did the same work with the same mores. In the city, however, the child and the parent have different work and different values. The child, influenced by other sources, rebels against the parent in order to climb in his own society. The example applies to the relationship of the laity to the clergy and the Church. The laity live in a world of values much different from the clergy and the official Church teaching. This difference in values fosters a break between groups. All this is saying that society no longer encourages and promotes the Christian message.[44]

It seems that the masses have been lost to
Christianity. Some hope to simply remove the
obstacles which are seen as mere prejudice against
the Church and the faith. In reality, however,
it is not simply prejudice. When the obstacles
are removed, faith does not follow, but indifference. There is mass dechristianization because
the elements of civilization that once supported
Christianity no longer do so. Inertia no longer
plays a role in favor of Christianity. The
communications media, so necessary to the urbanization process, present a plurality of values, and
do not stress continuity in Christian values.

In the United States and Europe, seculariza-
tion becomes the way of solving the problem of the
demise of Christendom. In Latin America, however,
this seems not the solution. There is still a
pastoral effort to bring the masses into the
Church. Beneath the surface of homogeneity and
immutability, however, there is noticeable
insecurity of the people, and a constant, losing
battle to win adherents to the Church in any
committed sort of way.

This desire to still be the religion of the
masses shows in the pastoral practice of the Latin
American Church. For one thing, the Church recognizes that it is in a consumer society. The only
way to be religion of the masses is by offering
something for consumption, by trying to sell
Christianity as a product. This inevitably leads
to binding people to an external institution in an
artificial way, and without real inner conviction.
It is a form of social pressure when society at
large does not provide that pressure. Thus, for
example, religion courses are made mandatory for
a business degree at a Catholic university; devo-
tional practices are used as springboard for
pastoral action; time, energy, and money are
poured into Church schools, hospitals, etc., in
the hope that the services rendered by institutions will also bring across the Christian
message.

Segundo observes that this desire to have people cling to the institutions and to the old religious customs is merely the dispensing of security to them. When the institutions and customs were formerly based on a uniformity of values in the culture, then the clinging to the institutions could in some way be a link also to the values. It was a positive help for the masses. Now, however, we must appreciate the differences in the adhesion of an uprooted society compared to the closed society of the past. "Certain forms of adhesion to Christianity in the open urban society of today cannot be regarded sociologically as a guarantee that a Christian conception of life has been transmitted. . . . The milieu no longer generates or substitutes for real personal conviction."[45] People will now adhere because of insecurity that makes them seek out the remnants of a previous closed society.

The effects of such a consumer Christianity or a desire for mass Christianity are evident, and mostly negative. First of all, most of the effort of the Church is not for real committed Christians, but for large numbers. The stress is not so much for quality as for quantity. Moreover, in trying to attain this quantity, there is a holding back of the demands of Christianity. The principle becomes "the minimum requirements for the maximum of membership."[46]

Another negative result of attempting to keep Christianity as a mass religion in Latin America is the alliance set up between the Church and the State. In Christendom the temporal authority was an automatic ally of the Church, since Christianity was interwoven into the very fabric of society, and was a major factor of unifying and facilitating the functioning of that society. The Church enjoyed the help of the State, which provided its powerful authority to aid it in Christianizing and in maintaining the society as Christian. At the same time, the State appreciated the influence of the Church, since its religious sanctions helped to maintain the social order and to maintain the State in its authority.

With the dechristianization of Latin America the alliance between Church and State has become detrimental. For one thing, the Church now has to actively seek out the support and the good pleasure of the State in order to receive its influence over the masses, and the protection for Church institutions. In effect, this means that the Church must cater to the existing government and accept the present social order as the given fact. This means an automatic acceptance of the status quo, a conservative political policy, a continuation of oppression of the poor. The Church fears being a real prophetic and critical influence in Latin America because it might hurt it economically and institutionally.

At the same time, the detrimental effect flows from the State's reliance on the Church for its acceptance by the so-called Christian masses. In its own way, often subtle, the temporal authority uses the Church as a means of giving security to the masses, to control their daily activities, to mechanize or automate their lives, and thus prevent their challenging the status quo of the political situation. Once again, the Church gains the reputation, not of being truly neutral in politics--an impossible situation--but of being the support for an oppressive and enslaving government.[47]

Finally, one further negative evaluation that Segundo would draw from this social analysis of the Church itself is that Christendom may have made the masses freer from obstacles to choice, e.g., by the facilitation of choices through a "second nature" of institutions, but that did not, by that very fact, make man or woman any more free. Real freedom comes from a personal adventure which involves humanity's own self-creation

in risk. Massive Christianity depersonalizes the
masses in the long run, or at least makes demands
only on the surface of commitment. It operates
under a manner of external pressure and does not
rely on the intrinsic persuasive power of the
gospel itself to win fully convinced and dedi-
cated members to Christianity.[48]

The end conclusion from such social analysis of the Church is that it will speak to the
Latin American person of today, and not contribute to his alienation, only when Christianity
is seen sociologically as a minority movement.
The gospel must speak of its own accord and be
persuasive. Men and women must act counter to
mechanization, with a freedom that is creative,
heroic, and deeply personal. It is not a question of a mass movement rediscovering a faith
as Christendom once lived it. It is, rather,
the recognition that a minority must actually
discover the faith on a deeper level for the
first time.

Such suggestions by Segundo lead to the
question of whether he is elitist in his view of
Christian membership. We will have to return to
this issue later. For the moment we can say that
Segundo rejects elitism at least to the degree
that he maintains that the minority must be at
the service of the masses. He does maintain,
however, that the masses will be affected only
by a minority that acts as leaven. The very
nature of the masses obviates their ever
embracing Christianity fully and completely:

. . . Between the Christian ideal and
mass-man there is something more than a
present-day opposition. Christianity, which
is mediated and anti-Manichean by essence,
appears to us as the call which must always
resound before mass-man, pushing him toward
his liberation. And, on the contrary, the
essential determinism which is at the
interior of the masses makes every sincere
adhesion to Christianity an undertaking

85

torn of authenticity, a challenge to the
massive force which weighs on history and on
man its inhabitant.[49]

With this sociological analysis of ecclesiology we thereby have the most complete illustration of the first steps by Segundo himself of
his hermeneutic circle. He begins with a concern
for Latin America and its oppressed masses. He
finds Marxist social analysis a convenient tool
for carrying out his commitment to the poor. He
applies Marxist and other social analysis to
theology about the Church, not to reject this
ecclesiology outright, but to create suspicion
that it has left out important data. This hermeneutics of suspicion lays the groundwork for
the next step of the hermeneutic circle, the
renewal of theology to take into account the data
previously left out of consideration.

The following chapter will be concerned
with the renewal of theology in the light of the
social analysis. We will see what Segundo posits
as theological tenets that will consider the
needs of the oppressed and work towards their
liberation. What we have seen so far about social
analysis and ecclesiology also gives us insight
into how Segundo views the relationship of the
Bible to human experience and can be applied to
morality as well. We will make that application
in the final chapter. As we begin the next
chapter we will again look at his ecclesiology,
but especially as that will bridge the gap to
eschatology and thereby provide insight not only
into how theology should be renewed, but also into
the second major question we have been asking
about the use of the Bible for Christian ethics.[50]

CHAPTER II

NOTES

[1]Juan Luis Segundo, The Liberation of Theology (Maryknoll, N.Y.: Orbis Books, 1976), p. 8.

[2]Ibid.

[3]Ibid., p. 9.

[4]Ibid.

[5]Juan Luis Segundo, "El posible aporte de la teología protestante para el cristianismo latinoamericano en el futuro," Cristianismo y Sociedad 8 (1970): 41.

[6]Ibid., pp. 43-44. From this point in the dissertation when quotations are taken from Spanish editions of Segundo's works, as indicated in the footnotes, translations are my own.

[7]Juan Luis Segundo, Masas y Minorías en la Dialéctica Divina de la Liberación (Buenos Aires: La Aurora, 1973), p. 92.

[8]Segundo, Liberation, p. 7.

[9]Ibid., p. 8.

[10]Juan Luis Segundo, "Social Justice and Revolution," America, April 27, 1968, p. 576.

[11]Ibid.

[12]Juan Luis Segundo, "Ritmos de cambio y pastoral de conjunto," Perspectivas de Diálogo 4 (1969): 133.

[13]Juan Luis Segundo, "Condicionamientos actuales de la reflexión teológica en Latino-américa," in Liberación y Cautiverio: Debates en torno al método de la teología en América Latina (Mexico City: Comité Organizador, 1975), pp. 95-97.

[14]Juan Luis Segundo, "Capitalism-Socialism: A Theological Crux," Concilium 96 (1974): 105.

87

[15] Ibid., pp. 106-7.

[16] Segundo, "Social Justice," p. 577.

[17] Ibid.

[18] Segundo, Liberation, p. 17.

[19] Segundo, "Capitalism-Socialism," p. 115.

[20] Segundo, Liberation, p. 60.

[21] Juan Luis Segundo, "Wealth and Poverty as Obstacles to Development," in Human Rights and the Liberation of Man in the Americas, ed. Louis Colonnesse (Notre Dame: Notre Dame Press, 1971), p. 23.

[22] Segundo offers a number of the reasons usually given for the underdevelopment. Among the "acceptable" reasons, i.e., those that can be talked about freely and without giving appearance of prejudice, are: low level of popular culture, demographic explosion, politics, incapacity for reasonable and sustained work, archaic social structures and work techniques. Usual "unacceptable" reasons, i.e., that usually cannot be declared publicly, yet are believed privately, are: Latin temperament, laziness, machismo. See ibid., p. 24.

[23] Ibid., p. 28.

[24] Juan Luis Segundo, De la Sociedad a la Teología (Buenos Aires: Ediciones Carlos Lohle, 1970), pp. 109-26.

[25] Ibid., p. 112.

[26] Juan Luis Segundo, "Hacia una iglesia de izquierda," Perspectivas de Diálogo 4 (1969): 36.

[27] Segundo, Masas, p. 21; Liberation, p. 218.

[28] Segundo, Masas, pp. 18-22; Liberation, pp. 216-18.

[29] Segundo, Liberation, p. 184.

[30] Segundo, Masas, pp. 28-29; see also

Liberation, pp. 225-26.

[31] Juan Luis Segundo, The Hidden Motives of Pastoral Action (Maryknoll, N.Y.: Orbis Books, 1978), pp. 3-23.

[32] Juan Luis Segundo, "Education, Communication and Liberation: a Christian Vision," IDOC International (North American Edition), November 13, 1971, p. 66.

[33] Ibid., p. 67.

[34] Ibid., p. 68.

[35] Segundo, Hidden Motives, p. 15.

[36] Segundo, "Education, Communication," p. 75.

[37] Ibid., p. 76.

[38] Notice that Segundo here supports conscientization, but criticizes the motif as it is presented by P. Freire and others. They liken it to a literacy program and intend it for the masses, while Segundo reserves it for a minority. See Liberation, pp. 209-11.

[39] Segundo, Hidden Motives, pp. 21-22.

[40] Segundo, De la Sociedad, pp. 16-18.

[41] Ibid., pp. 19-22.

[42] Ibid., pp. 23-26.

[43] Juan Luis Segundo, La Cristiandad ¿Una Utopia?, vol. 1: Los Hechos (Montevideo: Mimeografica "Luz," 1964), p. 4.

[44] Juan Luis Segundo, Función de la Iglesia en la Realidad Rioplatense (Montevideo: Barreiro y Ramos, 1962), pp. 51-52.

[45] Segundo, Hidden Motives, p. 30.

[46] Segundo, De la Sociedad, pp. 40-44.

[47] Segundo, Hidden Motives, pp. 37-44.

[48] Ibid., pp. 66-70.

[49] Segundo, ¿Utopia?, vol. 1, p. 42.

[50]Notice that ecclesiology has been the content out of which we have been able to draw our considerations for Segundo's hermeneutical methodology, and for insights also into the Bible and ethics. We use ecclesiology because that seems to be the preponderant topic in Segundo's writings. For a study devoted explicitly to that, see Gerald J. Persha, <u>Juan Luis Segundo: A study concerning the relationship between the particularity of the Church and the universality of her mission</u> (Maryknoll, N.Y.: Orbis Probe Books, 1979).

CHAPTER III

THEOLOGY AND IDEOLOGY IN SEGUNDO

Juan Segundo posits a second precondition
for his hermeneutic circle, complementing the
first precondition of social analysis that we
have just considered in the preceding chapter.
This second precondition is incorporated into
the third step of his hermeneutic circle. As
precondition it is described as the willingness
of theology and biblical exegesis to speak to
the real life situation in the world today.
As the third step of the circle, the precondition is translated into the ability of theology
to recognize its presuppositions as they are
unveiled by social analysis, and to change its
tenets on the basis of that critique.

Since Segundo is doing theology from
the perspective of a commitment to the poor in
Latin America, the presuppositions of theology
are seen also from that point of view. This
is best expressed in terms of ideology, which
we can tentatively define as the vision of
life, whether in conscious or unconscious
ideas, which is presupposed behind our reasoning and our acting. This vision of life is
analyzed by our author in reference to its
concerns for the poor. As we proceed, this
definition will take on two distinct meanings,
negative and positive. In any case, it seems
that our best way into this chapter of our
study is by examining the interrelationship
between theology and ideology.

Theology and Negative Ideology

When we talk in detail about ideology,
we refer to something which underlies in one
way or another all the social analysis that we
outlined in the previous chapter. In a more

91

negative definition, ideology is the force behind the massification of man and woman in Latin American society. Segundo does not, in his own writings, give a formal definition of ideology in this sense, but much of his writing assumes it. We will refer to this sense of the word as ideology^n. We can take the formal definition from several authors who provide various elements for it. All of these elements would go into what Segundo sees as ideology^n.

Ideology does not offer adequate and scientific knowledge of reality; rather, it masks it. Ideology does not rise above the empirical, irrational level. Therefore, it spontaneously fulfills a function of preservation of the established order.[1]

It is the distortion of reality due to the surreptitious efforts of a person or social group to protect a privileged position.[2]

[It is] a (more or less coherent, or partially modified) unified perception of the world. . . . people are themselves unaware of it. Their words and actions may intend something else. But in the context of a given situation they may in fact be supporting and buttressing a certain political and/or economic line . . . in the wider context of the total society.[3]

From these definitions we can gather the essential ingredients that Segundo would give to ideology^n. It is, first of all, not a reasoned view of life, but is prior to full reasoning. It is irrational at least in the sense that it flows from images, experience, social context, and other influences that are pre-rational, and that mask an accurate view of life. Generally these influences lead one to try to maintain the status quo of one's situation in life. As Segundo sees it, ideology generally pertains to a society. He is not overly concerned for the individual aspects of ideology. Moreover, the society in question need not be just one social or economic grouping, but can be any class in society, just as long as it seeks the path of the least resistance, maintains the status quo, and does this by the false consciousness of a pre-rational view of life.

Ideology in this negative sense also pertains to any group that is in dominance. It is the way of protecting this dominance, which is often economic, but can also embrace other areas of life. Finally, this false consciousness is usually vast enough to embrace a total view of life, so that all of social experience is interpreted in view of the same ideology.

In relation to the poor, ideology is the device used by first world powers to keep the third world in underdevelopment. It is the way in which the political function of a poor country artificially supports an economy to the advantage of a few and the oppression of the many. It is the means by which the crisis of mass urbanization is solved in Latin America, through the mass media, so that the majority are pacified and resigned to their lot of poverty. In all of these areas we are talking about the creation of the masses, so that ideology[n] becomes the making of mechanized, non-thinking members of a society, who act in support of the status quo of their social position.

Theology enters the scene in that it, too, is affected by ideology[n], so that it unwittingly contributes to the maintaining of the status quo of the poor in Latin America. "When we view religion under the lens of ideological suspicion, it shows up . . . as a specific interpretation of Scripture imposed by the ruling classes in order to maintain their exploitation--though this intention may never be made explicit."[4] We have already seen at the end of the preceding chapter how the Church in Latin America is struggling to be the Church of the masses, and how this sociological observation exposes it as maintaining

the status quo of the rich and the poor. Now we
have to develop further the theology of Church
and how it unwittingly grows under the influence
of ideology[n] which puts massification before all
else.

Segundo maintains that there are three
assumptions of theology about the Church which
make ecclesiology a hidden form of ideology[n].
First of all, there is the assumption that the
Church has been fashioned for the benefit of
those who belong to it as an institution.
Secondly, there is the assumption that the
universality of the Church is to be quantitative. Finally, there is the assumption that
the Church is always the best place for obtaining salvation. Our author maintains that these
assumptions are incorrect and must be altered.[5]

Basically, all three assumptions revolve
around the particular concept that one has of
universality, a quantitative concept, so that
the first and the third points are dependent
upon the second. Our author points out that in
recent times Karl Barth already saw the quantitative conception of ecclesial universality as
dangerous for Christianity. He showed that it
cannot account for the fact that a pastoral plan
in that direction has always failed, and it can
scarcely account for the contradictory situation of having so many in unbelief or indifference, so that they remain outside the Church
and, on this theory, outside salvation intended
for all.

I do not believe I am mistaken in
saying that Karl Barth, well into the
twentieth century, is the first important
theologian to recognize it as a contradiction, up to the point of breaking not
only with the Catholic tradition, but also
with the Lutheran, and to exclude the act
of faith, or simply faith, as condition
for justification, thus making it indication of justification, but not justification;

knowledge of justification, but not restrictive condition of justification, and thus giving it its total universality.[6]

A quick glance at history shows that the notion of the Church's universality should not be conceived quantitatively.[7] Even in the first centuries the pagans had the question of how a small, historically conditioned Church could be the unique source of salvation. For example, Celsus and Porfirius asked about the salvation of the people who came before the Church. Why did Christ come so late? Likewise, within the primitive Church there was the impression of being a small minority group. Even St. Paul says Christianity is a sect of Judaism.

It seems that from the first the Church is to be incarnate as Christ was, and that this incarnation is to be taken seriously. Incarnation is a compromise of abstract universality into the concreteness of history. Every serious incarnation is a placing of oneself in all the determinisms and all the limitations of time, place, and people within history. The Church has always been and always will be a particular group incarnate in history, and so it should not be conceived as universal in quantitative extension.

According to Segundo, the universality of the Church has to be understood in another sense, namely, that the Church was made for all men and women, even before it existed and independently of its numbers. The Church is destined for the service of humanity. "The providence of God in the previous centuries was not occupied with any other thing than the Church, with that Church which would comprise all men from the beginning of humanity, because all would have been created for it, although on the other hand it would be a particular reality and, by the same token, destined for the service of total humanity, as Pius XII said."[8]

In elaborating further on this service of humanity Segundo makes clearer the ways in which he wants to move away from a Church of the masses toward one of a minority. He speaks of a new kind of Christian universality, one that is a functional service. He conceives of three possibilities in this direction. The first is a kind of dialogue between masses and minorities on a religious level, separated from the political level. "It is that which situates the universal function of Christianity in the conversion of the heart, that is, in individual conversion."[9]

The presupposition behind this conception is that the change of structures will be meaningless without a change of heart. The change of heart will not necessarily be in each and every person, but will be in a good part of humanity. This change of heart will not itself have a political content, but it will have an indirect political "reflex" which "is the guarantee by humanism of the necessary political changes."[10] The role of the Church will be the role of this minority which can bring about the religious conversion of the masses, even if the masses do not themselves become the Church. "The religious conversion of a Christian minority constitutes a leaven and a leaven necessary for every political change which pretends, in one way or another, to walk toward the utopia of the kingdom."[11]

A second view of universality, which seems opposed to this first view, also maintains a dialectic between the masses and the minorities, but does not, in actuality, carry it out in practice. It really gives minority characteristics (creativity, decisiveness, complexity, etc.) to the masses, so that it moves from a pejorative view of the masses to a positive view. This comes about through an identification of the Church with the oppressed in such a way that genuine conversion must include the political realm and must include change of structures. However, this conversion and change do not come through the activity of a minority, but through the masses conceived with non-massive traits. Thus, we have in this view also an opposition to the quantitative universality of the Church, since the stress is on the qualitative. It does seem, however, that the numerical extension of the Church is present along with the qualitative. The minority dimension of the Church is identical with its massive dimension.[12]

Neither of the above forms of the Church's universality seem satisfying to Segundo. He opts for a third form which has the good elements of the other two, along with some differences. In common with the first view, he believes that the ecclesial function must be that of a critical minority. However, along with the second view, he believes that the critical function should not separate the transcendent aspects of the gospel from the immanent, political aspects. This gives him a third form of qualitative ecclesial universality which sees the reciprocity between conversion of heart and the change of political structures, but does not believe that the messianic mission of bringing this about can be achieved by the masses. It can only be a minority function.

We have here all the complexity of this third conception. Political organization on the level of the masses constitutes a fundamental Christian task. However, the distinctive element which the Christian brings to this work is a lack of confidence, based on revelation, in the tendency, because of the masses and massive conduct, to absolutize the structures obtained.[13]

We can see, then, that Segundo proposes a view of the Church that conceives it theologically as still universal in scope, but in a qualitative sense rather than in a quantitative sense. He is still strong for a Church that is composed of a minority in society, a minority that comprises committed, creative Christians who act as leaven and salt among the masses without ever hoping to extend Christianity numerically among all those masses. Only in this way does theology break away from ideological enslavement. Christianity conceived as a minority is a more fruitful theology which can refute the assumptions of Latin American pastoral practice regarding the Church's universal role, a practice that makes the Church a promoter of the status quo and the political oppression of the poor.

Segundo himself sums up his theology on this point:

1. The exigencies of the gospel message are minority exigencies by their very nature and definition.

2. This does not point towards the maintenance of the interests of a small, self-enclosed group but rather towards the liberation of humanity--of the masses.

3. The liberation in question does not entail destroying the quantitative proportion existing between masses and minorities, since that remains equally operative in the Christian life. Still less does it entail reducing the exigencies of the gospel message to some minimal mass level so as to win the adhesion of the masses.

4. This minority effort among the masses is not meant to impose elitist demands on the latter, nor is it meant to construct a society based on minority exigencies. The aim is to create, for oneself and others, new forms of energy that will permit lines of conduct that are necessarily mechanized to serve as the basis for new and more creative possibilities of a minority character in each and every human being.[14]

Theology and Positive Ideology

From all that we have seen thus far we might draw the conclusion that ideology is basically a negative ingredient of society, and that theology must try at all costs to avoid becoming a hidden ideology[n]. There are, in fact, some theologians who claim that all of theology must be deideologized. For instance, Segundo describes the attitude of Edward Schillebeeckx, who claims that theology can never be ideological in the Marxist sense of the term, because it must be simply the application of the pure word of God to the present life situation. "He seems to hold the naive belief that the word of God is applied to human realities inside some antiseptic laboratory that is totally immune to the ideological tendencies and struggles of the present day."[15]

On the contrary, Segundo holds that there is a positive side to ideology and a necessary link between faith or theology and ideology. In fact, he actually uses the same word ideology in a totally different meaning from ideology[n]. The shift of meaning behind the same word can lead to confusion, if one is not forewarned. We will refer to Segundo's positive meaning of the word as ideology[p].

Our author explains why there is need for ideology[p]. For one thing, Christianity is destined to be elaborated in history, and history supposes continuity. Now if history is to have continuity, then it requires the existence of the masses, even if they are not destined, as masses, to become Christian. For Segundo, it is a paradox that the masses are destined to reject Christianity, yet history, if it is to be recapitulated in Christ, requires continuity through these very same masses.

If there were no masses, there would be no sociological laws, no historical groupings, no continuity in history. "Yes, there is total failure of the message of Christ on the part of the mass (the opposition Christ-world), given that its inertia, its internal structure clashes with the essential structure of Christianity; but this failure has a function in history, and certainly in the history which leads to Christ."[16] Now if there is failure in terms of the masses, yet the masses are essential for the Christian message in history, then ideology^p is also essential, for it is the mechanism of action of the masses.

Thus, it is a question of criticizing the ideology^p, of bringing it to consciousness, of relativizing it, of changing it, but it is not a question of eliminating it. Likewise, theology must beware of becoming a hidden ideology^n, which can happen when it is not critical in attitude toward ideology^p, but it must always inevitably have to work hand in hand with ideologies^p.

Segundo gives a positive definition of ideology in this sense. "By 'ideology' here I am simply referring to the system of goals and means that serves as the necessary backdrop for any human option or line of action."[17] It is the recognition that every life has its presuppositions as to what is important and what should be sought at what price and effort. Our author himself gives the example of Caligula in Albert Camus' play, who tried to root out all physical and emotional bonds in his search for happiness, because he felt that human beings are never consistent in their pursuit of these goals in life. They are distracted by these human bonds. Caligula found that his giving up of all presuppositions regarding life finally left him uninterested in life itself, and brought his death rather than his happiness. Segundo's conclusion is: "No human being can experience in advance whether life is worth the trouble of being lived and in what way it might be worthwhile. . . . Real life for a human being presupposes a nonempirical choice of some ideal

100

that one presumes will be satisfying."[18]

Ideology^n becomes a negative and a harmful element of society when the presuppositions become absolute, distort the reality of life, and become a means of maintaining the status quo of a dominant group in society. It is to prevent this that theology has a role to play, if it functions well, and does not become a hidden ideology^n itself. In this regard it is interesting now to develop more at length the interrelationship between faith (and theology) and ideology^p. For although theology may be itself a hidden ideology^n, the contrary is not true: theology is not an ideology^p, and must work in a dialectical relationship with such ideology^p. They have points in common, they need each other, yet they are also to be distinguished.

Segundo feels that a phenomenological analysis of faith and ideology^p gives the sense of their dialectical relationship better than simple definitions which are artificial and which leave aside the complexities of real existence. Phenomenologically, faith and ideology^p have common origins, and diversify only as they develop in a person. To begin with--and recall Caligula above--every person has a conscious or unconscious structure of life which gives coherency and logic to what one does. Call it ideology^p, because it is a system of means and ends, often unconscious. Call the same thing faith, because it is not verifiable beforehand, and requires trust in other people. As Segundo sums it up at this first stage of life:

. . . It is the identification of faith and ideology. Both organize life in view of a meaning that makes it worth the trouble; both tell what is important and what is not; both mark the prices one has to pay in order to be happy. But both also proceed out of subjective risk, or as it were, out of faith in witnesses.[19]

Faith and ideology[p] begin to be distinguished as the vision of life gets more complex,
and as one moves away from the primary witnesses, such as parents, teachers, etc. Other
witnesses enter the scene who challenge the
objectivity of the initial witnesses or of the
initial structures of life. Sometimes, instead
of these witnesses, or accompanying them, is a
moment of crisis. One experiences failure, which
prevents coherency in the system, or one sees
failure in others, which brings the same effects.
It all leads to a search for objectivity and to
a movement toward systems where faith and
ideology[p] are distinguished but interrelated.

The search for more objectivity regarding
valuable life structures takes two directions.
One search is for efficacy, i.e., finding the
means to overcome failure and to truly arrive at
the values one desires. The other search is for
significance, i.e., arriving at what is truly of
value, even to the point of understanding the
value of failure itself. The first search is
for ideology[p]. Segundo defines it once again,
not really in a way opposed to the positive
definition we have already given, but simply
spelling it out in terms of efficacy: "Ideologies are always presented in history as coherent
systems in order to act in the direction of
efficacy."[20] The second search is for faith,
defined in this context as the search for truth
and for ultimate values of life within the
context of on-going history.[21]

Faith and ideology[p] need each other.
Significance would be stupid if one did not
search for efficacy. Efficacy would be frus-
trating if there were no significance to it.
Faith works only through ideologies, even as it
relativized every ideology[p]. First of all, it
works through ideology[p]. While faith is permanent and unique, and while it puts us in
touch with the absolute, it can only express
itself in terms of the changing and the relative
in history. "If someone were to ask me what I

102

have derived from my faith-inspired encounter as a clear-cut, absolute truth that can validly give orientation to my concrete life, then my honest response should be: nothing."[22]

What is absolute in Christian faith is the adherence of the person to Jesus Christ. "The search for significance is not a question of confiding oneself in something abstract, but in someone who in history gives himself as absolute value. In the ultimate term it is in God [through Jesus] who gives the absolute significance of human existence."[23] However, what this means in context is to be developed constantly in history. There is no fixed and final "deposit of revelation" in a static sense. In fact, the very adherence to Jesus can be affirmed and strengthened only as it strives to do this effectively in time and place. In other words, values of significance would not only have to be applied efficaciously, but would not even be significant if not also effective.

Segundo draws on H. R. Niebuhr to allay the fears that such relativism leads to subjectivism and to scepticism. One need not doubt the reality of what one sees just because one is conditioned by the standpoint from which one sees what one does. "It is not apparent that one who knows that his concepts are not universal must also doubt that they are concepts of the universal, or that one who understands how all his experience is historically mediated must believe that nothing is mediated through history."[24]

What we have been saying about faith and theology is Segundo's own way of enunciating a basic principle of all of liberation theology, namely, that theology is reflection on praxis. "Praxis, however, is not merely action. Praxis is action plus theory for action."[25] It is action with its ideologyᵖ, action with its coherent system that makes the action truly

103

effective. Now such ideology does not yet have its values in any explicit way. It simply pre-supposes the values and seeks to attain them. When it becomes a system that propounds its own value system as well as its means and ends, then it becomes ideology^n. Good ideology^p must look elsewhere for its system of values, and that can be the role of theology from a Christian's point of view.

Now, as Segundo has been emphasizing in all of the writing that we have analyzed, his perspective is from the point of view of commitment to the poor in Latin America. The praxis that we have been talking about is the praxis of liberating the poor. We are at a particular point in history, a particular time and place and circumstance. The ideology^p of this praxis can vary, but Segundo believes that the one most effective is Marxism, as the social analysis that we have done in chapter two has indicated.

It is to this praxis, to this historical situation, that Segundo believes theology must speak. He observes that Marxism does not prove its values. It supposes a fundamental harmony of values as reason for liberating the poor, e.g., the need for social justice, etc. Marxism as an ideology^p simply develops the effective means for attaining these values which it assumes. Marxism goes astray when it tries to become a total system and view of life, and seeks to formulate its own values. Segundo would not accept this attempt. He acknowledges Marxism as an ideology^p, and then turns to theology to formulate explicitly the values of life that are worth seeking on behalf of the poor.

The theology that he is talking about, therefore, is not abstract and ethereal. It must speak to history, and that means to the poor in Latin America. That means it must keep in touch with ideology^p, so that its significance may be efficacious to life.

104

It is an eternal tendency of Christians
to believe that in order to be Christian
they already have the effective solution to
human problems, or that they have a proper
ideology which is founded on the faith and
which would be contrary, for example, to
the Marxist one.
The gospel not only supposes values, but
makes them explicit. It gives objective
understanding of the significance of existence, . . . but it is not an ideological
system which says to me what I must do in
each concrete case in order to convert these
values into reality. . . .
However, from this we cannot conclude
that we must reject ideologies, but, to the
complete contrary, that Christianity is
nothing without ideology. It is made clear
by an ideology.[26]

In the rest of this chapter we will consider what theology says to Marxist ideology[p],
to the social analysis of the first chapter, to
the praxis of the poor in the Latin American
scene. According to Segundo, a theology that
speaks as he describes it to Marxism is the
only viable theology in the Latin American context. "It makes no Christian sense at all to
try to separate ideologies from faith in order
to safeguard and preserve the latter. Without
ideologies faith is as dead as a doornail, and
for the same reason that James offers in his
epistle: it is totally impracticable."[27]

Before we launch into this survey of some
points of Segundo's theology, however, we must
first make the point that this theology will not
only speak to and affirm Marxist ideology[p].
According to Segundo, it will also challenge the
ideology[p] and make it relative. We mentioned
before that faith and ideology[p] were in dialectic. Faith works through ideology[p], but it also
needs to be distinguished from it. It transcends ideology[p].

Our author makes the keen observation: "Every ideology seems to go through a similar process in history. It begins as a protest against the limitations and ineffectiveness of a prior ideology and it ends up as a crusty refusal to give way to some newer ideology that is on the rise."[28] Faith can help that movement to newer and better ideologies^p as an on-going process in history, because faith is the search for values which move human existence to higher and higher levels, toward ultimate value. It urges one not to remain in any ideology^p as ultimate.

This does not mean, of course, that faith operates independently of ideology^p. It needs ideology^p as the means to make its values effective. However, it does not rest in any particular ideology^p as ultimate. Hence, the dialectical relationship of faith and ideology^p: "Maintaining the structure of values [faith] one has to enrich the system of means [ideology^p], making this system more coherent, more complex, more efficacious for obtaining the goal which indicates significance."[29]

Continuity in Eschatology

To this point we have seen the third step of Segundo's hermeneutic circle from a negative approach (theology breaks the hermeneutic circle of renewed Scriptural exegesis by not renewing its own approach; it absolutizes one ideology^n), and we have seen the general statement that theology should renew itself in view of changing ideologies^p. Now we can study particular statements of theology that show its dialectic with Marxism's ideology^p, and its new statements of the Christian message in favor of the poor. We will illustrate how Segundo makes positive application of the third step of his hermeneutic circle in his own writings.

Our discussion of the Church in the end
of the last chapter of our study, and the ecclesiology that we have criticized at the beginning
of this chapter are a helpful start in the
formulation of Segundo's theology of liberation.
By taking an approach that accounts for the
social analysis of the Church, and that does
not look to a quantitative universality for the
Church, we have the beginnings of a renewed
theology that will renew also our exegesis of
Scripture and what it says to Christian ethics.

The central focus of the theology advocated by Segundo is concerned with eschatology.
One of the chief effects of renewing an ecclesiology in the light of social analysis and
ideology[p] is a stronger affirmation of this
world reality. This becomes clear if we compare
the two views toward the Church, which revolve
around whether universality is quantitative or
not. The view of the Church which sees its
mission as a quantitative extension of membership puts the emphasis on the Church itself as
the major reality of life, and diminishes the
importance of the world.

In this first view of the Church its own
functions are the unique and absolute values,
and all others are subordinated to these. All
problems are considered less important than
those of acquiring and accepting these values.
Church doctrine is taken seriously as a deduction from a rational view of the world, and is
applied to the world and its structures. The
dialogue is mostly one way. The Church is
assumed to have all the answers to life's
problems, and the world is not seen as having
value in itself. In fact, the important world
is seen as hidden and above this life. The
Church shows how to reach it through membership
in its external, visible structures. Segundo
sums up this position well:

Up to now we have insisted on what
appears to me as the radical, and certainly

107

the theological fault of the first position:
the unawareness of the religious in the
apparently profane, temporal and human. The
religious is distinguished from the profane
in order to deprive the latter of all decisive value, of all value for salvation.[30]

In contrast to this view of the Church and
its resultant view of the world, Segundo proposes
the view which puts more emphasis on the quality
of Church membership among a minority in society.
This makes the universal role of the Church that
of service to humanity. According to Segundo,
this becomes an affirmation of this world
reality in a continuous eschatology.

The Church is seen as one among many
functions in the world, all of which are important
and necessary. The Church is seen as having some
solutions to the world's problems, but these are
all part of the same reality which it shares with
the world. Church doctrine is less a deduction
of reasoning and more a sensibility to world
reality, without being illogical. It takes from
the social reality and responds to it. The
primary emphasis is not internal to the Church,
but is centered on the world, and the Church is
to live human reality authentically, without
categories that deform it. There is truly a
dialogue, for the world has value of itself, and
can teach the Church. In this view,

the great religious revolution of Christianity has been the abolition of the profane.
And this is not in favor of the religious, as
the first conception would demand, but in
favor of the absolute religious value of what
we call profane.[31]

In this second view of the Church there is
a delicate balance to be maintained between the
Church and the world. It is the balance between
the Church as "little flock" and as universal
community at the service of humanity. The two
dangers that this view encounters are, firstly,

not taking the Church seriously enough in its role before the world, and secondly, making the temporal so autonomous that it is not sacred in its own way, and does not allow the Church to enter into its history. Both of these dangers lead to a theory of progress which makes a radical separation between the sacred and the profane. That theory removes the Church from history. In the long run it leads to the same problem as the first view of the Church, seeing the religious sphere as just one sphere of life, and denying the revolutionary aspects of Christianity as transforming this world and being involved with historical tasks and realities.[32]

Pastorally, the false theory of progress shows in the laity working with non-believers in the temporal sphere as if this sphere had no connection with their Christian faith. They do not want to live their daily life simply as obedience to the institution of the Church, as if the authority of the Church dictated what was to be done in the temporal sphere (the first view of Church in the world as quantitatively universal). Yet, neither do they see how their Christian faith brings anything of relevance to the world. Thus, this continuity in eschatology, in Segundo's vision of liberation theology, must be a delicate balance--a dialectic--between the true autonomy of the temporal in this world reality, and the universality of the Church within that history.

If I am of the Church in order to be able to be more perfectly man among men, I cannot prescind from the Church when I work with men among men. And on the other hand the Church cannot pretend to reduce me to her specific function as the only worthwhile task, given that her very mission is to be at the service of all the people of God.
This is the essential dialectic, the tension without which the Church cannot be understood nor live.[33]

Another way of describing this emphasis on the continuity in eschatology and on this world reality is in terms of the relationship between the natural and the supernatural. Segundo believes that a better response of theology to social analysis and praxis of the poor is a revision that has taken place in present days of the theology of grace. In the past there was a tendency to oversimplify the view of the supernatural. One saw it as departing from what is already human to another state. This sort of "higher existence" comprised an entire system of realities: instruments, habits, values, and hopes. "And, by supposition, only one step separates this conception from the other in which the merely human values and the merely natural hopes are declared of second rank and as a consequence, compared with the supernatural, are declared false."[34]

Since Vatican Council II this separation of the natural and supernatural into separate or autonomous spheres has been changed, so that they are really seen as one reality. That does not mean that the natural has been suppressed. It is simply recognition of the supernatural as a gift that orders all of humanity's life and existence toward its goal.

Thinking of the supernatural as gift leads one to associate a "before" and an "after" with the gift, and this is what has created a dichotomy between nature and grace. In the past we assumed that we could see a change that grace worked in a person, or could compare one who was graced with one who was not. (One assumed this was the difference between a Christian and a non-Christian.) The idea of gift also bespoke scarcity, and so it was simply assumed that not all shared it, again leading to a separation of nature and supernature.

In reality, however, gift can be part of every person's existence without being any less a gift. Likewise, it can be possessed from the

110

beginning of one's existence, so that there is no "before" or "after" in chronological terms. In this way, the concept of supernatural is simply a way of saying that man and woman's nature is gifted with a reality that moves it more surely and more deeply toward the goal of its existence. "In other words, the purely natural is a limit-concept (a possibility which it is necessary to keep in mind in order to understand and remember that the gift is a gift), but not a concept which has a real, historical content, which means a concept that aims at something which it would be possible to come across or to imagine concretely in our history."[35]

Now the end product of such a unity between nature and grace is the affirmation of this world reality and a continuity in eschatology. The supernatural is not a goal outside of humanity's present life, nor is this natural worldly existence something to be superseded entirely. There is only one reality, the present, and what is most gratuitous is also internal to humanity's own structure and is most necessary for ultimate human happiness. "Can it not be said, with apparent right, that the essence of personal being consists precisely in being ordained, by (concrete) nature, to personal communion with God in love, and to be able to receive this same love as free gift? But does the same not happen in earthly love?"[36]

Segundo offers some specific instances of what the world offers to the Church and the Christian message, thus fostering a renewal in theology with a stress on human values. He begins such considerations with the statement stressing that the Church must truly dialogue, and not just cooperate with the world as if the Church already had full possession of the truth. Moreover, the dialogue is with the world in its concrete reality. "The world in general is not [concrete interlocutor]. It is rather this precise world in which we move, which supposes

111

that one day even near it might have in its hands the power to destroy itself."[37]

This particular world is constantly moving in history, so it is not possible to enumerate all that it says to the Church as some static presentation. Segundo selects some points that have less particularity to limited situations, and which seem to be the more decisive today in the world. All of the points are realizations of the human value of love, and challenge the Church to deepen its own awareness of this central Christian virtue.

First of all, the world today shows a constant acceleration of energy with which humanity works to solve its problems and to meet its needs. Humanity searches and finds more and more hidden resources. As a consequence, the world is being made more and more artificial, more "human," more dependent on humanity itself. It also means that there must be more respect for one's fellow person. The interdependence of humanity also takes on a global aspect, not out of caprice or ideology[n], but out of necessity. "For the first time in human history, people scattered all over the world can be the object of our love because now they are no longer faceless entities. We know how they live, how they think, how they suffer."[38]

Another necessary dimension of today's world is the growing need for placing the fate of all in the hands of all. The world can destroy itself now. It is also put together in such a way that the resolution of a problem in one place can create disequilibrium elsewhere. Geographic isolation is no longer possible. Human love, therefore, becomes a shared responsibility. It leads to its fullest expression in world socialization. We are all interconnected, and can no longer be neutral in our actions. We are either collaborators in the true meaning of love today, or accomplices in its absence.[39]

As Segundo analyzes all this, the world presents to the Church a presence of Christ more fitting than his continued physical presence. It is a world more mature, presenting a Christ who is more and more the center of history through love. What the world brings, however, is incomplete, and offers questions which the Church needs to answer as part of the total theological picture. For one thing, the movement of love has risks. When one moves beyond the first stages, one loses autonomy and comes to depend on another. The question arises as to whether this is worth the risk. It is Christian faith which answers yes to that question. Likewise, the search for love is never quite completed, and one wonders whether perseverance is possible. Once again, Christian faith brings with it a hope and a certainty, even while it searches along with the rest of the world for the solution to human problems.[40]

Eschatology and the Kingdom

It is not difficult to see the jump that can be made from the Church-world dialogue or the natural-supernatural synthesis to the concerns of the poor and oppressed. In that way we can already see how, for Segundo, social analysis prepares the way for theology, and theology speaks to the concerns of social analysis and ideology[p]. However, what we have seen thus far still does not seem to capture completely the links between theology and ideology[p] as Segundo would want them.

His concern is that the links might be seen as the joining of two separate fields, which still remain extrinsic to one another in essence. His preference is that theology must in the long run choose one particular ideology[p] or social analysis, and cannot remain aloof to any or all political choices. Theology and ideology[p] are distinct, but they have interests which bind them intrinsically to each other.

Study of this element of Segundo's thought leads us further into his eschatological views, especially as they concern his concept of the kingdom of God.

Our author's views toward the kingdom of God are in line with what he believes about the Church, the supernatural, and the life of grace. None of these realities is divorced from this life and history. Neither is the kingdom of God. It is not an other-worldly reality, although it cannot be identified with just this world. Thus, Segundo disfavors the view that holds for a difference of finalities between the kingdom of God and temporal progress. He sees it as less tenable from the documents of Vatican Council II and from the Bible.[41]

In terms of H. R. Niebuhr's categories, there seems to be an ambiguity in Segundo's position. We will see later in his treatment of some biblical themes, that he seems to propose a Christ-transforming-culture model. In his treatment of the teaching on the kingdom, however, he seems to opt for a Christ-of-culture model. According to Segundo, a better view of the kingdom of God would be to see it as sharing the same finality as temporal progress.[42] Both have the same identical goal of eternal life which begins now and culminates in eternity. The Christian may know this explicitly, but it is the same progress for the entire universe. Segundo objects to distinguishing temporal progress from the growth of the kingdom of God:

Does the Council [Vatican II] not define by chance the reign of Christ as a reign of justice, of love and of peace? And what else seeks the construction of history made precisely out of our efforts in the order of human dignity, of love, of fraternal union, of freedom, all that which we are going to meet on the new earth? To what then does temporal progress refer? What is this human progress which has to be

114

distinguished carefully from the coming of
the kingdom of God?[43]

Our author cites Harvey Cox in his Secular
City as a further warning against taking a
theology of history away from a theology of the
kingdom. He points out that Cox gives three
reasons why the two theologies are often
separated. First of all, the kingdom of God is
seen as God's work alone, while the secular city
is seen as human work. Secondly, the kingdom is
seen as a demand for repentance, while the
secular city is the place for abilities and for
aptitude. Finally, the kingdom is seen as above
and later, while the secular city is in this
world.[44]

These false views toward the kingdom can
be overcome by recognizing the supernatural as
perfection of the very human, and not beyond the
human. Eternal life, the culmination of grace,
is the final goal of the human life itself, and
is joined intrinsically to this life. Segundo
points out, for instance, that we do not, and
cannot know anything about the next life apart
from this one. One is in some way predisposed
to react against the placing of another life as
a reward for living this one. It is as if it
were no reward at all. Eternal life must be in
some way the putting on of immortality of this
being and existence rather than some totally
new existence separated from now.[45]

To make the same point, Segundo also
observes a psychological fact, namely, that
the offering of only another life as a consolation for the disappearance of this life would
be no real consolation at all. No one, for
instance, who loses a loved one would find that
as a consolation. Nor would it be a genuine
service of Christianity to mankind to offer a
substitution for the problem. Christian hope
must say something about this life of ours, and
the kingdom must speak to this life in some
way.[46] Christian hope would be disinterested,

115

but only in the sense that it has no other interest than the results of what human life should achieve. It does not mean lack of interest in this life, or interest in another result beyond this life. As our author observes, "One who constructs seeks passionately that construction. And, for all that, he is not interested."[47]

In trying to develop an adequate concept of the kingdom, Segundo tries to balance an incarnational approach with that of the so-called eschatological approach. In this definition of the terms, the eschatologist would deny the role of history, would claim that we are in the end times, would see all of life now as under judgment, and would see no progress in history. According to our author, this view must be balanced or modified by the incarnational approach, which says that historical process is not yet terminated, although it is complete in its roots in Christ. It says also that we are in the end times, and each individual stands in judgment before Christ. Yet, there is room for more universal possibilities of love in each succeeding generation. We must distinguish what can accumulate in history from what cannot. The theology of the kingdom is ultimately a synthesis of the eschatological and incarnational views of the world. The kingdom of God must be the continuation of what we live now in history.[48]

Once we have appreciated this definition of the kingdom of God as being the continuation and completion of what we live now, then we have the basis for which Segundo says a true theology of the kingdom demands that we also make political choices. Theology cannot remain indifferent to any or all ideologies[p]. Thus, he cites with partial approval the statement by Johannes Metz: "Then indeed, what has been said up to now draws us to the conclusion that 'it is necessary, from the theological point of view, to reunite what has been unfortunately separated in the theological

conscience for a long time, namely, <u>transcend-</u>
<u>ence and the future</u>,' or, what is the same,
eternal life and the building of history."[49]

"According to Metz, '. . . what distinguishes "Christian eschatology" from the
ideologies of the future in the East and West,
is not that it knows more, but that it knows
less about the future which mankind is trying
to discern, and that it persists in its lack of
that knowledge.'"[50] In this view a theology of
the kingdom relativizes every ideological^p
system and knows less about capitalism or
socialism than any of the theorists in either
system. The claim of every political theology
or theology of revolution is that we must beware
of a premature desire for the kingdom of God and
that we must relativize everything in the face
of that absolute reality. Now every ideology^p
is the risk of such absolutization, so the
theology of the kingdom cannot settle on any
particular ideology^p.

According to Segundo, this fear of abso-
lutizing an ideology^p ends up by being a conservative ideology^n maintaining the status quo.
Moreover, humanity must construct the kingdom
from within history now, so ideology^p must be
chosen. Otherwise there would be no causal
relationship between the kingdom and humanity's
work for it.

German political theology chooses with
the utmost care the terms which indicate
this relationship between a relative political order and the absolute eschatological
order: anticipation (Moltmann), analogical
image or analogy (Weth) and outline (Metz).
All these terms systematically and expressly
reject every idea of causality.
But who consecrates his life to an
"analogy"? Who dies for an "outline"?
Who moves a human mass, a whole people, in
the name of an "anticipation"?[51]

On Segundo's view the eschatology of
kingdom does not affect the content of theology,
so that it rejects every ideology^p as relative.
Rather, particular ideologies^p are drawn into
the absolute nature of the kingdom as affecting
it. The eschatology of the kingdom affects the
form of theology, i.e., the way in which it
accepts absolute commitments. It avoids having
the ideology^p degenerate into rigidity, or
sacralizing of the present order, but it does
make particular commitments in the present
order.

Much of political theology's aloofness
from any particular ideology^p stems from the
application of Luther's theory of justification
by faith alone. Rudolf Weth is cited as an
example in his discussions of the kingdom. He
says the kingdom is totally God's work. It is
already prepared for humanity, and the work of
humanity is simply to prepare itself to enter
this kingdom. This is obtained by faith alone,
and not by works. According to Segundo this
excludes automatically any options among socio-
political systems which try to prepare the
kingdom in a causal relationship. It seems
also that Roman Catholic theology in Europe is
moving closer to this kind of political
theology. Henri de Lavalette is cited as an
example.[52]

In contrast to this approach, Segundo
maintains that, whatever its merits for the
individual Christian, the Lutheran theory of
justification by faith alone cannot be used for
all of theology, especially for the communal
demands of building the kingdom of God. First
of all, it does not pay enough attention to the
New Testament idea that faith is worked out in
love. Nor does it pay sufficient attention to
passages such as the Last Judgment parable,
where those who enter the kingdom are those who
do something and those who have a causal link to
the kingdom.

Segundo observes that, if the kingdom is to be torn away from utopian notions and placed squarely among men and women, then the biblical passages "have no meaning if one begins from an *a priori* position that the kingdom is already built in all its perfection, and only awaits the entry into it of every man by faith."[53] That means political choices and particularly ideologies[p], even if they are incomplete and need to be criticized and constantly reformed. "What is at stake [in political options], in a fragmentary fashion if you like, is the eschatological Kingdom itself, whose realization and revelation are awaited with anguish by the whole universe."[54]

As a final conclusion of all of his considerations of the kingdom, Segundo can assert that there is a difference between the Church's involvement with the political right or political left. Segundo makes the claim that one cannot assert, as de Lavalette would want to do, that Christian theology teaches an indifference to the right or left in the same way that it teaches an indifference to male or female in Christ Jesus.[55] Eschatology does not lead one to find a middle course. It should rather lead to political choices. According to Segundo, given the present options for alleviating the poor, especially after the failure of the theory of development and after the other social analysis that we saw in chapter two, the choice should be for the left or for Marxist socialism, at least in the present history.

Segundo defines the left as: "the conquest of that which is still without form, of that which is still unrealized, of that which is still in a state of utopia."[56] In other words, it is a permanent openness of society to the future and is centered on historical sensibility. "For that very reason the sensibility of the left is an intrinsic feature of an authentic theology."[57] And so, the eschatology of the kingdom leads to an even more necessary link between theology and ideology[p]. The question arises of whether this is an adequate definition of the left, and of just how tightly theology must be linked with such politics, but we defer this discussion until later.

Revolution and Violence

In this chapter we have been analyzing the second precondition of Segundo's hermeneutic circle, the ways in which theology can change its presuppositions and can dialogue with social analysis and ideology[p] as part of concrete life today. Before we conclude this analysis we do well to consider one specific area of theology and ideology because of its importance to liberation theology. Since this theology speaks from the perspective of commitment to the poor, and since it involves such an emphasis on political action, it touches of necessity the area of revolution and violence. While Segundo does not speak at length to this topic directly, we will consider his basic stance toward this very sensitive subject.

Segundo poses the question in the form of whether or not there is a specific contribution of theology to the evaluation of violence prior to actual ideological involvement in a revolution. On the basis of his view of theology as reflection on praxis, it would seem that theology cannot be prior to ideology[p] and action itself. In a debate with Hugo Assmann he agrees with this other liberation theologian that theology must be expressed in an ideology[p] before it can have anything to say to violence and revolution.

He agrees with Assmann, first of all, in a theoretic way. Recent studies in the historical conditionedness of the Bible and of theology itself have shown the need to demythologize these texts. Segundo says we also have need to deideologize these texts. All of our theological views toward revolution, especially when

120

they try to be "neutral" and to judge the action beforehand, tend to be hidden ideologies[n]. If we wish to get to a more deideologized form of theology, it makes more sense to begin with reality and with involvement in the life situation, and then have the Christian message speak to that. It is not really theology totally devoid of ideology[p], since that is impossible, but it is theology conscious of its ideology[p] rather than deceived by hidden presuppositions. It is theology deideologized from ideology[n] with conscious relation to ideology[p].[58]

Segundo also agrees with Assmann from an analysis of praxis that there is no specific theological contribution to violence and revolution before involvement in a specific revolution. Praxis involves means to ends. If a Christian were to anticipate beforehand what kind of praxis he would look for, he would seek one that could be critical of its ideological foundation, that could dialogue with other ideologies[p], and that could proceed in general from a minoritarian approach to action. Segundo says that the problem with this is that the Christian would want guarantees beforehand for this kind of praxis. Seeking the ideal as previous condition would prevent his involvement in any revolution, since such condition could never be guaranteed. Thus, theology of revolution cannot be fully formulated before involvement in revolution.[59]

The theology of the kingdom of God as Segundo develops it also necessitates involvement in praxis and in a specific ideology[p] of revolution and violence, since it would not be fully a theology of kingdom if humanity were not involved in it in a causal way. Violence and injustice already exist as a matter of fact in history, and the kingdom is to eliminate them. That will happen only if humanity works toward that. Theology of the kingdom does not spell out how that is done, but ideology[p] does. Thus,

If by supposition Christianity is not a prescription of cult, neither is it, therefore, indifferent in the face of violence, injustice or the alienation of man. The Christian message is a powerful call to man to oppose everything in society which negates, exploits or alienates the human being. Nevertheless, it has no special system to make these necessary changes, but sends the Christian to the world in order to seek with others, and among existing or possible undertakings, what seems the most effective for this end.[60]

On the other hand, while theology needs and expresses itself only through ideologies[p], it does also enter into dialectic with ideology. For one thing, it does relativize any particular ideology[p] of revolution and violence. Thus, Segundo parts company with Assmann and asserts that there is a specific contribution of theology to ideology[p] even before involvement in any particular revolutionary movement. "The text of Assmann suggests a special degree of sensitivity as previous condition for such evangelical understanding, which leads to commitment to 'the (singular) concrete revolutionary process,' . . . Why would a Marxist commitment be privileged as evangelical preunderstanding?"[61]

The Christian can and must collaborate in a revolution, but by virtue of his or her theology the Christian can only do this to a certain point. That limit will in fact save the Christian to give the best to one's fellow man and woman, and will help one draw the best out of the revolution itself. For every revolution tends to forget its high goals. It degenerates into revenge, or it oversimplifies the facts and becomes a hidden ideology[n], perpetuating the automatic functioning of the masses. Theology reminds every revolution, even a Marxist revolution, of its relative value. It recognizes the need for action by the masses, but acts always as a critical minority among the masses. The

122

Christians hold on in a balance between exaggerations, not overthrowing everything, while at the same time searching for true change.

Segundo sums up the way in which theology needs ideology[p], but relativizes it:

> On the one hand, there will not be lacking the unhappy person who shouts "Communist" when he sees that the communists applaud when he speaks of social reform. On the other hand, there will not be lacking also the unhappy person who comes to thank him: "Thanks to what you said on social reform I am now a revolutionary and am affiliated with the Communist Party."[62]

In developing the interplay between theology and the ideology[p] of revolution and violence, Segundo posits some points which show the role of violence, and some points which qualify it. We will look first to the positive side, where our author says violence is a necessary part of human values and of Christian love.

It is a part of human values in that it may be necessary to attain human rights. Our author observes that often human rights are declared as a way of maintaining possessions already attained by some at the expense of others. The rights are usually declared by those in possession of some privilege, and a quasi-Manichean mentality is established: the good are those who recognize the rights, and the bad are those who deny them. In such ambiguous circumstances, violence may be the only way of achieving the ideal that is still lacking for some. "The hero, if he is to be a real man, must give up the instruments of law and right and let his fate and that of his family depend on the speed of his draw. San Francisco 1948, forgetting the Wild West!"[63]

In accurately analyzing Christian love, we find that violence is a necessary ingredient.

Segundo finds the following as a disembodied absolutization: God is love, <u>therefore</u> the Christian is nonviolent, <u>therefore</u> he must not make use of violence. His observation is that in genuine incarnate love, even that love of Jesus, the exclusive opposition between love and violence is not historical.

The main reason for this denial of full opposition is that no love is totally love, and no egotism is totally egotism. Pure violence would be egotism, but no incarnate situation is sheer egotism. Thus, no concrete love can exist without some violence. Some examples are given of this violence as part of love.[64]

First of all, any denial of the unique and irreducible worth of each individual is a kind of violence. Now man and woman are in history that consists in developing more and more complex systems of interpersonal relationships in which the love for each individual can be created and sustained. However, this history is still in process, and to begin it one creates relationships with those neighbors close at hand. This often means the reduction of others to the status of things, to some kind of impersonal relationship. It is a necessary violence because even Christian love is imperfect.

There is also a violence in Christian love in that it must overcome the evils that block genuine interpersonal relationships. At the same time there is a sense that one cannot overcome all the evils at any given time, and this leads to the violence of having to choose some over others. By the same token there is the violence of having to restrain the egotistic desires of those whose evils are being overcome. They would have the tendency to want more and more of the effective powers of love for their own personal, selfish advantage.

Finally, there is the violence in love that comes from not having the resources to give each and every individual the fullest attention all the time. This necessitates having to judge people en masse, without knowing their personal history, background or attitudes. In summary, the basic problem with human love is that it is incarnational, which means that it is limited in time and place. That means violence at the very heart of love. It was the case even for Jesus, who was incarnate. "When the God who is love became man, he revealed himself as love in history. And, like any and all love in history, it sought fulfillment in the best possible proportion between its two inescapable components: violence and personal acknowledgement."[65]

The place of violence in theology, then, is not rejected. It is a question of degree. Segundo also offers some qualifications which restrict the use of violence without eliminating it altogether. He says, for example, that one should recognize that violence is a disturbing reality, and should not be covered over by polite use of words.

Who denies that these tasks are "dirty" and sad? What doubt is there that they are inhuman? That the responsibility for them falls principally on those who made them necessary is a truth which we admit in general. But it is not enough to "clean up" these tasks before the conscience of the one who has to execute them. For evident reasons politicians do not employ, in order to describe these tasks, words such as murder, treason, torture, vengeance, cruelty, because the final cause, the common good, the remote responsibility and the tragedy of everything cover--always in general--with a mantel of abstract value and tragic nobility each individual concrete act.[66]

Our author cites Karl Rahner concerning what should be the ingredients of Christian deportment, and concerning what should be considered even in violent revolution. Christian behavior should defend humanity from the fever of achieving its projects by brutal force, sacrificing one generation to the next. It recognizes that a person keeps dignity even if he or she is not able to make a visible contribution to the future. It does this even while recognizing that Christianity confers on work towards the future a radical and supreme seriousness, since it is the way of salvation itself.

The main point is whether or not the final demands of a revolution--the points made by Rahner--are already present in the first violent stages. Segundo does not answer this question definitively, but he does point out the difficulties of an affirmative answer.

The classical solution, one already knows, consists in imagining in the same man a doubling between today and tomorrow. It is in imagining that a man who has put his whole life to making the future come puts this in parenthesis in order to put the finishing touches to a victim, to throw a bomb among women and children. . . . Of course, this is not only the guerrilla. But it is him also. And in this is also the problem. Is this doubling real?[67]

Segundo points out that there are difficulties, morally and psychologically, in living two levels. He asks if there is enough justification to judge against the violence and injustice of a situation, and at the same time use the same methods of violence and injustice. He does not answer this, but shows the ambiguity involved with the use of violence.

Finally, our author points out that violent revolution also has the problem of hurting the innocent. Often enough a justification for violent revolution is that it will prevent the harm of many others who would suffer under unjust situations for many years to come. Segundo asks, "What greatness or smallness of humanity would suffice to personally justify the use of means which do not go directly against those responsible for the injustice?"[68] One cannot simply trade off some people for others, and so once again violence becomes an ambiguous activity.

With this final concrete example of violence and revolution we conclude our study of the second precondition for Segundo's hermeneutic circle, and the third step of his process toward renewed interpretation of the Scriptures. Social analysis and ideology[p] challenge theology. They bring ideological suspicion which leads theology to revise its formulations in the light of these analyses. Theology must speak to the life situation through particular ideologies[p], while at the same time relativizing any particular ideology[p]. Many of the same questions return to this section of our study that we raised in chapter two concerning social analysis. Does Segundo allow enough of a role for theology or does he put too much emphasis on ideology[p]? Is ideology[p] always the start or always prior to theology? Where is revelation? We will take up these questions in chapter five. For now we continue with Segundo's methodology. With the two preconditions and three steps that we have studied we can now approach the particular biblical passages used by Segundo to see how he concretely applies his hermeneutics from the perspective of commitment to the poor in Latin America. This is the topic of the next chapter.

CHAPTER III

NOTES

[1]Gustavo Gutierrez, A Theology of Liberation (Maryknoll, N.Y.: Orbis Books, 1973), p. 235.

[2]Roger Shinn, "Faith, Science, Ideology and the Nuclear Decision," Christianity and Crisis, February 5, 1979, p. 5. In this article Shinn offers a number of definitions of the word ideology. In fact, the view that he takes toward the word in the body of his article is not negative at all. We are borrowing here only what will help define Segundo's meaning.

[3]Jose Miguez Bonino, Doing Theology in a Revolutionary Situation (Philadelphia: Fortress Press, 1975), p. 94. We should observe here that Miguez Bonino also has a positive definition of ideology, which we are not using here. In this regard he is like Segundo and different from Gutierrez, cited in note 1, who uses utopia instead of ideology positively.

[4]Juan Luis Segundo, The Liberation of Theology (Maryknoll, N.Y.: Orbis Books, 1976), p. 16.

[5]Juan Luis Segundo, The Hidden Motives of Pastoral Action (Maryknoll, N.Y.: Orbis Books, 1978), pp. 70-77.

[6]Juan Luis Segundo, Masas y Minorías en la Dialéctica Divina de la Liberación (Buenos Aires: La Aurora, 1973), p. 9.

[7]Juan Luis Segundo, "La Función de la Iglesia," Perspectivas de Diálogo 1 (1965): 4-7.

[8]Ibid., p. 7.

[9]Segundo, Masas, p. 56.

[10]Ibid., p. 58.

128

[11] Ibid.

[12] Ibid., pp. 59-62.

[13] Ibid., p. 64.

[14] Segundo, Liberation, p. 231.

[15] Ibid., p. 7.

[16] Juan Luis Segundo, Función de la Iglesia en la Realidad Rioplatense (Montevideo: Barreiro y Ramos, 1962), p. 71.

[17] Segundo, Liberation, p. 102.

[18] Ibid., pp. 103-4.

[19] Juan Luis Segundo, "Fe e Ideología," Perspectivas de Diálogo 9 (1974): 228.

[20] Ibid., p. 231.

[21] Segundo, Liberation, p. 110.

[22] Ibid., p. 108.

[23] Segundo, "Fe e Ideología," p. 232.

[24] The Meaning of Revelation, cited by Segundo, Liberation, pp. 176-77.

[25] Juan Luis Segundo, "Statement by Juan Luis Segundo," in Theology in the Americas, ed. Sergio Torres and John Eagleson (Maryknoll, N.Y.: Orbis Books, 1976), p. 283.

[26] Segundo, "Fe e Ideología," p. 233.

[27] Segundo, Liberation, p. 121.

[28] Ibid., p. 126.

[29] Segundo, "Fe e Ideología," p. 232.

[30] Segundo, Rioplatense, p. 41.

[31] Ibid., p. 35.

[32] Ibid., pp. 55-63.

[33] Ibid., p. 49.

[34] Juan Luis Segundo, "La Vida Eterna," Perspectivas de Diálogo 2 (1967): 109.

[35] Ibid., p. 112.

[36] Karl Rahner, _Theological Investigations_, vol. 1, cited by Segundo, ibid., p. 113.

[37] Juan Luis Segundo, "El Diálogo: Iglesia-Mundo," _Perspectivas de Diálogo_ 1 (1966): 3.

[38] Juan Luis Segundo, _The Community Called Church_ (Maryknoll, N.Y.: Orbis Books, 1973), p. 100. This statement by Segundo needs to be compared with other statements such as the following from _Liberation_, p. 159: "We are able to love our neighbors to the extent that we keep other human beings from showing up as neighbors on our horizon." If we are not to accuse Segundo of contradiction here, we can interpret these statements as contrasting possibilities with actualities. In the first statement he is saying that our neighbor can be found from practically anywhere on the globe. He is not saying that we will love each and every individual all over the globe. In fact, the second statement says that when we actually love, we must make choices which limit whom we designate as neighbor. At least now the choices are not restricted geographically or culturally. We will treat the limits of love in the section on violence later in this chapter.

[39] Ibid., pp. 102-3.

[40] Ibid., pp. 50-58.

[41] Juan Luis Segundo, "Evangelización y Humanización: Progreso del Reino y Progreso Temporal," _Perspectivas de Diálogo_ 5 (1970): 10-12; 15.

[42] Segundo's idea of temporal progress is, of course, different from what is normally considered progress in Western culture and in the idea of progress of the first world theologians in the first half of this century. His notion is not tied to the theory of development or to capitalism. Rather, he borrows heavily from Teilhard de Chardin and adapts Teilhard's insights to a socialist perspective. More specifically, he uses what Teilhard said about the higher synthesis of energy into life and adapts that to

the Marxist concepts of masses and minorities. According to this theory, energy in the universe remains constant, but changes in its distribution. Superior bodies have a better distribution of energy, while at the same time are fighting the tendency of energy to degradation, i.e., to return to simpler and less usable forms. The primary expression of this higher synthesis is in life itself, which recapitulates the lower thresholds already attained in evolution, but also enables energy to be creative of new thresholds. The quantity of hominized energy is small, but is qualitatively greater. Another way of putting this is to say that life is a minority movement, and that inorganic matter is massive and, because of its tendency to degradation, is constantly against the probability of life. Mutations are improbable but are a step upward in evolution.

Now, what can be said of life can also be said of economics, and hence we come against the law of masses and minorities as further movement in evolution. Finally, all of this reaches its culmination in Christ who shows the ultimate possibilities for the personalized minority in the universe. Christianity is the "reflectively Christified portion of the universe," moving against the status quo and showing the improbable and the exceptional and the absolute future as final synthesis of evolution.

With this approach Segundo seems to combine evolution with revolution (the improbable and exceptional), but all within a framework of progress, since Segundo is optimistic about the synthesis as part of the destiny of this world reality. See De la Sociedad, pp. 155-73.

[43] Juan Luis Segundo, "Hacia un Exegesis Dinamica," Vispera 1 (1967): 83.

[44] Segundo, "La Vida Eterna," p. 88.

[45] Ibid., pp. 113-14.

[46] The case of the Thessalonians may serve as an example. In 1 Thessalonians Paul does

console the community with the offering of
another life. However, he also comes to
realize that true human consolation cannot
escape this life altogether. In 2 Thessalonians Paul needs to remind the community of
the obligation to work in this life as part of
the dimensions of Christian hope.

[47] Ibid., p. 114.

[48] Juan Luis Segundo, Grace and the Human
Condition (Maryknoll, N.Y.: Orbis Books, 1973),
pp. 122-27.

[49] The statement by Metz is contained in
an article by Ingo Hermann in Concilium, no. 16,
cited by Segundo, "La Vida Eterna," p. 114.

[50] Juan Luis Segundo, "Capitalism-
Socialism: A Theological Crux," Concilium 96
(1974): 110.

[51] Ibid., p. 112.

[52] Segundo, Masas, pp. 68-73.

[53] Segundo, "Capitalism-Socialism," p. 122.

[54] Ibid., p. 123.

[55] This claim by Segundo does not seem to
take into account passages of Scripture such as
the story of Jesus and the coin of tribute.
Perhaps Segundo's point would have been clarified
if he had dealt explicitly with such texts, but
he does not. We will have to discuss later on
whether he overstates the identification of the
gospel with a politics of the left. In any
case, his basic point here does not have to
ignore texts such as that of the coin of tribute.
Even though Jesus himself showed a relativity
toward any political system, he did not refrain
from criticizing authority. His indifference
to politics seemed of another kind than his
indifference to gender. For an interpretation
of Luke 20:20-26 that demands political judgments and not indifference, see Richard Cassidy,
Jesus, Politics, and Society (Maryknoll, N.Y.:
Orbis Books, 1978), pp. 56-60. Cf. a passing

reference in Liberation, p. 70.

[56]Segundo, "Capitalism-Socialism,"
p. 123.

[57]Ibid.

[58]Segundo, Masas, pp. 76-78.

[59]Ibid., pp. 79-81.

[60]Juan Luis Segundo, "Camilo Torres,
Sacerdocio y Violencia," Vispera 2 (1967): 71.

[61]Segundo, Masas, p. 93.

[62]Segundo, Rioplatense, p. 79.

[63]Juan Luis Segundo, Our Idea of God
(Maryknoll, N.Y.: Orbis Books, 1974), p. 163.

[64]Ibid., pp. 164-69.

[65]Ibid., p. 169.

[66]Segundo, "Camilo Torres," p. 74.

[67]Ibid., p. 75.

[68]Ibid.

CHAPTER IV

SEGUNDO'S SCRIPTURAL EXEGESIS

Now that we have seen the two preconditions
set by Segundo for his renewed biblical interpretation, and now that we have examined the ways in
which these preconditions are met in the three
steps of his hermeneutic circle, we are ready to
make the fourth and final step. In this chapter
we will examine the specific use of Scripture
which Segundo makes in his own writings. We will
look at the passages with which he works, and see
how he arrives at new interpretations on the basis
of his social analysis and on the basis of the
challenges which this analysis makes to previous
theology and exegesis. This will help us study
how Segundo thinks the Bible speaks to Christian
ethics, and will enable us to compare his views
with other models.

General Observations on Exegesis

Before we examine specific biblical texts
we do well to consider more general observations
which give insight into Segundo's hermeneutical
methodology for Scripture. The first important
observation sheds insight into a question that has
kept recurring in the preceding chapters. In
both the sections on social analysis and on
ideology we have been wondering whether revelation is in the gospels or the sociology. A partial answer is offered by Segundo. When he
speaks of the Bible directly, he makes statements
often enough to verify that he finds objective
truth in the text itself. Such statements offer
a balance to the preceding chapters of our study,
which could easily lead to the conclusion that
one only draws subjective meaning from the Bible
depending on ideology[p].

Of course, what we have seen previously also leads to the conclusion that one cannot derive the full message of the Bible without proper preunderstanding that should include commitment to the poor. Nevertheless, Segundo does say things often enough to warrant our concluding that he finds this preunderstanding an element of exegesis and not eisegesis. The message is in the text and not just read into the text. It may be that Segundo still overstates the role of commitment to the poor or social analysis as preunderstanding, but he does not seem to slip entirely into a subjective reading of the Scriptures.

Our author observes, for instance, that social analysis and the ideology[n] that it uncovers warrants a return to the basic message of the gospel. He makes a prophetic call for evangelization on the Latin American continent, and claims that true evangelization can center on an intrinsic, essential message of the text itself. "Evangelization means offering Christianity to individuals in such a way that by its own content, its intrinsic value, it calls forth a personal, heroic and interior response."[1]

Segundo's basic contention is that Latin America is not being evangelized today. The massification of humanity, accompanied by the pastoral desire of the Church to remain quantitatively universal, has blocked genuine preaching of the good news. On the whole, the pastoral program of Latin America presumes that people have the basics of the gospel message, and it preaches what flows from the basics. In the long run, it is maintaining the status quo of a society of the masses, and does not liberate the poor and oppressed.[2]

In a further elaboration of this observation, Segundo says explicitly that the objective message of the Bible needs the subjective preunderstanding of one's life situation. He says that evangelization must have three characteristics. It must limit itself, first of all, to proclaiming the deep substance of Christianity, removing the accidental, the adventitious, the superfluous. But this message cannot be an abstract theory, and so, must be formulated in view of the problems of humanity today. For Segundo, of course, these problems are perceived from one's own life situation and, for himself, come out of commitment to the poor. Finally, the evangelization must be a prudent and progressive exposition, leaving time for people to absorb each point at their own pace. Even this final characteristic calls for pre-understanding, since it means listening as well as speaking.[3]

Besides observations which attempt to maintain the objectivity of the Bible along with the need for ideology[p], Segundo is also concerned with keeping legitimate distance between the biblical context and the present situation. He seems quite sophisticated in his use of the Scriptures, avoiding tendencies often criticized in liberation theologians. Such theologians often make too facile a connection between the biblical text and its solving a particular contemporary problem, or they are quite selective in using only particular biblical passages for their purposes. Segundo seems to recognize these criticisms and is careful to speak to them in his writings.

Our author addresses himself to two difficulties which confront the theologian and necessitate respecting the distance between the biblical and the contemporary life situations. The first is the problem of written language, and the second is the problem of choosing passages for any particular topic.

In addressing the difficulty of the Bible as written language, Segundo makes the usual observations about the need for clear translations and for polished language that can remain faithful to the text without becoming too erudite or scholarly. Nevertheless, even after these aspects are cared for, there remains the gap between present culture and past history that is hidden within the very nature of language and that must be allowed for in our use of the Bible.

We must recognize that the literal verbal message does not exhaust all the meaning conveyed in language. There is much that is implicit, a kind of metalanguage or metainformation that derives its meaning from the concrete context and brings with it an entire network of nuances and relationships above and beyond the mere words themselves. An example of metalanguage can be seen in considering even just one hypothetical phrase from a prophet, such as "Kill the king." Although the verbal meaning would be the same, there is already a world of difference between that form of the imperative and some literary or polite way of expressing the same thing, such as in the use of third person imperatives in the romance languages.

The fact that we are speaking of a king also removes us from the full involvement in a concrete plot, since we are not politically involved with kings. For this phrase, as for so many others in the Bible, it is like hearing the words in a formal context, as in a play, rather than in concrete reality of every day. Segundo points out how in the recent past we began every passage of the gospel with "At that time," already giving the text somewhat of an abstract or theoretical nuance. Notice also how we sometimes reserve certain words for biblical passages, as if ordinary day-to-day words would not suffice. We call Mary a "maiden" but not a "girl" and in French we set aside the word "cêne" instead of the usual "dîner." All this says that in using the Bible we must try to capture the metalanguage as well as the language itself. Otherwise we remove much of the actual meaning of the text.

It is symptomatic that when we reach
some conclusions on this, ecclesiastical
conservatism is alarmed with this biting
fact, considering it catastrophic and
supremely compromising that the words of
the prophets want to castigate actual
things and attitudes and persons with name
and surname among us, and considering with
allergic reaction or frank repugnance the
fact that Jesus wants to sow division
between religious or "Christian" groups
which frequent the same temple. In a word,
they have to excuse themselves before the
weighty message by a bold criticism of the
Scriptures themselves.[4]

There is a second difficulty in using the
Bible, namely, that of the choice of passages for
any particular topic. Segundo recognizes that
the Bible is a series of writings extended over
history. It is a process of revelation rather
than a single record of information. The danger
in trying to derive a contemporary message from
all of the Bible for a particular group, whether
poor or otherwise, is the danger of distorting
its message. There is the danger, first of all,
of looking just for those passages which speak
to the group, and of taking one stage of biblical teaching as the meaning for all stages.

This danger of oversimplification is one
of the reasons why Segundo will not single out
the Exodus event as the full message of the
Bible for liberation theology. That is often the
tendency of liberation theologians. "The . . .
more naive explanation maintains that the Exodus
event is the key to the interpretation of Scripture as a whole, including the Gospels and the
rest of the New Testament. . . . We could maintain that liberation was the only theme of the
New Testament, I suppose, but only if we were
willing to go in for a great deal of abstraction."[5] Our author points out, for instance,
that the sapiential literature in the Old Testament took a turn toward individualistic,

inner-directed, apolitical theology which contrasts with the Exodus theology. In the same way, the New Testament shows not only continuity, but also correction of the Old Testament.

Another danger of using the Bible for any particular topic is that of simply maintaining the status quo of a given social situation. A particular group would simply presume that its position is correct and would then proceed to find verification for it from Scripture texts. "Every intention of translating a complex and dialectical process into a univocal and concrete orientation by a determined and situated group of men leads, in the short or the long run, to a conservative position, given that the process is open, while every summation, application or translation of it to a given situation allows one beyond possibilities which at such time today would not be necessary, but would be tomorrow."[6]

Recognizing these dangers, Segundo offers some general approaches to Scripture to resolve these points. These approaches make further use of his insights regarding ideology[p] but apply them to the historical conditionedness of the biblical personalities and biblical authors, rather than to the preunderstanding of the Bible reader. Our author speaks of the Bible as a process, which is his way of saying that the revelation of the Bible is conditioned by time and place in a long history, and is his way of extending the historical conditionedness of the text to its application in a contemporary, non-biblical time and place.

In speaking to the problem of meta-language, Segundo discusses the Bible as process in terms of the text itself having been developed in time and place over history. He suggests that one can guard against the loss of meta-language by capturing as much as possible the context around the texts. One must grasp the historical situation which gave rise and meaning

140

to the text. This will also help prevent the taking of any particular texts as the whole message of the Bible.

Segundo is strong for the entire process of the Bible, so that he does not want to take just the last stages of biblical teaching as normative, telescoping all the previous stages. Rather, he finds an educative value in the previous stages that makes them necessary for the full message. For example, he suggests that there is something to learn from the movement from syncretism to idolatry to legalistic worship to egotistic worship to internal worship.

Thus, for our author the problem is not the criticism from conservative theologies which fault liberation theology for being "horizontal" in view and translating all into social terms. The problem is rather that the sociological interpretation is itself part of a biblical process. It is a valid discovery, but even the social analysis of the Bible cannot be reduced to an instant of flat information divorced from the process.[7]

To put all of this into the vocabulary of Segundo's hermeneutic circle, social analysis and ideology^p are necessary preunderstanding to dis-cover the liberating message of the Bible, a message that is objectively there but needs the ideology^p to be uncovered. Nevertheless, even the biblical text itself is influenced by its own ideology^p, so that what is uncovered must be seen as part of a long process. There is no biblical text totally neutral in ideology^p. The danger is that this ideology^p will not be recog-nized and will evolve into an ideology^n. "An ideology absorbed unconsciously at the origin of a manipulation is converted, more or less in the long run, into a conservative element. Only a continual deideologizing [from ideology^n] is, in the final count, liberating."[8] Many texts are not liberating in the immediate, but only in the process of the whole Bible.

Segundo sees the Bible as process, not only in the historical development of the text itself in time and place, but also in the application of the text from its own history to the present, non-biblical time and place. He employs again his concept of ideology[p] to respect the gap between the biblical and the contemporary life situations. It is also in this context that he speaks of Christ as part of a process.

According to this view, there are not only different ideologies[p] in different texts of the Bible, but there are also different ideologies[p] behind present applications of the biblical text. Our author gives examples of ideologies[p] at various stages of the Bible, which are helpful not only for the point we are making now, but also for what we have just previously elaborated. In the early stages of Israel's history, "the extermination of enemies was the ideology that faith adopted, with or without critical thought, at that moment in history."[9]

Jesus himself is part of a process of revelation because he belonged to a specific historical context. "When Jesus talked about freely proffered love and nonresistance to evil, he was facing the same problem of filling the void between his conception of God (or perhaps that of the first Christian community) and the problems existing in his age. In short, we are dealing here with another ideology."[10] We may also be sure that there were ideological elements that influenced the early Christian community in its putting together of the gospels. Finally, even Paul seems to show ideologies, e.g., in his teaching that slaves remain as they are.[11]

In terms of our present history we recognize the biblical teaching, and even the teaching of Christ, as part of a process and we try to deideologize any elements that may have evolved into an ideology[n] in present application. Nevertheless, we also recognize that we can never totally free ourselves from ideologies[P], and in fact, our goal is not to find the message freed from ideologies[P].

Is there anything left in Scripture once we have discarded the ideological element? It is too easy to say that what remains is precisely the conception of God that runs through the centuries and that the various ideologies attempt to relate to specific historical circumstances. It is too easy because that conception of God is never found separated from the ideologies that attempt to interpret God by applying his demands to a specific historical situation. Both processes are inextricably linked. You cannot get rid of one without emptying the other of content.[12]

Segundo suggests that perhaps the way out of the impasse is by recognizing that we are speaking of two different levels of learning. We may be confusing a proto-learning, the information we derive from the Bible as faith-content in the context of ideology[P], with a deutero-learning, the application which we make of the faith content to the solution of new problems through new ideologies[P].

There is a first level of learning in which information is added or subtracted in a person. A child, for instance, will be able to solve any problem that he has been taught to solve, or any problem that is a copy of the one he has studied. Even animals have this level of learning in their reaction to stimuli. A human being, however, will move to another level of learning. He or she will soon be able to solve problems that were not studied, and that are not mere duplicates of what were studied. On this level information is not just added. It is multiplied. If there are errors, knowledge is not simply subtracted, but divided.

143

Segundo suggests that the reading of the Scriptures operates on these two levels of learning. "Ideologies present in Scripture belong to the first level. . . . Faith, by contrast, is the total process to which man submits, a process of learning in and through ideologies how to create the ideologies needed to handle new and unforeseen situations in history."[13] It means that we read Scripture not just to learn the solution to a problem, since it is more complicated than simply making application of a text to a present situation. Instead, we read the whole Bible as a process, both to learn what it says, and to "learn to learn."

The Scriptures can and should be examined and studied from both points of view since both processes are in the sacred writings and do not compete with each other over content. This means that fighting one's way out of bondage in Egypt is one experience and turning the other cheek is another experience. Someone who has gone through both experiences and has reflected on them has learned how to learn; he has multiplied his faith-based information, not subtracted it to zero.[14]

Two corollaries flow from this method of learning-to-learn. First of all, the whole Bible has a place in this process, including that which might seem outmoded in the Old Testament. When one is learning to learn, one must have confidence in the educator. One cannot simply select what one wants from the process. Often in the initial stages, the full truth is not given, because the learner is not disposed to receive it yet. Even error has a role in real learning, and this must be said of the Bible as well as any other work. Thus, for example, wisdom literature may have been mistaken about the nature of life as simply a test for an afterlife, but it did prepare the way for Jesus, as is attested by Job's questions about suffering.[15]

A second conclusion that is also important to this method is that we cannot derive our concrete answers to today's questions directly out of the Bible. If learning to learn is a creative process and prepares to be creative, then the answers must in fact be creative. We cannot seek them from the Bible. Thus, Segundo observes that the prophets did not cite the Scriptures to confirm their theology. They made the Scriptures by means of their theology. He also faults some Protestant writers for a tendency to compare in simple and direct ways the facts of today with a group of facts in the Bible.[16] Finally, we have the reason why Segundo says that instead of trying to "invent an ideology that we might regard as the one which would be constructed by a gospel message contemporary with us," we should be more creative and see that "it is becoming more and more obvious to Christians that secular inventiveness and creativity is more appropriate and fruitful."[17]

Our author thus gives valuable insight into how to keep the distance between the biblical times and our own, while at the same time making application of the Bible to the present. It may also explain how Christ can be part of a process of revelation and yet be a definitive norm of revelation. He is definitive norm on the level of proto-learning, and he is part of a process on the level of deutero-learning. Whether we can pin Segundo down to a more specific indication of the ethical significance of Christ seems doubtful. We have previous statements about the objectivity of Scripture which could be applied to Christ as well. However, the interpretation of Christ and the application of his message seem to hinge on ideology[p].

We can ask ourselves again whether Segundo overstates his case concerning the role of social analysis, ideology[p] or Marxism, but we must credit him with the sophistication of stating that none

145

of these comes from direct application of the
Bible. He sees no particular text that gives
arguments for Marxist ideology or social analysis, for example, but sees such observations as
conclusions from a process that includes a
historically conditioned Bible and historically
conditioned applications. As far as the whole
question of making application of the Bible to the
present is concerned, Segundo notes that his
suggestions may be inadequate. He admits: "No one
would be able to deny that there exists here, if
not an impasse, then at least a difficult problem
for which, as far as I am concerned, practically
no one has among us an appropriate response or
an easy solution."[18]

With these general observations about
objectivity in the biblical message and the need
for distance from the biblical context in applying Scripture to the present, we have a background
for examining particular points of exegesis suggested by Segundo. We will look at those texts
where he sees especially the convergence of social
analysis with exegesis that can speak to that
analysis. In other words, we will highlight those
texts which seem to support the theological presuppositions of the previous chapter which were,
in turn, formulated to dialogue with Marxist
ideology and its statements in favor of the poor
in Latin America.

The "Flesh" and Mass-Man

Perhaps the most central texts of Scripture
for Segundo, which enable exegesis to speak to
social analysis, are those texts which deal with
sarx or the flesh in St. Paul's epistles, and
cosmos or world in St. John's writings. We will
see what Segundo draws from each of these terms.
As we shall see, the basic interpretation
revolves around seeing Christianity as a minority
movement, without necessarily eliminating its
dialogue with the masses.

146

In examining the word sarx in St. Paul,
Segundo recognizes that it does not come from the
Greek culture, and does not mean simply the
material body as opposed to the soul of a person.
This meaning would be reserved on occasion for
soma, although Paul is not always consistent in
his use of words. In any case, in order to appreciate the usual meaning of sarx for Paul we must
examine the Old Testament antecedents. In doing
so we begin to notice problems with Segundo's
analysis. We will return for a more thorough
critique of his exegesis in the next chapters,
but we will make some brief observations as we
attempt to describe his own thought now.

We notice, to begin with, that our author
does want to find objectivity in the biblical
data, and for that reason he seeks the meaning of
sarx as it has been developed by scholars over
the years. However, we also find a tendency to
overstate the case for his ideological concerns
with liberation. This shows in a paradoxical
stress of Western philosophical concepts that
would be somewhat foreign to most of biblical
thought. We use the word paradox advisedly.
Segundo says that sarx does not derive its meaning from Greek culture. His ideological suspicion moves him to be critical of reading
Western first-world meaning into the biblical
text. Yet, most of his treatment of sarx presupposes a Greek, rationalist perspective, and,
as we move into New Testament analysis, a first-
world personalist and individual existentialist
philosophy.

Segundo dwells on the Hebrew word basar,
which has the more metaphoric meanings of flesh,
and he sees this word as the intermingling of
two basic meanings: "The word flesh is used in a
metaphoric sense in two different ways: flesh
comes to signify the concrete sensitivity of
each man, while all flesh designates passivity
or receptivity essential to the creature with
respect to the Spirit of Yahweh."[19]

147

The first concept reads rather Hellenistically. Flesh is humanity's space for sensation. Things could enter into a man or woman's flesh insofar as they entered or not into the sphere of his or her interest and his or her existential space. The second metaphorical meaning developed out of the exile and after the discovery of Yahweh's transcendence. It refers to humanity's position as creature. Since Israel had no word for creature, it evolved all flesh to mean the totality of living beings. As Segundo treats the meaning, however, the connotation is one of impersonal and purely external relation to the Creator. There are overtones of existentialist philosophy and the individual quest for freedom.

This existentialism becomes even more prominent in the New Testament analysis. Segundo stresses that movement out of the flesh into the spirit entails a dynamic which abandons impersonal, external ties with God and creation, and struggles for liberating, self-creating, personal relationships on all levels of existence. So strong is he for this ideological reading [possibly an ideology[n]?], that he overstates salvation and liberation as humanity's own effort and accomplishment, and leaves little room for the divine action and redemption. In what follows we will present Segundo's description of sarx in Paul, leaving further evaluation to chapter five, and hoping that the presentation will also offer some insights valuable for biblical interpretation, even if overstated.

According to Segundo, the word flesh has no pejorative sense in the Old Testament, but acquires one in Paul because Christ changes radically the relationship of God and humanity. The change is described in personalist terms. In the Old Testament the relationship was external and impersonally on the level of creature to Creator. As Paul presents the New Testament message, the ties are now internal to humanity itself and create humanity into the life of God

himself. This brings man and woman to the
realization of their own existence as persons,
with all that this implies of human freedom,
and moves them far beyond relating to the
divine in terms of nature only.

Paul is said by Segundo to work out this
dynamic of the flesh in Galatians especially.
There the tendencies of the Judaizers are equated
with the works of the flesh which render vain
the cross of Christ. The desires of the
Judaizers to keep the works of the law, circumcision, the "elemental spirits of the universe,"
are all attempts to remain as creatures in the
face of a Creator. As Segundo intends this, it
means serving God in a natural way, i.e., doing
what nature determines should be done, without
any personal relationship behind it. For Paul
this ignores the newness of life that Christ
brings.

> . . . If God in the Old Testament sum-
> moned man to a relationship centered around
> the difference in natures between creature
> and Creator, he did so because man had not
> yet reached his adulthood. . . . Christ
> fulfilled and proclaimed the full maturity
> and adulthood of man as a son of God. . . .
> Man is no longer under the law. . . . If he
> chooses to remain under it, it is because he
> is still fleshly, because he does not choose
> to assume the maturity of his new personal
> and creative relationship with God. So we
> can see why the fleshly outlook nullifies
> Christ. The whole transformation he ushered
> into human existence centers around this
> transition from a determining nature to a
> nature determined by liberty.[20]

Segundo shows that he is influenced by
his hermeneutic preconditions and the previous
stages of his circle, for he says that this
theology about the flesh is simply another way
of talking about the dialectic between the masses

and minorities. Living in the flesh is equivalent to acting as mass-man, determined by the nature around him, dominated by the instruments which should serve as his mediations with the divine. It is the law of least resistance that sociological analysis describes, but written up in biblical vocabulary. "The Christian allows himself to be led to convert these means [of relationship to God] into mechanical, deterministic conditions. . . . Living according to the flesh means allowing oneself to be dominated by it."[21] Christ brings a new life, however, which enables humanity to break out of this deterministic pattern, and--as Segundo would overstate the case by apparently ignoring divine initiative--to freely create itself as son of God. It establishes the creative minority of society.

Segundo returns to this same section where he has treated sarx in Galations to develop three antitheses that can provide a context for the term. We have here, most likely, an instance of reading the Bible as historical process. This context also helps to qualify Segundo's optimism about humanity's self-creation and freedom, and stresses divine activity and humanity's freedom as a gift. The first antithesis is faith-works, seen as a more concrete form of flesh-spirit. This is found especially in Gal. 3:6-14. Faith in this section is not intellectual adherence, but abandonment to God. As Segundo analyzes the relationship, faith and works are as two traits in humanity's relationship to God. However, we act by faith, and only thanks to faith do we perform works. Works are the results of faith, not on the same level. As Segundo words it, "The opposition is encountered between those who have faith in God and those who have faith in their own works."[22]

A second antithesis is that of promise-contract (Gal. 3:15-19). There are two ways of

150

expressing intention regarding a gift. One is as a unilateral and unconditioned promise; the other is as a bilateral conditioned gift or contract. As Segundo sees it in Galatians, humanity's relationship to God is not a contract. The law comes after the promise, and Judaizers--even the Jews themselves--should not make it a condition of the promise. Moreover, the promise of the Old Testament has been fulfilled in Christ, so that the law has reached its term and now yields to Christ. "If, on the one hand, the law has never been a condition previous to the conceding of justice, and if, on the other hand, the promise has been fulfilled and realized in Jesus Christ, those who pretend to reintroduce the law as condition of salvation, make themselves evidently culpable of a double negation before Christ."23

A third antithesis, found in Gal. 4:1-11, is that of slavery of child as heir-freedom of adult as heir. Paul contrasts sonship to servitude which submitted humanity to creaturely elements, to mediations of this world, to the law of the world and to nature. He points out in verses 8 and 9, that man as son has entered into personal contact and intimacy with God. Segundo interprets this especially from the biblical connotations of "to know" and "be known" as personal relationship. If such is the case, then this freedom through Christ should remove the attitudes of the flesh that are characterized by fear. To refuse to leave fear is to reject the New Testament. One must now build on the possibilities of humanity as consisting of persons, as substitute for attitudes based on one's nature as a creature.

The end result of all these antitheses is an acknowledgement of the Christian religion as response to God's work, not humanity's achievement. Nevertheless, as far as Segundo is concerned, the response brings in human activity which results in self-creation as God calls one to it. It is the paradox of the Christian

message. Nothing efficacious for salvation comes
from the human as such, while at the same time
Paul can say, "All things are yours."

Segundo makes use of other Pauline passages
to reinforce this paradox. In 1 Cor. 3:3, Paul
applies to the Church itself the false confidence
in its own structures, which ultimately dominate
the members, and create a human determinism. In
the long run it leads to living by the law of
least resistance and to mechanical behavior. In
Paul's words this means living by the flesh, and
in Segundo's words it means acting as mass-man.
This text applies to the pagans the same dangers
encountered by the Judaizers in Galatia. In this
case in Corinth, it is overstressing the importance of baptism by prominent figures. Centering
attention on Church institutions is just as
dangerous as being determined by what flows from
one's nature as a creature. "You are still of
the flesh. For while there is jealousy and
strife among you, are you not of the flesh, and
behaving like ordinary men?"

On the other hand, "whether Paul or
Apollos or Cephas or the world or life or death
or the present or the future, all are yours"
(1 Cor. 3:22). The newness of creation that
Christ brings enables humanity to make use of
all of this world as means to its own movement
in freedom.

Man must not begin by submitting himself to
any created "human" thing whatever, as if
his own value consisted in adapting his being
to an axiological norm pre-existent and
superior to him. The law which comes from
nature, the Church and its institutions, can
and should help man by permitting him to be
himself, that is to say, free, since without
these norms, as we have seen, he would turn
back to enslaving himself. But its place is
not above freedom.[24]

Segundo thus believes that his hermeneutic circle
enables him to read Paul in such a way that the
apostle supports his claims that Christianity
requires a minority exercising its freedom in
relativizing and criticizing the masses of
society. The full and concrete working out of
how this minority is to function would be derived
through deutero-learning from Paul, but it seems
that Segundo does believe that human freedom and
Christianity as a minority movement exercising
this freedom can be found objectively in Paul
when he is read with the hermeneutical suspicion
of social analysis.

As Segundo continues his description of
freedom as a personal trait, he brings it into
metaphysical dichotomy with nature, rather than
simply a psychological one. A key text for him
is Rom. 7:14-24, and Paul's description of
freedom through the human experience of concupiscence. The apostle speaks of the law which
dwells in his members. It is his way of speaking
once again as he did about the flesh, but here
emphasizing the threats to freedom. Because of
this law within him, "the evil I do not want is
what I do." If it is certain that man and woman
have a personal principle of freedom (his "inmost
self"), a principle moving him or her to determine
things in life, it is also true that the natural-
ness of the universe seems to ignore this principle. Humanity is often treated like a machine.
There are certain functions, of course, that
freedom cannot touch, although it is affected
by them, e.g., digestion, etc., but even human
projects seem to threaten freedom.

Segundo sees this passage of Paul as highlighting this threat from the law of nature. So
strong is he for freedom that he again makes a
statement that seems to exaggerate the claims for
human involvement in redemption. "We are in the
full center of the Pauline image. All of us men
possess an incipient freedom which seeks realization, but encounters in the power of nature which
inhibits us something which, if it is foreign to

the most intimate core of our being, still pertains to us and conditions all our realizations."[25] Humanity must seek all that will move
it past nature as universally determined order,
and must seek what will make man and woman
persons. In effect, Segundo's sociological preconditions are brought to bear here as he interprets Paul as saying that we have <u>things</u> within
us that threaten to make us <u>things</u>.

This description of things is what Segundo
calls Paul's experience of concupiscence. It
sheds light on what Paul sees as the metaphysical
dimensions of freedom, as opposed to just psychological. By this Segundo means that human
freedom does not consist so much in choosing
between good and bad actions, but hinges on how
much humanity can determine itself in choosing
any actions. How much are a person's acts truly
one's own, according to his "inmost self"?

Once again we have overstatement about
human freedom as self-created, but at the same
time we find a helpful distinction about real
freedom coming from inner decision and not simply
exterior choices between good and bad actions.
As Segundo sees Romans 7, Paul does not consider
freedom as dependent upon external laws which
determine good and bad actions. The only law is
love, creatively construed, and that flows from
within humanity as genuine gift of self. The
only problem is that often we pass imperceptibly
from love which is a gift to an exterior action
similar to love, but which is not a gift of self.
In effect, we change to egotism to achieve love
more easily. This is the constant threat of
what we call concupiscence, and it thus highlights also Paul's meaning of freedom. The
natural should serve love, but in fact betrays it.

Segundo sums this up as follows:

Effectively, man has no original, intimate,
personal motivation which does not impel him
to love, that is, to take that which he is and

154

to give it to another person. This is the
true law, the divine law (Paul calls it
spiritual in order to differentiate it from
that which points out things permitted and
prohibited). In the intimacy of man this law
is unique: on this level man does not decide
between good and evil. Every inner man is
in accord with this law which comes from God.
However, there arises the task of realizing
love, of translating it into external reality.
. . . And there the law of facility, of least
resistance, offers a thousand occasions to
egotism in order that it might seize love and,
under pretext of realizing it, might stop and
eliminate it. . . . And therefore, we are
inside or outside of the law, we are doing
things "permitted" or "prohibited," we are,
in reality, denying love and doing evil.[26]

And so, we are before Segundo's analysis of
Paul in which he thinks social analysis and exegesis converge. His most invaluable insight is
his social analysis of massification and the
ideological suspicion that it casts against
reading Christian universality quantitatively.
This suspicion in turn enables him to read Paul
as offering insights that call for the creative
and personal stance for freedom that belongs to
a minority in society. If we can move Segundo
past the inadequacies of his analysis of the
flesh--his underestimation of the Old Testament
which leads to too much of a distinction between
nature and person, and his too liberal a dose of
self-determination in human freedom--we can
derive and maintain his helpful interpretations
of Paul regarding the social dimensions of the
flesh and its link to massification. An attempt
toward a more adequate exegesis will be made in
chapter five.

As a final point we must also say that
some of Segundo's exegesis concerning sarx seems
to be misdirected. It is an attempt to derive
from the text what one wants to find. The concern for ideology[n] or for formulating biblical

interpretation to speak to the present situation leads in this instance to reading into the text. Segundo tries to parallel the ambiguity of the masses in his social analysis with ambiguity of the flesh in Paul. In the same way that he drew from social analysis that the masses are an opposition to the minority and at the same time a necessity, so Segundo draws from Paul the insight that the flesh is opposed to freedom, but is not sinful. It is the destiny of all humanity. "The work of the Word, that is, the communication of the possibility of truly loving, is realized in the measurement of proximity--neighbor--that is to say, in the measure in which men constitute a single body among themselves, a single flesh."[27]

Segundo is playing with the concept of determinism. He says that if all were totally sinners--or determined--the body of Christ would fall apart. On the other hand, the body of Christ could not operate if all were totally free and without any determinisms. For love can only function concretely when it knows the concrete and foreseeable needs of a person, and that means needs that are determined in some way. Now the flesh in Paul is, according to Segundo, this area of determinism. One seeks to be free from it, but also needs it so that the body of Christ can truly exist as concrete human love of foreseeable human needs.

The problem with this is that it must either identify sin with all determinism, which is not the case, or it must separate the concept of flesh from the concept of sin. It seems that Segundo chooses the latter--otherwise he would make sin a necessary ingredient of the body of Christ--but then he fails to grasp the eschatological dualism that Paul teaches, and the ultimate opposition that Paul places between flesh and spirit.

Segundo cites other texts, such as Gal. 4:4 and Rom. 8:3, to show that Christ lived under

the law and in the flesh in order to free from
the law and to achieve what the flesh could not.
The way in which he uses the texts, however,
ultimately removes living under the law as something negative and ignores "living in the flesh"
as the equivalent of "being made sin for us."
There is an eschatological opposition operating
in the concept of flesh that cannot be accounted
for when flesh is seen as a necessary determinism
of the Christian life dissociated from sin and
simply part of the day-to-day evolving maturity
of the Christian. So, while Segundo's insight
into massification may be valid, its application
to Paul's notion of the flesh seems to be more
eisegesis than exegesis, at least in this particular aspect.

The "World" and Mass-Man

As the term flesh in Paul is useful for
Segundo's insights in the background of social
analysis, so is the term world a central consideration from the writings of John. According
to Segundo, this term is more of a Greek term
and is less complicated in meaning. "The term
world is sometimes synonymous with humanity and
sometimes with creation in general. And right
off we can see that the same thing happens to
it in John's writings as happened to 'flesh' in
Paul's writings. It acquires a pejorative
connotation."28

This pejorative meaning for world arises
again in the New Testament context as a result of
the descent of the Word. In the measure in which
the life of God with its deep and total meaning
invades humanity, world takes on the dimensions
of a collective, impersonal, massive force that
can be described, according to Segundo, as human
inertia and mass-man. We will describe the ways
in which world can take on these qualities seen
through the hermeneutical presuppositions of
social analysis and the need to speak to the life
situation of the poor, but we will also have to

qualify some of the exegesis of Segundo to keep
it in touch with the objective meaning of the
Scriptures and avoid eisegesis.

Our author concentrates on the prologue
of John's gospel, where he sees all the meanings
of world and where he sees description of the
descent of the Word of God as precipitating
rejection by a majority of humanity and acceptance by a minority. "At each approach of the
Word-Light, there corresponds an accentuation
of the distance which separates the masses from
the minorities."[29]

Segundo accepts the majority of exegetes
in describing the first five verses of the prologue. He says that it tells of the Word in
the presence of God and the Word in its relation
to creation, but it does not yet speak of the
descent of the Word into humanity. This begins
in verse 9.

At this point Segundo makes two observations that seem unwarranted by the text. He
says that ēn erchomenon in the imperfect in
verse 9 designates that the Word came only
progressively in history. This does not seem
borne out by the text, since the imperfect
designates duration or repetition in the past,
but does not say anything about progression.
Secondly, he says that the Word comes as light
and that this means coming as full truth, not
on an impersonal, objective plane, but in terms
of our own personalities and freedom. Once
again, we seem to have Segundo's exaggerated
distinction between nature and person, a reading
of personalist, existential philosophy into the
text which does not seem supported by the
biblical context of John. Beyond these somewhat
dubious interpretations Segundo does then give
insight into how the Word challenges the world
to response and thereby begins to effect a
majority and a minority.

Verse 10 contains the key text for Segundo in defining the various meanings of the term world for John. "He was in the world" refers to the term in a neutral sense of a place or the ensemble of mankind. "The world was made through him" refers to this same term as including all the universe, but in a more positive sense. It is a sign of God, a world that should be in its entirety as God demands it. "The world knew him not" begins to show the pejorative sense of the term, while also narrowing down its contents. It comprises all those who do not meet the demands of God. It refers to all those who make the option of "no" before God. It cannot be the ensemble of humanity, since in subsequent verses part of the world will be "his own" who do recognize him in some way. In this third case in verse 10, the world must refer, therefore, to the majority of humanity.

Segundo asks why this majority must be called the world, and not the minority, or why this majority is not called "a greater part of the world" rather than world as such. He does not answer the question, but states the fact that "whatever the answer may be, it is obvious enough that the term world has acquired a pejorative connotation. Those who deny the Word, and only they, are 'the world.' One can say that the whole Gospel of John does nothing else but depict a battle between Jesus and this world."[30]

In developing this point further Segundo speaks of verse 11 in the unfortunate terminology of a "second descent of the Word" into the world. It seems more faithful to the text to see verses 11 and 12 as further specification of verse 10, all of them speaking of the same descent of the Word of God. It is also doubtful that "coming to his own" in verse 11 is reference to the Old Testament. It seems that the insertion of verses about John the Baptist in 6-8 already introduces us to the New Testament, so that the succeeding verses 9ff. are all references to the one descent of the Word in the incarnation of Jesus. "Coming to his own" would mean the Israelites of Jesus' time who did not believe in him, while "those who received him" would indicate the disciples who did believe in him. Raymond Brown observes that verse 10 gives a summary statement, with verse 11 summing up the first half of the gospel, the "Book of Signs," and verse 12 summing up the second half, the "Book of Glory."[31]

In any case, whether speaking of the Israelites of Jesus' time, or, as Segundo believes, of the Israelites of the Old Testament, one can read tendencies toward massification in their conformity to law, institutions, and other worldly determinisms, all designed to provide the path of least resistance for a majority which will reject Jesus and his demands for concerns of liberation. "The law, without force to resist the inertia of the world, is transformed into a law like the others, physical and exterior."[32] Those who are part of the world are trapped in the mechanisms of "flesh and blood" (see verses 12-13) and become determined by their institutions rather than making creative decisions as a minority for freedom. Segundo's hermeneutics of suspicion enable one to read John's concept of world in a way that speaks to liberation.

Moving to a wider context, our author illustrates from the Johannine writings (gospel and epistles), three characteristics of the world, uncovered from the text when it is read with the presuppositions brought by social analysis.[33] The first trait is described as the incapacity of the world to await the truth and its ambassadors. Besides the text of the prologue, other passages show this trait, e.g., John 7:7: "The world cannot hate you, but it hates me because I testify of it that its works are evil"; John 14:17: "Even the Spirit of truth, whom the world cannot receive, because it neither sees him nor knows him; you know him."

160

When we ask where the incapacity comes from, we reach the second trait of the world, its essentially conservative social mechanism. There is a closed circle of understanding within the world, a structured totality that is closed in on self, and does not let the Spirit or the truth penetrate. In 1 John 2:16, we read: "For all that is in the world, . . . is not of the Father but is of the world." The world seems to have one essential principle: to avoid knowing what it should not desire. The world listens only to its own, and pushes toward mass ideology, to facility of action, to the simplest and customary way of acting. "They are of the world, therefore what they say is of the world, and the world listens to them" (1 John 4:5). It ends up being a vicious circle of error and slavery, blocking sight, hearing and knowing (cf. John 8: 43-44).

To break this vicious circle is to enter into crisis in the etymological sense of the word, i.e., into judgment. John develops this theme in terms of Christ bringing light and exposing our darkness, as for instance, in chapter 3 of his gospel. Segundo interprets this darkness as not so much hiding the distance between actions and moral laws, as losing freedom to the facilitation of actions or to determinisms. Christ exposes these automations of life and enables a minority to move out of its massification into true freedom.

The world, however, has loved the darkness rather than the light, and does not come to the light, lest its deeds be exposed. Coming to judgment--or, as Segundo says in his overstated stress on human freedom, "judging oneself"--is already the first step of liberty, so that the world is incapable of even doing that. Its day-to-day desires are transformed into a system which denies judgment and continues to do what it is doing and to love what is loved. "Only he who does what is true comes to the light" (John 3:21). Segundo defines truth as "the coherence between the plan and the act; the authentic."[34] The free man or woman, then, is the one who does what he or she really wants to do, moving away from determinisms to what creates the person, and one must accept judgment in order to make this move.

Part of the problem of the world and part of what is exposed in judgment is the ahistorical character of its activity. Caught in its own circular movement, the world sees all time as the same. Segundo brings insight here from what he has said about process in biblical development and in the application of biblical texts. Here he considers process in terms of human experience itself, the fact that humanity is historically conditioned and that human existence is a process of growth. He is again, perhaps, over-optimistic in seeing the process as a gradual maturing in history, and he again presents a Christ-of-culture model, but he does seem to have valuable insight into human life as having creative moments of time. In terms of John's gospel he shows Jesus breaking the circular movement of the world by having his creative moments of freedom and opportunity. He says that John sums this up through the term hour toward which Jesus works.[35]

In John 7:4, Segundo finds the ahistorical character of the world. The relatives of Jesus desire his miracles again and again, and want Jesus to become part of the world's expectations. It is the subtle working of the world to coopt freedom into its system. Jesus resists. He prefers waiting for his time as opportunity. No opportunity exists for a closed system (John 7: 6-7). To have an hour is to live a fully human life, to grow in freedom.

In John 12:19, according to Segundo, we have one of the last attempts by the world to neutralize Jesus by drawing him into their system. The statement is made that the whole world has gone after Jesus, and then the Greeks approach to represent the world. Jesus answers by saying that his hour has come, his moment for true freedom and authenticity, but that this encompasses his death. It is the ultimate resistance to the world's determinisms, that brings the world to judgment (12:31), and Jesus to glory (12:23).

The hour is a death because death seems to triumph and to make vain the decisions of freedom. The world gathers its supreme forces to remain intact and it always seems to win against the light destined to expose and question it. This produced the death of Jesus. At the same time, the hour is one of glory, not as a reward, but as the realization of the full gift of self in freedom.

From John 13:1 and the passage which follows, we learn that the real movement of Jesus in freedom, and the coming of the hour means the final movement of Jesus in love. It is the supreme instant of the gift of self. Christ crosses the last barrier of love and loves to the end. It is the final overcoming of temptation. Moreover, the enemy is not external. It is the weight of our own being, the part of each of us which is world. The supreme hour of love is not recognized by its beneficiaries, and becomes an hour of loneliness caused by the alienation of the very ones being loved (John 16:32).

In another point which he makes, one similar to what he attempted for flesh in Paul, Segundo seems again to misread the eschatological dualism of world in John. He tries to show that world, like the masses, is something negative and yet is something necessary for freedom and love. He points out, for instance, that Jesus says he comes to judge the world (John 12:31), and at the same time says he is sent to save the world (John 3:17). He says that Jesus, on the one hand, does not pray for the world, but for his disciples, as if they are not to be part of the world. On the other hand, the disciples are told that they are

163

not to be taken out of the world. (Cf. John 17: 6, 15, 18).

Segundo seems not to give enough attention to the fact that John is here using world in two different ways. Jesus' entrance into the world and the disciples' mission to the world are reference to place of activity and refer to world in a neutral sense. It does not mean that Jesus or the disciples are to share in the world in terms of attitude. When world is used in this sense it is negative and is associated with sin. Hence, Segundo has the same problem here as he did for flesh. He must either equate all determinism with sin or he must separate world from its association with sin. This would again underestimate the eschatological dualism of the biblical text. Segundo has valuable insights into John and has valid insights into massification. The social analysis may even help in reading John, but this particular aspect seems again to be a reading into the text and not a good application of his hermeneutic circle.[36]

One final point that may be helpful in interpreting John in view of liberation and the poor, is the way in which Segundo brings minority presuppositions to the reading of John 1:29 and 1 John 2:2. Segundo defines the "sin of the world" as "the structure by which the actions of man are hidden from the same man in their true meaning. We would be able to translate this, without fear of equivocating, by saying the alienating sin of the world is 'ideology.'"[37] Jesus comes to expose this ideology[n] of the masses, of the world. He acts as minority force in the world.

Of all the Scripture used by Segundo, the most explicit and the most central seem to be the word studies of Paul and John that we have outlined. Word studies are, of course, dangerous in that they run the risk of pulling terms out of context and imposing meanings. They can be helpful if they respect authors and context.

164

Segundo seems to recognize this. Qualifications
of his exegesis seem necessary more out of ideological debate than out of criticisms often
associated with this form of biblical theology.

In terms of methodology, these word studies
are the application of Segundo's hermeneutic
circle, doing theology and exegesis especially
from the perspective of commitment to the poor.
They offer opportunity to bring social analysis
to the text, concentrating especially on the
dialectic of the masses and minorities in society
that lead to the oppression of the poor. They
seem to support this social analysis and show
Christ as one who came to overcome the inertia
of the masses by the creation of a committed
minority who would work for freedom. It is the
major way that Segundo sees the biblical basis
for his liberation theology. We can now look at
several other word studies that he offers, and
that do show an element of present, this-worldly
eschatology as Segundo stressed it in the previous
chapter of our study.

"Salvation" and Eschatology

Most of the vocabulary that Segundo considers to show his eschatological teaching is
concerned with the description of salvation. We
begin with the words he uses to describe salvation as something new. In the preceding sections
we pointed out that the terms flesh and world
took their pejorative connotations in the New
Testament. Much of this was due to the influence
of Iranian dualism in the intertestamental period,
but such dualism lent itself to the New Testament
context because of the radical newness that Christ
brought to human life. Segundo gives direct
attention to that newness and uses it to show
that there is continuity in biblical eschatology,
as well as discontinuity. In his study he draws
on much of what seems traditional exegesis, but
we may presume that he sees his ideological
concerns as giving these traditional points an

added emphasis. Such studies help us confirm that Segundo does not want to oppose the presuppositions of social analysis to objectivity in the Bible.

In John 3, in his conversation with Nicodemus, Jesus stresses the radical newness of the Christian life. According to Segundo, Nicodemus certainly went beyond the attitudes of the other Pharisees who had stagnated into purely external forms, living by pretence and facile submission to ideologies[n]. Yet, even he came seeking only to add something to his already achieved power, virtue and knowledge.[38] That is what is implicit in his praise of Jesus as teacher. Jesus, however, gives clear, precise terms for entering the kingdom, and these all demand a new birth and a new creation. This new birth is described by John in the Greek term anothen (3:3).

This word has a double meaning of again and above. According to Segundo, this ambiguity stresses the continuity and the discontinuity of eschatological salvation. Above designates the divine intervention, a transformation, a discontinuity, but again signifies a continuity. It is renewal of something that already exists. While it is doubtful that Segundo's distinction can hold up--even being born again comes through the Spirit and is a radically new intervention-- his ultimate point may hold in that John sees both birth from above and birth again as something that takes place already in this life, as well as something that is beyond this life. "Thus it is the earth which we hope for and which is identified with eternal life. It is nothing else: it is ours, that of our history, that of our work, transformed."[39]

Paul treats of new creation which renders the life of the flesh as inappropriate. For Paul this new creation shows both continuity and discontinuity with this life. The Christian stands between two epiphanies: grace and glory

(Tit. 2:11-13). This comes about especially through the resurrection of Jesus. It means that, having in a certain manner already risen with Christ, we are also elevated to see on our horizon the point of arrival of all our history. "This means also that we have to join two indivisible things, that is, our construction of human history in Christ, and the acceptance concretely and existentially of his gift."[40]

The treatment of the resurrection event in Paul should lead us to appreciate the two poles of our existence, one pole being the keen involvement of the Christian with history and this life, and the other being an appreciation of the gratuity of a life wholly beyond our wildest hopes. Segundo cites 1 Cor. 15:20 to confirm this. He also points out that the resurrection passages in the gospels show this same reality. "Thus the risen Jesus among his friends is new, distinct, glorious, and his intimate friends delay in identifying him, in being sure that it is he. And, of course, he is profoundly and plainly the same."[41] The disciples of Emmaus recognize him when he does something very human, breaking bread. The disciples often recognize him when he joins them in the fruit of daily work in this life, eating fish and bread with them. Thus, there is continuity along with discontinuity in the salvation that Jesus brings.

The newness of life, and its eschatological implications are brought out by Segundo through a study of the very word new in the Bible. First, he spends a short while on the connotations of the word in current language. It can mean two things, which are actually interrelated. New connotes something recent or modern in time, and it connotes something qualitatively different, unforeseen and unexpected. The meanings merge in that the qualitative connotation always implies a temporal before, although it does not stress it. The temporal element tends to disappear as the profundity of an experience takes over. Thus, the word has a sense of discontinuity

within a framework of continuity. "This 'new'
something, which makes the previous situation
'old,' was possible thanks to the old even though
the latter does not explain it."[42]

   In looking to the word in the Scriptures,
as it goes through the whole biblical process as
Segundo defines it, we find both meanings for
new as we have been describing them. Both the
Septuagint and the New Testament use the word
neos to express temporal categories, and kainos
to express qualitative categories, especially for
descriptions of God transforming his people.
In the Old Testament the concept went through a
process of interiorization. Newness was first
perceived as the rhythm of nature. Eventually,
the liberation of spring came to be moved to the
liberation of humanity from slavery. Cyclic time
came to be converted into history. As Israel
came to appreciate more and more its infidelity
and Yahweh's fidelity, newness took on its
fullest meaning as the progressive manifestation
of mercy and new creation. It is a reencounter
with God. (See Jer. 31:31-34 and Ezech. 36:
25-29.)

   By the time of the New Testament the word
reaches its fullest sense with the final manifestation of God's grace and truth in Christ. The
word kainos is used for eschatological salvation,
and it takes on the two senses of discontinuity
within continuity. (See Gal. 6:15.) "'Newness'
is an historical category which expresses the
complex experience of love. . . . history . . .
acquires a new import. It becomes the slow,
progressive unfolding of all that which, in
germinal form, was definitively given to us in
Christ."[43]

   Segundo believes that a study of the word
grace in the biblical process reveals similar
conclusions. This word has complex meaning
derived from the Greek and the Hebrew, charis and
hen. In the Old Testament the Hebrew usage
seems more consistent in always using the word

168

for the benevolence of a superior towards an
inferior. It acquired a number of meanings:
enchantment, benevolence, mercy, gratitude.

As with most words, it began with a
corporeal reference and ended up with a more
spiritual, analogous meaning. It had the sense
of corporeal enchantment, then went to qualities
of soul in terms of an individual, and finally
arrived at spiritual qualities for human relations. When it came to describe human relations,
it spoke of benevolence only insofar as this
connoted at the same time the sense of enchantment. Benevolence with enchantment involves the
aspect of gift, since, as Segundo says, "Nothing
which is rigid, predetermined, mediocre, mild,
exact is enchanting. And on the contrary, the
enchanting always raises with it an abundance,
a freedom . . . , a gift."[44] Thus, in the theological sense in the Bible, grace took on the
two meanings of the enchanting aspects of human
relations and unmerited gift.

In the New Testament the word is not used
much in the gospels. Luke uses the word four
significant times (1:30; 2:40; 2:52; 4:22), but
not on the lips of Jesus except for two vulgar
uses (6:32, 34). Even these two uses, which
are probably not from Jesus in any case, according to Segundo, prepare the way for the theological meaning of abundance and gratuity.
Paul takes over the word grace for its one meaning of unmerited gift to describe the new reality
of salvation brought by Christ. He does this in
light of his own conversion and the realization
it brought that all came from God and nothing
from himself (Gal. 1:13-16). Once again, we are
led to the conclusion that salvation is both
continuous and discontinuous with this life.
It is the transformation of this life, but it is
the transformation of this life.[45]

Segundo provides further observations on
his eschatological interpretations of Scripture
through the analysis of the word salvation in the

Bible, and the other cognate words around sozo.
His major conclusion is that Christ gave his
message of salvation basically within the context
of extramundane salvation, but implicitly introduced elements that might correct this. Paul and
John spelled out the implications in terms of the
construction of human history. Detailed study of
the words for salvation will illustrate Segundo's
conclusions.[46]

To begin with, even the profane use of the
words save, savior, and salvation offers some
helpful meanings in the Scriptures. Segundo
follows the basic pattern of asking three questions answered by these words: Saved from what?
Who saves? How is one saved? In terms of what
salvation saves from, the profane usage indicates
any kind of evil, most often sickness, with
indications also of fear and even death.
Matt. 9:22 shows that the words for salvation
can be interchanged often with the words for
healing. Matt. 14:30 and John 12:27 show other
kinds of evil. In any case, in this aspect salvation and liberation are mixed together.

As for who saves, the answer is always
"another." Even in the profane sense there is
the idea of the unhoped-for. The passive voice
is used or the transitive form with subject and
object being different persons. Contrasted with
liberation, salvation makes another point: "To
be freed from something is to see oneself free
from an evil. On the other hand, and above all
in biblical language, to be saved is to be
object of an action which comes from another
agent."[47] Even outside of a religious sense, God
is frequently the subject. (See Mark 7:26;
John 12:27.)

In asking how one is saved, we are really
asking what the relationship is between savior
and saved. If there is something passive in the
one who is to be saved, so that he or she is the
object of benevolence, that quality is nevertheless quite personal and positive. It is best

described as faith in the sense of confiding oneself to the action of salvation. Faith is the
only word not a person that could be the subject
of save because it does not eliminate the person
in fact.

With these observations as background we
can look to the religious uses of the words for
salvation, beginning in the Old Testament. For
most of this literature what we have said holds
for the religious uses of the word as well as
the profane. What makes the word religious is
God's intervention and not any extramundane
reality. Any perusal of biblical passages would
show God saving from current human evils, so that
we are very much involved with this world
reality.

Another vision opens up with the wisdom
literature of the Old Testament, and its appreciation that God could not work his justice
totally within the limits of this earth. It
seems that evil triumphs too often in this life
for God's justice to be fully vindicated.
Wisdom solved this dilemma by seeing all of
this life as having relative evils, and saw
extramundane condemnation as the only absolute
evil. Salvation came to be associated then with
extramundane reality. We move towards a discontinuous eschatology. This life comes to be
a testing ground, measured especially in terms
of conformity to law, to prepare humanity for
rewards of the after-life. (See Wisd. 1:12-16;
2:11-20.)

When we turn to the New Testament, we find
that many texts seem to continue the themes
developed by wisdom literature, especially texts
close to the Hebrew mind. 1 Peter 1:3-5 seems
to stress that salvation is absolute and is concerned with the next life. James 2:4 talks of
works which are humanity's test in life in order
to achieve absolute salvation. Heb. 6:7-9 seems
to confirm these thoughts. However, Jesus begins
to make statements that put salvation in the next

171

life, but at the same time associate it with this life. Segundo compares Matt. 19:25-26 and Mark 16:16, which seem to indicate salvation as successful completion of a test, with Mark 10:26-30 and Luke 18:26-30, where salvation is also spoken of in terms of this world. Luke 9: 55-56, and the idea of not destroying this world, also links the temporal with the absolute of salvation.

What is subtle and indirect in the Synoptics and the teaching of Jesus is made more explicit in Paul. Like the use of the word salvation in the profane sense, Paul asks from what we are saved. His answer sometimes seems to talk about salvation in the absolute, without an object, and would then mean something extramundane. However, when we look more closely, we see that Paul also specifies evils from which we are saved. Segundo lists four from Rom. 8: 14-24 (after also noticing salvation in the absolute sense): inner slavery, fear, corruption of the surrounding universe, and subjection of our body. Salvation from these evils leads to liberation, to real freedom, and in this world.

Paul juxtaposes verbs in his epistles that show the interplay of this-worldly eschatology with the other-worldly. In Rom. 5:10, he uses future along with present and even past. "If while we were enemies we were reconciled to God by the death of his Son, much more, now that we are reconciled, shall we be saved by his life." Salvation is a prolongation of a change already in the present history. In the same passage that we just treated in Rom. 8, we are said to have already received adoptive sonship, and at the same time to hope and to groan interiorly for that sonship.

In asking who saves, Paul comes firmly to the answer that it is God (see 1 Cor. 1:18-21). Salvation must be seen as gratuitous. This relates to all we said previously about the antithesis of faith and works, and promise and

172

contract. It says that even the intramundane
aspects of salvation must not depersonalize
salvation and make it a question of determinisms
through defined works. It must remain the free
movement of persons, with God as ultimate agent.

Finally, Paul answers how we are to be
saved by God, and says it is through faith. In
a passage such as Phil. 2:12-13, he says that
salvation is a question of fear and trembling,
meaning that we cannot rest in our own security
and forget God's call to move in creative freedom.
On the other hand, he also says that we must work
out our salvation, showing that it is an intramundane activity.

From the several word studies that we
have done, we find that social analysis can
help derive insights into the biblical texts,
illustrating Segundo's hermeneutic circle. This
in turn draws an eschatological teaching from
the Bible that can support renewal of theology
and seek liberation of the poor in this world.
With this section we have completed our study
of Segundo's circle. In the next chapters we
will appraise his methodology, especially in
terms of ethical implications, and then compare
him with the other ethicists whom we have previously introduced, in order to show his contribution to the use of the Bible for Christian
ethics.

CHAPTER IV

NOTES

[1] Juan Luis Segundo, "The Church: A New Direction in Latin America," Catholic Mind 65 (1967): 44-45.

[2] Juan Luis Segundo, The Hidden Motives of Pastoral Action (Maryknoll, N.Y.: Orbis Books, 1978), pp. 120-32.

[3] Juan Luis Segundo, "Problemas teológicas de Latinoamerica," paper delivered at one of the first international Latin American conferences during Vatican II, Petropolis, Brazil, 1964, pp. 6-7. Cf. also Segundo, Hidden Motives, pp. 109-10.

[4] Juan Luis Segundo, "Teología: Mensaje y Proceso," Perspectivas de Diálogo 9 (1974): 264.

[5] Juan Luis Segundo, The Liberation of Theology (Maryknoll, N.Y.: Orbis Books, 1976), p. 112.

[6] Segundo, "Teología: Mensaje," p. 268.

[7] Ibid., p. 265.

[8] Ibid., p. 266.

[9] Segundo, Liberation, p. 116.

[10] Ibid.

[11] Ibid., p. 11, and footnote 9, p. 123.

[12] Ibid., p. 118.

[13] Ibid., p. 120.

[14] Ibid.

[15] Segundo, "Teología: Mensaje," p. 268.

[16] Juan Luis Segundo, "America Hoy," Vispera 1 (1967): 56.

[17] Segundo, Liberation, pp. 117-18.

174

[18] Segundo, "Teología: Mensaje," p. 268.

[19] Juan Luis Segundo, La Cristiandad: ¿Una Utopia?, vol. 2: Los Principios (Montevideo: Mimeografica "Luz," 1964), p. 27.

[20] Juan Luis Segundo, Grace and the Human Condition (Maryknoll, N.Y.: Orbis Books, 1973), p. 79.

[21] Ibid.

[22] Segundo, ¿Utopia?, vol. 2, p. 33.

[23] Ibid., p. 34. These observations about the law should also shed some interesting light on the role of Marxism or any political activity to bring justice to the earth. They show that any human effort must remain relative and ultimately inadequate to the full task. We will make observations that qualify Segundo's this-worldly eschatology in the next chapter.

[24] Ibid., p. 37.

[25] Juan Luis Segundo, "La Condición Humana," Perspectivas de Diálogo 2 (1967): 57.

[26] Ibid., p. 60.

[27] Segundo, ¿Utopia?, vol. 2, p. 75.

[28] Segundo, Grace, p. 80.

[29] Segundo, ¿Utopia?, vol. 2, p. 2.

[30] Segundo, Grace, p. 80.

[31] Raymond Brown, The Gospel according to John (New York: Doubleday, 1966), pp. 29-30.

[32] Segundo, ¿Utopia?, vol. 2, p. 4.

[33] Juan Luis Segundo, Masas y Minorías en la Dialéctica Divina de la Liberación (Buenos Aires: La Aurora, 1973), pp. 40-48.

[34] Segundo, ¿Utopia?, vol. 2, p. 51.

[35] Ibid., pp. 52-61.

[36] Ibid., p. 7.

[37] Segundo, Masas, p. 38.

[38]Nicodemus may be a poor paradigm for Segundo's hermeneutic circle. He can certainly be said to have his ideological presuppositions which block his hearing the message, but conversion comes not through deideologizing, but through the message of Christ. We will return to this point later.

[39]Juan Luis Segundo, "La Vida Eterna," Perspectivas de Diálogo 2 (1967): 116. Cf. also p. 85.

[40]Ibid., p. 116.

[41]Ibid., p. 117.

[42]Segundo, Grace, p. 119.

[43]Ibid., p. 122.

[44]Juan Luis Segundo, "¿Que Nombre Dar a la Existencia Cristiana?" Perspectivas de Diálogo 2 (1967): 6.

[45]Notice that in this regard Segundo makes one of his rare presentations of a model of Christ-transforming-culture. Cf. page 114 of this study.

[46]Juan Luis Segundo, De la Sociedad a la Teología (Buenos Aires: Ediciones Carlos Lohle, 1970), pp. 77-106.

[47]Ibid., p. 79.

CHAPTER V

A CRITICAL APPRAISAL

When one begins a critique of a liberation theologian, one already feels on the defensive. This entire study is in the academic realm. It seeks to establish principles rather than practice. It is done in the context of first world theology, by an author who lives in the context of the capitalist economic system. Let me begin, therefore, by stating that the entire study was undertaken because of the merits which I perceived Segundo to have, even for first world theology and ethics. His thinking is sophisticated and cannot be described as simplistic or myopic. It bears out the warning that Robert McAfee Brown gives against oversimplified or pseudo-issue critiques of liberation theology.[1]

At the same time, the method of this theology is newly elaborated and can only grow in sophistication through dialogue and critique. As much as is possible in this chapter I will try to take the position of the liberation theology of Segundo and will try to identify in some way with the perspective of commitment to the poor in Latin America. By the same token, I assume that concern for the poor does not necessitate my accepting all the methods and conclusions of Segundo. It is only by dialogue and critique that his own theology avoids becoming an inbred, sterile and factious reflection. It is that same dialogue and critique that will make Segundo speak even more clearly to the first world as well as to the third.

It must be noted, at the same time, that our study is not concerned with an overall view of Segundo or of liberation theology.[2] It seeks to penetrate his specific methodology for biblical hermeneutics and its relationship to Christian ethics. As we undertake our critique, therefore, we will direct it toward various aspects of the methodology as we have outlined it in the preceding chapters. It seems best to follow the general outline of the chapters on Segundo himself. Therefore, we will begin with an evaluation of his social analysis and then proceed to evaluate the relationship between faith and ideology. This will give us a view of his biblical exegesis modified by our critique. In the last chapter we will engage Segundo in a dialogue with first world exegesis and then, finally, compare him with the ethicists presented in chapter one. It will show Segundo's contribution to the debate over the biblical role in ethics.

Marxist Social Analysis and Revelation

We have stated that our evaluation does not embrace all of Segundo's liberation theology. In that case it will not be a detailed study of the content of Marxism. However, our critique will begin with some observations on the use of Marxist social analysis and the adequacy of social analysis in general as starting point for biblical hermeneutics.

Time and again in our presentation of Segundo we have come against the same basic question regarding his methodology. If social analysis is always the starting point, then where is the revelation? Does not the use of sociology in Segundo's fashion dictate that revelation is a human determination rather than a divine initiative? Our answer is that this is not necessarily so, although Segundo may be guilty of excess in his use of sociology in such an exclusive way.

Segundo seems to be building on the theory of revelation propounded by theologians such as Karl Rahner and others who claim that God reveals only through the human and that good theology is ultimately good anthropology. Rahner writes:

As soon as man is understood as the being who is absolutely transcendent in respect to God, 'anthropocentricity' and 'theocentricity' in theology are not opposites but strictly one and the same thing, seen from two sides. Neither of the two aspects can be comprehended at all without the other. Thus, although anthropocentricity in theology is not the opposite of the strictest theocentricity, it is opposed to the idea that in theology man is one particular theme among others.[3]

As Rahner unfolds his explanation of this principle, he links the objective knowledge of God to the subjective possibilities and limits of the knowing human person. "Whenever one is confronted with an object of dogma, one inquires as to the conditions necessary for it to be known by the theological subject, ascertaining that the a priori conditions for knowledge of the object are satisfied, and showing that they imply and express something about the object, the mode, method, and limits of knowing it."[4] According to Rahner, it is not a question of humanity dictating the revelation, but it is a question of God revealing himself in and only through human existence. Moreover, if this reality is not to leave humanity on the level of an abstract, unhistorical transcendent being, then the same process must unfold in history as humanity struggles to bring its a priori, prereflexive knowledge to the status of a posteriori, reflexive knowledge in history.

What Rahner expresses in rather complicated philosophical language Segundo describes in simpler terminology: "The passages [of the New Testament] which allow theologians to discourse on what God is in himself, independent of our life and history, can be counted on one's fingers; and it is even doubtful whether they can be separated from a context wherein God consistently reveals himself in dialogue with human existence."[5] The particular merit of Segundo is to make explicit that socio-economic and political influences affect how humanity sees itself and, therefore, how it conceives the revelation of God. "Thus it does not take too much imagination to realize that the infinite, inaccessible God-as-nature, the creator of an order prior or indifferent to the existence of each individual, is at the same time the projection and justification of our desire and our effort to rigidly structure other people within our societal life."[6]

What Segundo says about starting his hermeneutic circle from social analysis, then, may not necessarily remove divine initiative from revelation. Nevertheless, once we move from the level of a priori, pre-reflexive knowledge to that of a posteriori and self-conscious knowledge of God there is the need for criteria to safeguard that the insights derived are truly objective and not just projections of human subjective needs. Segundo himself demonstrates the concern for objective truth: "We cannot go along with the idea [of Marx and Freud] that reason is totally dominated by practical interests. Nor can we agree that the idea of God is merely the projection of some more or less hidden intention of the individual or society. But their suspicion helps us to realize that while the idea of God can be liberative, it may also be the source of much hypocrisy."[7]

We are back again to our question of objectivity. While Segundo does say often enough that he seeks objectivity in the Bible, he does not seem to ever center in on the exact criteria for theological, exegetical or ethical truth. It remains a shortcoming of his hermeneutic circle. Nevertheless, he does make some cryptic statements that we can enlarge on, and which may perhaps give us some criteria for objectivity. At the same time, they will require that we qualify the hermeneutic circle as we have presented it in the previous chapters.

180

Early in his presentation of the hermeneutic circle Segundo writes: "A hermeneutic circle in theology always presupposes a profound human commitment, a <u>partiality</u> that is consciously accepted--not on the basis of theological criteria, of course, but <u>on the basis of human</u> criteria."[8] He never spells out what these human criteria are, but we can attempt that in our critique. The human criteria are the totality of other ideologies[p] which give insight into human existence, which provide context and balance to socio-political analysis, and which relativize it and prevent its becoming an ideology[n].

To phrase this in more classical theological terms, revelation comes through the human historical situation. We cannot escape this reality in searching for objectivity, but we can use it to approach objectivity. Every human situation, because it is historically conditioned must be relative and, therefore, in danger of becoming subjectively distorted as the full vehicle of divine revelation. What prevents this distortion is the balance of other historically conditioned insights. We can never attain absolute objectivity, but we can approach it with greater assurance by the totality of human experience as vehicle of revelation.

Use of this criterion requires more than anything else an evaluation of the ideology[p] to see if it genuinely describes human reality and is thus a fitting vehicle for revelation. It also demands that we place a particular ideology[p] into the context of other ideologies[p] in order to see it in proper perspective and to come closer to the authentic revelation. We will do this with Segundo's own ideological perspectives, especially with his Marxist social analysis. There seem to be some weaknesses in his approach that can be pointed out by a testing of the ideology.

Another criterion that we may find helpful is built on what Segundo has said previously about Christ as part of a learning process. It may be that application of the text of Scripture is a second-step procedure based on deutero-learning, but Christ still performs some normative function as part of proto-learning. One is not free to by-pass the first steps or to construct an ideology^p just out of human experience. Previous human experience--albeit couched in an inevitable ideology^p--has already captured an insight into divine revelation which must be normative in some way for future generations.

What we are saying ultimately is that if Christ is to function in any fashion as norm, as part of proto-learning, then there must be a true dialectic between text of Scripture and human experience or ideology^p. Christ does not negate human experience, but he does relativize any particular human experience. The danger with identifying theology with anthropology is that one can shift too easily to the side of immanence in revelation and lose the transcendence. The genuine Christian path is a delicate balance and a dialectic between immanence and transcendence.

If and as long as these historical mediations are really mediations to the presence and acceptance of the mystery of God, and while retaining their relative nature yet prove themselves even in this way as unavoidable for the historical being of man in this aeon before the direct vision of God is reached, history and transcendence will never be subject in Christianity to an ideology of immanence, i.e., to the idolisation of intramundane powers, or to an ideology of transmanence and transcendence, i.e., to the idolisation in empty, formal abstractions of man's transcendentality by grace.[9]

Segundo himself has said that faith relativizes every ideology^p, but one wonders if in practice he acknowledges this. If one begins

182

always with social analysis and ideology^P, then one does not have a dialectic. In almost all that we have exposed of Segundo's circle we have reiterated over and over that social analysis is the foundation, the beginning, the challenge and the precondition to exegesis and theology. It may be a good thing overstated, for theology and the Bible must also be the foundation, the beginning, the challenge of social analysis from a Christian perspective. There must be a dialectic. Segundo seems not to accept this.

On the other hand, it is quite conceivable that Segundo recognizes the dialectic and is simply presenting one side of the picture because of his commitment to the poor. After all, it is not simply an academic question. He says explicitly in one place, "We have seen that the notion of God stemming from revelation and our interpersonal relations in societal life condition each other mutually."[10] He explicitly states that the divine revelation must be something which transcends the human and would, then, seemingly be in dialectic with the human: "If there is no divine intervention in history, not only is the biblical account mythological, but the interpretation of it is merely human."[11] My guess, therefore, is that Segundo himself, if pressed, would admit that the hermeneutic circle is a valid methodology for partial insight into the biblical text, so long as a dialectic can be maintained whereby Scripture challenges the preceding stages and relativizes the insights of social analysis and ideology^P. Later in this chapter we will offer some ways in which it seems theology (perhaps based on other ideologies^P) gives perspectives which modify Segundo's ideology^P and social analysis as well as confirm it.

With this background on the nature of revelation, its dialectic with social analysis, and the criteria for determining its objectivity, we can undertake more specific critique of Segundo's hermeneutic circle. Granted the validity of using social analysis as vehicle of revelation, our first question is over the adequacy of Marxist social analysis as this vehicle. Of course, as we mentioned previously, our question is not concerned with an evaluation of Marxism as such, but rather with Marxism as interpreted by Segundo.

To begin with, Segundo does bring to Roman Catholic theology a less fearful approach to Marxism, an approach which allows the possibility of dialogue. Vatican II gave some initiative in that direction by vaguely dialoguing with modern atheism through its document on The Church in the Modern World. However, the general attitude has been one of misgivings about Marxism and the denial of any possibility of dialogue. Some of the staunchest critics of liberation theology reflect this viewpoint within Roman Catholicism, for their chief argument is that Marxism is necessarily linked to atheism and is therefore inimical to any theological use.[12] Segundo is more optimistic and thus opens the door to an area of thought that has influenced an entire sphere of the globe and that must be reckoned with in the modern world.

Our author is able to take this approach, which seems valid in our analysis, for several reasons. The first reason is summed up well by Robert McAfee Brown: "If Aquinas could create a medieval theology by responding to a non-Christian (Aristotle), there is no reason why theologians today could not create a contemporary Christian theology by responding to another non-Christian (Marx)."[13] In addition, the use of Marxism becomes even more of a possibility when we consider that there are many versions of Marxism, all of which owe something to Marx and none of which merely repeat him. Segundo himself observes,

Those who identify themselves with Marx and his thinking have a thousand different

184

ways of conceiving and interpreting "Marxist" thought. Aside from that fact, the point is that the great thinkers of history do not replace each other; rather, they complement and enrich each other. . . . After Marx, our way of conceiving and posing the problems of society will never be the same again. Whether everything Marx said is accepted or not, and in whatever way one may conceive his "essential" thinking, there can be no doubt that present-day social thought will be "Marxist" to some extent: that is, profoundly indebted to Marx.[14]

With such broad possibilities of interpreting Marx there are no a priori difficulties of using him for theology, and we have seen adequately enough the points that Segundo has derived from his version of Marx. It may be a question of overusing Marx or emphasizing him excessively that needs to be challenged, rather than the use of Marx as such. We will treat that question in the next section.

If we are maintaining a dialectic between biblical text and the social analysis then we must also ask if there are any aspects of Segundo's use of Marx that would be inimical to use by theology. Does theology challenge anything that must be rejected in Marxism? In this regard Segundo again gives indication that he recognizes a genuine dialectic between text and human experience, for he addresses what appear to him to be problems in Marx that would make it impossible to use him for theology and exegesis.

We have already seen how Segundo addresses himself to the accusations that Marxism is necessarily atheistic or that it is necessarily linked to materialistic determinism.[15] He refutes both charges as not being essential to Marx and so, enables Marx to be useful for insights into the Bible. As Segundo presents Marxist social analysis, therefore, it can be an adequate vehicle

for revelation and it can serve well as the first
steps of the hermeneutic circle offering insights
that affect how we read the Bible. We must
address now, however, the question of overstatement and the question of objectivity through the
testing of ideology^p in the light of other
ideologies^p.

The Testing of Ideology

Our reservations with Segundo's hermeneutic circle throughout this study have centered on
the problem of verifiability. His observations
are well taken about the impossibility of arriving at absolute truths as the content of faith,
and about all faith having to work itself out
in particular ideologies. The problem is in
controlling the ideology so that it does not
evolve from ideology^p, an efficacious means of
faith, into ideology^n, an all-consuming system.

We have already noted how Segundo's
methodology calls for Marxist and other social
analysis as the starting point for theology
and exegesis. We also have other explicit
examples of how he assumes that his Marxist
sociology is accurate and an always valid
starting point for theology. He says, for
example, that eschatology requires an opening
toward the future, and then draws on definitions
of the political left which define it as the
conquest of that which is unrealized, as the
openness toward utopia. With this definition
of the left, our author can then make the claim:
"For that very reason the sensibility of the
left is an intrinsic feature of an authentic
theology."[16] It seems on the one hand that this
definition of the left is too broad to verify
that Marxism must underlie theological analysis,
for there can be many versions of the political
left. On the other hand, the definition is too
narrow in saying that only the left is open
toward the future. Right-wing politics can
have the sense that the future must embrace past

traditions. It can be open to the future in another way. In other words, Segundo's assumptions are not totally verified, and not always valid. Once again, this critique does not eliminate his methodology, but it does qualify it. There is a problem of verifiability.

On the same occasion Segundo made a claim similar to the one above, a claim which we presented in an earlier chapter: "[Liberation theology] is theology seen not from one of the various possible standpoints, but from the one standpoint indicated by Christian sources as the authentic, privileged one for the understanding of divine revelation in Jesus Christ."[17] If faith must work itself out in relative ideologies, then how can there be one privileged standpoint? This seems to deny the hermeneutic circle itself. It points to the need for verification of the first steps, and not the simple assumption that they are an accurate view of life.

Finally, on this same point, we can question the statement of Segundo cited previously in another section of our study: "Evangelizing, then, presupposes . . . that we ourselves find and communicate the essential of the good news."[18] We can ask ourselves how it is possible to get to the essential without any ideology? Put another way, why should we assume that Segundo's perspective from commitment to the poor, a perspective of Marxism, is the essential message of Christianity? It is the problem of objectivity or verifiability.

As we try to verify the ideological positions of Segundo, we can make some observations that qualify his social analysis and thereby modify the presuppositions that we would bring to the hermeneutic circle. We can notice, for instance, that the problem of massification is a real danger within socialism as well as within capitalism. Segundo himself observes how Lenin needed to posit the existence of the masses even within the socialist state, but he seems to accept that as an integral part of political and social analysis. He is negative about massification only when it is seen as oppressive capitalism massifying the poor in order to enslave them in their oppression. It seems to me that massification is a negative element in any situation, although it may not be totally inescapable in this world. Even within socialism, therefore, there is the danger of depersonalizing individuals for the sake of the collectivity. It is a danger which trades one form of massification for another.

We find an invaluable insight in the notion of massification. However, the verifying of that view leads us to root it in a pluralistic social analysis. It seems not the insight of Marxist sociology alone, and is not overcome by Marxist sociology alone.[19] It does not necessarily lead us to an anti-capitalistic reading of the Bible, although it may lead us to a political reading of the Bible which opposes massification of humanity.

These qualifications that we bring to Marxist social analysis also lead us to ask if there is not still some hope for a theory of development. While Marxism may have some insights into the way capitalism leads the underdeveloped countries more and more deeply into poverty, it may not have the full truth in saying that socialism is the only way out. For one thing, the initial process of socialism simply perpetuates a discrimination between classes, for it merely reverses the dominating and the dominated. "The people" can be as unjust as the rich property owners whose possessions they take over. As Pierre Bigo observes:

Why have a revolution if it simply means denying to some what has been for all too long kept from others: the right to be judged according to a norm of justice not defined simply on the basis of class interests?

Every human being, every group attains
equity only through a hard struggle against
all that masks and alters justice in the
human heart.[20]

It seems, moreover, that even when Marxism
attempts to remedy the problems of poverty and
massification, it achieves success only by also
incorporating capitalist techniques. As Bigo
observes, "Marx himself accepts the creativity of
capital in at least one instance. His thesis on
qualified work, a multiple of simple work, is
well known. . . . And if qualified work has a
right to a higher revenue, is it not as one sort
of capital?"[21]

In similar fashion, the socialist reality
is inclined more and more to recognize the creativity in humanity's tendency to save and to
invest. This leads to compensating efforts which
promote these tendencies, and ultimately says
that absolute equality is counterproductive. In
the same way, initiative and real interest in work
comes from a genuine participation in the fruit
of that work. A total collectivity dampens
initiative. For this reason we find socialist
nations reorganizing enterprises to give relative
autonomy to each unit, with workers sharing in the
decision-making. It becomes a modified type of
property ownership. Once again, Segundo may have
a valuable insight into the problems of the poor
and may bring valuable presuppositions to this
theology and exegesis, but the first steps of
his hermeneutic circle need verifiability and
cannot simply be assumed as accurate views of
life. When verification is attempted, his views
need modification, although they do not seem to
have to be rejected outright.

Even granting the need to posit a plurality
of political analyses behind the phenomenon of
massification, another question arises as to the
extent to which masses and minorities should be
used as sufficient categories of society. It is
one thing to divide humanity into masses and

minorities, oppressor and oppressed, on a theoretical level. It is another thing to form these categories in the concrete. Segundo may thus be guilty of not extending the categories enough, while in other ways overusing the categories.

We have just seen that Segundo may be too restricted in using masses and minorities because he relies much on Marxist social analysis, at least derivatively through Lenin. We can now add that he may be too restricted in keeping only to the economic realm in any social analysis. There are other forms of alienation besides the economic, whether the latter be from capitalism or socialism. Consideration must be given to sex, race, creed, nationality, etc., and all of these would contribute to massification of society. Thus, Segundo may have valuable contributions in positing presuppositions to biblical exegesis, but his hermeneutic circle is incomplete in that he has only limited presentation of what these presuppositions are.

On the other hand, where he does use masses and minorities, he may be guilty of overuse. Can one, for instance, conveniently divide the world politically into oppressors and oppressed? The view is partially true, but cannot be an adequate category by itself. Moreover, there seems also to be a danger of elitism in the way Segundo uses this category of the minority. For one thing, he seems to think that on the concrete level, the effective minority is the one that operates on Marxist social principles of analysis. It is too exclusive a view of masses and minorities, as we have seen, since the Marxist minority is not totally free from oppressing the masses, and since a minority could operate effectively on other than Marxist social analysis.

An indication of this elitist tendency through a too heavy reliance on Marxist sociology appears in what Segundo expects from the Latin American bishops. He criticizes their support of existing governments as maintaining the status quo,

and implies they should take specific political
stances based on the Marxist social analysis.[22]
This may actually be expecting too much from the
bishops, since the social and political analysis
is much more complicated than that, and since
the Christian message can operate authentically
through a plurality of political analyses.
Segundo may be correct in criticizing the bishops
for maintaining the status quo, but he moves
toward elitism in asking them to make a specific
Marxist declaration as the Christian minority
message.

In the last chapter of The Liberation of
Theology our author gives four expressions of the
tension between masses and minorities. He speaks
of an ecclesiastical formulation (Christendom vs.
little flock or leaven), a socio-political
formulation (Marxist-Leninist presentation of the
masses), a scientific or biological formulation
(Teilhard de Chardin's view of life as an overcoming of inertia in matter), and a biblical
response to the other three (e.g., in the concept
of flesh and world). He suggests here again the
hermeneutic circle in that the first three
formulations suggest what to look for in the
biblical text, and the biblical text can speak
to the previous formulations. In this particular part of his writings he gives the impression
of a wide view of masses and minorities, with
the Marxist application simply as one among many.
However, in other sections of his works, where
he speaks of these formulations, he gives the
impression that the Marxist-Leninist social
analysis is the practical application of the
other expressions of masses and minorities, and
is the foundational insight (precondition) that
helps uncover the others.[23] In this overuse of
one particular social analysis he runs the risk
of elitism.

The idea of masses and minorities can tend
toward elitism also when Segundo relates them too
strictly to numerical categories. The valid
concept of masses concerns a qualitative

ingredient, massification as the path of least resistance. It is immaterial whether or not massified humanity is a quantitative mass or a small segment of a society, although the process is more generally related to the desire to keep large numbers under domination. In any case, the concept of minority does not have to be linked to quantitative categories. If one can act creatively, decisively and with appreciation of the complexity of motives required, then one functions in a minority capacity. Thus, Segundo's categories are extremely helpful in highlighting the dehumanization of society, but they become elitist when he links them to specific numbers of people.

The concept of minority runs the risk of elitism especially when Segundo speaks of ecclesiology and the problems of mass Christianity. While the desire for numbers may have led to the massification of Christians, it is not necessarily true to say that they can be de-massified only by being reduced in numbers. Where does one draw the line? To speak of small numbers seems to make Christianity in the concrete a religion of the few, and discriminates against the numerical masses of society. This is not necessary to maintain the valid point that Segundo makes about massification, even within Christianity.

Segundo does seem to acknowledge the possibility of the minority being a quantitatively large number. He likens this "popular messianism" to Marx's "proletarian messianism," whereby the masses themselves change attitudes and structures. He also says in the same section of his book, "From a more strictly methodological viewpoint, a 'theology of the people' [i.e., the masses with minority traits] would seem to lead us towards a hermeneutic circle that could very well enrich such a theology and keep it vital."[24] Nevertheless, when he gives more extensive treatment to masses and minorities in Christianity, he does not seem to apply this possibility, but treats the minority rather like a quantitative few.[25]

At minimum, therefore, Segundo's concept of masses and minorities runs the risk of elitism if it is not actually guilty of such. We will make application of it when we compare him with other ethicists, but the cautions we have elaborated must be kept in mind. Segundo may be conscious of his own ambiguity, for he says, "It is worth noting here that Marxism has never really solved this basic issue either [of masses and minorities], not in an explicit and convincing way at least. . . . So we are left with a major issue that must still be explored."[26]

What we have seen thus far shows the necessity of verification of the first steps of the hermeneutic circle, and also offers modification in what Segundo brings as his analysis of the life situation. We have been trying to apply the "human criteria" for objectivity, the balance of other ideologies[p] and views of life, as we proposed to do at the beginning of this chapter of our study. In what follows we wish to come back briefly to the other criterion proposed earlier, i.e., the need for a true dialectic between text and life experience. We have already mentioned that if revelation is to maintain its aspect of transcendence as well as immanence, then what the Bible says must somehow challenge the life experience as well as being influenced by life experience. We can now reiterate this same point by taking up the distinction Segundo makes between ideology[p] as efficacious means and faith as value system.[27]

Segundo makes a good distinction in contrasting faith and ideology[p] and in saying that faith relativizes every ideology[p]. The difficulty seems to be that he does not allow for this in his concrete applications, when he uses his hermeneutic circle. For him to say that he always begins with social analysis or ideology[p] is to hide the fact that he is making hidden value judgments as to which ideologies to use. What determines that some ideologies are negative and some positive? Why begin with some and

193

not others? It seems that the very use of an ideology[p] is already a value judgment, and, on Segundo's terms, that must come from faith. On the other hand, the full appreciation of faith is influenced by the ideologies operating. In other words, we have much more of a dialectic than Segundo's hermeneutic circle calls for. His methodology gives valuable insight, but it is a partial insight within the dialectic.

We can ask Segundo why commitment to liberation is the entry into the hermeneutic circle. My guess is that he overstates his point precisely because that is the nature of a commitment. He is rightly convinced that the situation of poverty in Latin America--and elsewhere for that matter--is of such proportions that it is intolerable for Christianity to let it continue. He finds that many attempts to solve the problem up to the present have been futile and he sees Marxism as offering a ray of hope--at least a new possibility. Marxism is to be taken seriously, and so Segundo undoubtedly feels it will not be taken at all unless he insists only on that approach.

But what is to prevent us from merely reversing the conflict or inverting the problem? If the difficulty in the past has been that the Bible has been interpreted through the prejudiced optic of the rich and the dominant, what is to prevent the same thing from happening through the poor or dominated? What will prevent their reading the Bible through prejudiced views? It seems to me that it can only be avoided through a dialectic in which faith and the Scriptures themselves relativize any reading of the text, even while life situation determines how one is reading the Scriptures.

This judgment may appear to coopt all that Segundo and liberation theology are trying to accomplish. I hope not. I hope that their commitment still comes through, especially to

encourage our own. Nevertheless, commitment is
one thing, and academic formulation of a
methodology is another. As Segundo uses the
term "hermeneutic circle" it is only a geometric
figure of speech for stages of interpretation
that he does not think can be switched around.
As we have been presenting our critique, the
"hermeneutic circle" is a genuine statement of
the interrelationship of the stages. The fourth
step is also the first step in a dialectical
relationship. One can really enter on the level
of the text or the ideology^p--or other
ideologies^p for that matter--but each influences
the other.

In what follows we will consider not what
ideology^p offers to biblical interpretation, but
what the text says to relativize the (Marxist)
social analysis of Segundo. We will look to some
biblical exegesis that relates to what he has
suggested for the changes in theology at the
third step of the hermeneutic circle. We will
look to biblical exegesis to see how it qualifies,
as well as supports, his claims that theology can
meet social analysis by refining its eschatological teaching. Our critique will be an
attempt to complete the dialectic.

Biblical Teaching on the Kingdom

A rapid survey of the wealth of literature
that has been devoted to the teaching of the
kingdom in the life of Jesus reveals a myriad of
opinions and conflicting viewpoints. The questions are still not resolved. Segundo's own
approach to the topic would certainly find home
with one group of exegetes, even if they would
probably not agree with the Marxist social
analysis to which the eschatological teaching was
addressing itself. I am referring to the group
of American exegetes who tend to see Jesus as a
prophet, to stress that his eschatological
teaching is in terms of this continuing world

order, and who therefore put the emphasis on the present dimensions of the kingdom. This group would include those of the liberal theological tradition which prevailed at the beginning of the century, and is highlighted in Walter Rauschenbusch. We will return to his particular theology and ethics later in the chapter which follows. The group is also represented by exegetes who write well after the eschatological debates precipitated by Schweitzer's studies, and are represented by Amos Wilder.[28]

Nevertheless, some modifications will have to be made in Segundo's views, even as they are proposed for this school which de-eschatologizes the message of Jesus into this-worldly prophetic teaching. As Norman Perrin summed it up:

In many ways this work represents the last stand in the Anglo-American theological world against the movement towards the recognition of the essentially eschatological nature of the Kingdom in the teaching of Jesus which began with the impact of konsequente Eschatologie. It represents the last of a number of attempts that have been made to show that Jesus 'transformed' the eschatological concepts that he used. But like the remainder of these attempts it breaks down on the hard fact that it cannot be reconciled with the evidence in the New Testament.[29]

We have now to look at some of the New Testament evidence as it will help us dialogue with Segundo's eschatological views.

There is still debate as to what distinguishes apocalyptic preaching from other eschatological teaching, but several elements seem more obvious than others. Apocalyptic preaching seems cast in a dualistic mold and makes more definitive the opposition between good and evil. It deals with the final period of world history and is concerned with the end of the present age and

196

the introduction of a new age. It is cosmic in outlook and pictures world catastrophe at some final stage of history. Finally, it views the last days as the work of God and his intervention, and not as the achievement of humanity in any way.[30]

When one considers passages such as Matt. 12:28 ("If it is by the Spirit of God that I cast out demons, then the kingdom of God has come upon you."), and Luke 17:20-21 ("The kingdom of God is not coming with signs; . . . [it] is in the midst of you."), both of which, in one form or another, are usually accepted as authentic sayings of Jesus, there is no doubt that he used apocalyptic language about the kingdom. The question now is whether Jesus retained only the language of apocalyptic or also the meaning. The fact that some of the sayings of Jesus refer to future expectations, and the fact that they can scarcely be explained away, supports the view that Jesus did acknowledge the apocalyptic expectations of Judaism.

In Mark 9:1, for example, there have been various unsatisfactory attempts to eliminate the future orientation or the apocalyptic color of the statement. C. H. Dodd originally claimed that the sentence could read, "There are some of those standing here who will not taste of death until they have seen that the Kingdom of God has come with power."[31] His claim, in this interpretation, was that the kingdom had arrived in the life of Jesus and that the disciples would recognize its power later on. When criticism of this exegesis mounted, Dodd himself offered another view, one shared by those who would see the kingdom almost totally in terms of this world reality. He said that the coming referred to the time after the resurrection and the conferral of the Spirit, when the kingdom would be seen "in power" in the life of the early Church.[32] This second opinion seems as unlikely as the first, because the early Church never saw its age of the

Spirit as the fulfillment of kingdom. We are led
to the conclusion that the passage has apocalyptic reference, a point made explicit by the
interpretation of the parallel statement in
Matt. 16:28 (". . . see the Son of Man coming
in his kingdom").

Other sayings of Jesus confirm his apocalyptic teaching. The sayings about the Son of
Man are shown by Jeremias to be authentic to
Jesus himself, at least in the essentials.[33]
These point to a new order of things, and reach
their culmination in the confession by Jesus at
his trial that God's final intervention in history was yet to come, but was inevitable.
Though these titles used at the trial scene in
Mark 14:61-62 may show the work of early Christian redactors and may be secondary to the
authentic sayings of Jesus, nevertheless they
seem to rest on a basic historical nucleus which
says that Jesus was put to death for distorted
accusations resting on his apocalyptic claims
for the coming of the kingdom of God. W. G.
Kümmel believes the statement itself is authentic to Jesus.[34]

The apocalyptic teaching of Jesus is con-
firmed also by his claims that the temple will
be destroyed, whether spiritually or physically,
and the new temple established as sign of the
eschatological community. The historicity of
this claim by Jesus rests on the accusations
brought against him at the trial before the
Sanhedrin, accusations which corroborate the
other sayings of Jesus about the temple. See
Matt. 23:37-39 ("O Jerusalem, . . . your house
is forsaken. . . . you will not see me again
until you say, 'Blessed is he who comes'");
Mark 11:15-19 (temple cleansing); 13:1-2 ("There
will not be left a stone upon another"); 14:58
("We heard him say, 'I will destroy this
temple'"); 15:29 ("[Mockers derided him,] 'You
who would destroy the temple, . . . save your-
self'").

Finally, a number of parables stress the future element in Jesus' teaching, and confirm the apocalyptic content of his preaching. J. Jeremias offers two specific categories to describe this. The four contrasting parables (the Mustard Seed, the Leaven, the Sower, and the Patient Husbandman), as well as the parables of the Unjust Judge and the Man Asking for Help in the Night, all point to the future coming of the kingdom as a preaching of "great assurance." On the other hand, parables such as the Children in the Marketplace, the Unfruitful Fig Tree, and other sayings speak of the future coming of the kingdom as a preaching of "imminent catastrophe."[35]

Nevertheless, while we must call Jesus a preacher of the apocalyptic message, we cannot label him completely an apocalypticist. Norman Perrin showed that Jesus stressed only certain aspects of apocalyptic teaching, namely, that the kingdom was God's work in history, and that it represented a final stage of redemption for mankind.[36] Jesus was not interested in showing history moving in a predetermined course to a predetermined climax, nor was he interested in outlining the sequence of events leading to the climax or the signs and calculations related to the end. As Kümmel sums it up: "Though it cannot indeed be denied that Jesus shared these apocalyptic conceptions, yet it can also be stressed that he felt very little interest in them."[37]

That Jesus wanted to stress God's intervention in history is evident from a number of sayings on the kingdom. Mark 1:15 ("The kingdom of God is at hand; repent!") is disputed as to whether engiken means present or imminent, but in either case it depicts the kingdom as an advancing force on God's part. Other sayings of the kingdom also use the word coming as an indication of an invading force, a symbol of God's initiative. See, for example, Mark 9:1;

Matt. 12:28; Luke 17:20-21, all already referred
to. Other sayings tell of God giving the kingdom,
of it being inherited or received, so that the
initiative once again is God's. Mark 10:15
("Receive the kingdom like a child"); Luke 18:29
("There is no man who has left . . . for the sake
of the kingdom"); Luke 12:32 ("Fear not little
flock, for it is your Father's pleasure to give
you the kingdom"); Matt. 8:11-12 ("Many will come
from east and west and sit in the kingdom");
Matt. 25:34 ("Come, O blessed of my Father,
inherit the kingdom") are instances. Finally,
the parables which were erroneously described as
parables of growth are seen more as parables of
the secret workings of the kingdom, the power of
God's invading force that is working certainly
and imperceptibly in history. These are parables
such as the Mustard Seed and the Leaven.

Jesus does seem to take apocalyptic preaching seriously in stressing that the kingdom is
the final inbreaking of God into our history, so
that it brings the end of time and this world
reality. This teaching is highlighted by sayings
that stress the radical newness of the kingdom,
such as Mark 14:24 ("I shall not drink . . .
until . . . I drink it new in the kingdom");
Luke 11:20 ("If it is by the finger of God that
I cast out demons, then the kingdom of God has
come"); Matt. 11:11b ("Who is least in the kingdom is greater than [John]"). Sayings which
speak of the kingdom as a coming banquet are also
concerned with the end of time. "From its origin in Isa. 25.6-8 the concept of an eschatological banquet as a symbol of participation in
the final blessed communion with God is used in
apocalyptic and it plays a real part of the
teaching of Jesus."[38] Examples would include a
passage such as Matt. 8:11 ("They will come from
east . . . and sit at table"). In the same vein
sayings which convey a reversal of values also
convey the eschatological finality of the kingdom.
See Matt. 5:3,10 ("Theirs is the kingdom");
Mark 10:23b, 25 ("How hard for those who have

200

riches to enter the kingdom. . . . It is easier
for a camel to go through the eye of a needle");
Luke 18:29 ("No man who has left . . . for the
sake of the kingdom"); Matt. 21:31 ("Tax col-
lectors and the harlots go into the kingdom").
Finally, once again a group of parables, such
as the Wheat and the Tares, and the Fish Net,
present the kingdom as the time of consummation.[39]

In the light of the biblical data and
what it seems to present, Segundo's contention
that the kingdom is a symbol of this-world
achievement would have to be modified. Doing
theology from commitment to the poor, or bringing life situation into the interpretation of
Scripture cannot simply make the Bible say what
it is not saying. Especially if the hermeneutic circle can be entered by beginning with
the boundaries that Scripture sets, then the
social analysis of reality must be qualified
by an eschatology that has apocalyptic dimensions.

What we have seen up to this point about
the biblical teaching of the kingdom does not,
however, totally eliminate Segundo's perspective of a present and realized eschatology in
this world reality. In fact, doing theology
from the perspective of commitment for the poor
draws our attention more sharply to that particular aspect of Jesus' teaching. Indeed,
while Christ preached an apocalyptic aspect of
the kingdom, he also proclaimed quite clearly
that there is a present aspect of the kingdom
of God.

When one looks at the sayings about the
kingdom, it is surprising that there can be any
claim that the kingdom is seen as wholly
future. A great number of sayings make it clear
that the kingdom is seen in some form as a
present reality bursting in upon humanity in
this world. Such sayings center especially upon

the response expected of man and woman for entrance into the kingdom. They intimate that the kingdom is within man and woman's grasp and require proper dispositions lived out in terms of this world reality. These passages show that the kingdom already has its effect in this history. See, for example, Mark 10:23-25 (difficulty of riches for the kingdom); 12:34 ("You are not far from the kingdom"); Matt. 6:33 ("Seek first his kingdom"); 11:12 ("The kingdom has suffered violence and men of violence take it"); 19:12 ("There are eunuchs for the sake of the kingdom").

Even some passages which show the apocalyptic dimensions of the kingdom--passages which, as we saw, stress God's work and relativize human achievement--even these passages often have a present dimension. They speak of God beginning the work of the kingdom in the present world reality, so that it affects human history. Such passages would be Matt. 11:11b; 11:12; 12:28; Luke 12:32; 17:20-21. Finally, some of the parables also stress the present reality of the kingdom, e.g., the Hidden Treasure and the Pearl of Great Price.[40] As Norman Perrin pointed out, even after putting a stress on the apocalyptic elements in the preaching of Jesus,

the apocalyptic understanding of history is presupposed in searching for signs of the end or calculating its coming, and in rejecting this approach in Luke 17.20f, Jesus is rejecting the understanding of history which it presupposes. The coming of the Kingdom cannot be calculated in advance, nor will it be accomplished by signs such as apocalyptic sought, because the Kingdom is the sovereign power of God breaking into history and human experience in a manner to be determined by God, it is not history moving inevitably to a climax predetermined in accordance with a divine plan to which apocalyptic seers have had access. In effect, we have in this saying a rejection

of the apocalyptic understanding of history
and a return to the prophetic understanding.[41]

If there is, in fact, a modification in
some of the aspects of Jesus' apocalyptic teaching, and if there is a present dimension to the
kingdom, then it will show itself in moral demands
in the present. Are we not, then, converging on
Segundo's claim for a realized and present
eschatology that shows itself in social justice?
Segundo himself summed up this view of eschatology, rejecting a full dichotomy between
history as humanity's work and eschatology as
God's work: "We do not think that the eschatological is only a negation of the historical,
but a construction, in the historical, of something which surpasses historical possibilities."[42]

That statement of Segundo can stand and
can fit in well with what we have been developing
here. It all depends on what Segundo means by
construction and how many possibilities he
thinks can be realized in the historical. He
does speak of the life of grace as gift and he
does say there must be a balance between an
eschatological and an incarnational approach in
the concept of the kingdom. However, his linking of the kingdom to Marxist social analysis
and to political ideology gives the impression
that it is human achievement and that all is
ultimately possible in the historical. We have
seen that the concept of kingdom is interpreted
by his own version of a theology of progress and
by a "Christ-of-culture" model.[43]

Are we not again confronted with a problem
of overstatement because of commitment to the
poor? Our suggestion is that Marxist ideology[p]
can be helpful as part of our hermeneutic circle
and that the present dimensions of kingdom can
speak to this presupposition. But we must also
allow for the influence of future eschatology on
the present, and we must allow for the relativity
of any human action or ideology in history.

The kingdom is in dialectic with social analysis.

What we have been developing in terms of the concept of kingdom in the gospels is taught by Paul in his presentation of this world or the present age and similar vocabulary. Paul's theology both confirms and qualifies Segundo's eschatological claims. Segundo's hermeneutic circle must be seen as a dialectic process. Commitment to the poor will draw our attention to certain aspects of this world reality which we might be prone to overlook, but the Pauline teaching will also warn us not to make commitment to the poor an occasion for distorting the other dimensions of the Christian revelation.

Paul's presentation of the present age or this world in the present reality fits into a broad vision of history that modifies the Jewish eschatological picture. For the Jews history was divided into three epochs: the age of creation, the present age, and the age to come. There was a distinct division between the present age and the age to come, so that their eschatology was totally future oriented. Paul knew, on the other hand, that the coming of Christ was a turning point in the history of humanity, beginning the time of salvation while by the same token looking forward to the complete victory. It led Paul to enlarge on the picture of history, so that he posits five epochs to the Jewish three: the age of creation, the time before Christ, the present age which rejects Christ, the present age of which Christ is Lord, and the age to come in which the Lordship of Christ is fully achieved.[44]

Paul not only has deeper insight into the epochs of history, but he views the chronology of the epochs differently as well. Whereas the Jewish view saw a linear movement in chronological order, Paul sees an interpenetration of the present and the future ages

of Christ and a dialectic between these two ages
and the present age of evil. Thus there is a
concurrence, an overlapping, and a simul-
taneity of the last three epochs. For that
matter, as far as Paul is concerned, it is often
not a question of chronology at all, but of disposition and attitude within a person or community.

This complex schema puts a complex context around this world or the present age, while
not depriving these terms of their basic negative meaning. "The word [the world] appears
thirty-six times in Paul's letters. Sometimes
there is in the term a reference to creation,
and sometimes it describes the totality of space
and objects; but in the majority of cases it
pertains to a realm or order of being that
stands over against God."[45] This world or this
present age is that which rejects Jesus and his
message. See, for instance, Rom. 12:2 ("Do not
be conformed to this world"); Gal. 1:4 ("Jesus
gave himself . . . to deliver us from the
present evil age"); 1 Cor. 2:8 ("None of the
rulers of this age understood this").

In terms of Segundo's concerns, this
world is characterized by injustice, poverty and
oppression. It is also of interest to note that
the term flesh is associated with Paul's concept
of this world. We will elaborate more fully in
a later section of our study how flesh can take
on some of the notions of massification that
Segundo proposes through his hermeneutic circle.
However, we must also note here that precisely
because flesh is associated with the powers of
this world, it cannot be very easily divorced
from the idea of sin, as we indicated Segundo
seems to allege in his analysis of massification.[46]

With the coming of Christ this world or
the present age continue to keep their negative
qualities, but a new dynamic unfolds. Christ
brings through his death and resurrection the

power of God which alone is capable of overcoming the powers of this world. "The power of
God is not a this-worldly power, but is
transcendent of this age and will have its
full effect only in the age to come when the
present powers are finally subdued and
abolished."[47] Jesus offers salvation as a
future reality, primarily in hope (cf. 1 Thess.
5:8: "the hope of salvation"). Paul's
eschatology and his vision of history remain
with a future orientation. "The undeniable
elements of his futurist eschatology are the
parousia (1 Thes 4:15), the resurrection of
the dead (1Thes 4:16; 1Cor 15:13ff.), the
judgment (2Cor 5:10; Rom 14:10; Eph 6:8), and
the glory of the justified believer (Rom 8:18,
21; 1Thes 2:12)."[48]

    With this emphasis it seems difficult to
agree completely with Segundo's claim that there
is continuity in eschatology, and that social
justice is to be achieved in this world reality.
This emphasis in Paul also shows why there is an
eschatological dualism behind the concepts of
flesh-spirit in Paul that will endure throughout
this worldly existence and that will be resolved
only in the age to come. Segundo's hermeneutic
circle would then have to be challenged by the
biblical data, since this eschatology rejects
his ideology[p]. Nevertheless, there is another
dimension to Paul's view of history and to his
eschatology. "Along with this future aspect
there is also the present aspect, according to
which the eschaton has already begun and men are
already in a sense saved."[49]

    Paul, for instance, is clear in announcing,
"Now is the day of salvation" (2 Cor. 6:2), and
"If any one is in Christ, he is a new creation;
the old has passed away" (2 Cor. 5:17). Even in
1 Thess. 5, where he talks about the day of the
Lord as a future age, he also says the Thessalonians "belong to the day" (v. 8). One of the
significant ways in which Paul describes how the

eschaton can already be present--a way that sheds
light on his concept of flesh--is that of the
gift of the Spirit. This Spirit is the first
fruit of the kingdom, the seal and guarantee of
the coming age of salvation (2 Cor. 1:22; 5:5).
As Furnish describes it, the Spirit "does not
just precede the coming age but actually bears
it and represents the power of that age (i.e.
of God himself) already at work."[50] In some way,
the future impinges on the present. Humanity
does not just stand between the present and
future ages, but rather at the point where they
interpenetrate. That is also why this present
age is already in dialectic with the age of
Christ. The flesh is already being overcome by
the spirit, even if not completely.

This particular aspect of Paul's teaching
offers possibilities for Segundo's hermeneutic
circle. It can be called forth by the challenge
of social analysis and ideology[p], and it can
lend itself to application through Marxist
political theory. If flesh can bear the interpretation of massification and social injustice,
then that aspect of this present age can begin
to be conquered through the working of justice
and minority movements of liberation already in
the present reality. (We assume, of course,
the qualifications that we have already brought
to the adequacy of social analysis in the preceding sections of our study.)

Like the concept of kingdom, Paul's concept of this world has a complex context around
it, some of which converges on Segundo's claim of
realized, present eschatology that shows itself
in social justice. However, also like the concept of kingdom, this world reality has a context which also enters into dialectic with
Segundo's hermeneutic circle and qualifies it.
We have always to ask who does the constructing
and just what are the historical possibilities.

Furnish makes an important observation: "Neither Paul nor any other early Christian writer ever refers to God's future rule as 'the new world,' for the term kosmos in itself suggests alienation from God."[51] The transformation of the world is so radical and total that it is a new creation. In other words, the power of God, even while it operates proleptically in the present, always remains transcendent to humanity. The transformation is God's work and not humanity's and the final achievement of the work is in a new age that makes any accomplishment here quite relative and incomplete.

The danger with Segundo's hermeneutic circle, then, is that he overstates the possibilities or at least runs the risk of exaggeration, especially when the circle is presented as a formal methodology. When he constantly says that the movement out of the flesh of this world reality is a self-creation in freedom, he downplays the divine initiative.[52] When he presents Marxist social analysis as the authentic application of the texts, he implies that social justice will be fully achieved in the present reality. Our suggestion is that these points of Segundo be put into a more relative context, and then the hermeneutic circle will be of value within a genuine dialectic of text and social analysis.

There is a fruitful example of how Segundo's hermeneutic circle, when kept in proper context, enables biblical exegesis to dialogue with social analysis by stressing the present dimensions of eschatology. The example is in the way Paul's use of dikaiosyne or righteousness has been interpreted over the years, and how some scholars are suggesting new interpretations now. We will briefly consider this point in this section of our study, since it follows well on the concepts of kingdom and this world that we have just examined. (Matthew tells us the kingdom of God requires righteousness, and Paul says God transforms this present age by the working of righteousness.)

John Donohue is one example of new interpretation of dikaiosyne that seems made in the light of challenge from ideological presuppositions. Ernst Käsemann is another who does this even more thoroughly. Donohue makes an impressive point about Scriptural exegesis in this time in history: "It is a paradox in contemporary discussions of faith and justice that while the Old Testament and the teaching of Jesus are called on to construct a theology of social justice, Paul . . . who struggles with the relation of faith and justice . . . is rarely treated in this context."[53]

Donohue thus makes the point that exegesis up to now has largely missed the position of Paul on social justice, and he suggests that righteousness should be interpreted in that direction. We have no quarrel with that point, but what we should notice is that sociological or ideological presuppositions seem to influence his finding this meaning in Paul. Donohue is writing an article in a book dealing with social justice and concerned with oppression and poverty. As Segundo would observe, doing theology from the perspective of commitment to the poor leads one to renew the exegesis so that it speaks to what life situation presents to it. Now that concerns for the third world and for the poor in all the world become a central issue, we find in Paul a new line of teaching that we did not notice previously.

Donohue makes an explicit overture toward the realized eschatology that Segundo advocates as the need for theology, so that it may be renewed in view of the hermeneutic circle. He shows how Paul's eschatology is a tension between the "already" and the "not yet."[54] Whereas he speaks often of this age as transitory in comparison with the age to come (1 Cor. 1:20; Rom. 12:2; 2 Cor. 2:6-8; Gal. 4:3), he also speaks of

Christ as already initiating a new era of salvation (Gal. 1:4; 1 Cor. 10:11; 2 Cor. 5:17). In any case, there is a present dimension of eschatology and when righteousness is seen in this context, it bespeaks social justice and redemption in this world reality:

When a discussion of justice in Paul is put in the context of his eschatology certain conclusions are suggested. . . . Then justice is not simply the quality of God as righteous judge over against sinful man, but the relation of the saving power of God to a world captured by evil. God's justice is his fidelity which inaugurates a saving victory over the powers that enslave and oppress man. Paul's eschatology suggests a Christian response to being in the world.[55]

Ernst Käsemann is an even better example of some of Segundo's observations because he is more thorough and more explicit than Donohue in his development of dikaiosyne. For one thing, Donohue did not explicitly speak of presuppositions, whereas Käsemann does. In fact, some of the observations that Käsemann makes seem to harmonize with the presuppositions of social analysis that Segundo wants to bring to the text. Käsemann points out that "the intrinsic value of the Bible is universally stressed, but its exposition is regulated and confined by considerations of edification or by the self-understanding which is prevailing at any given moment."[56]

As a verification of this contention, he shows the background of the debate as to whether justification in Paul is best understood as an individual existentialist view or as a more corporate concept as a salvation history. Krister Stendahl accuses the existentialist view of being too introspective and ending in individualism. On the other hand, the view of salvation history presents problems because it threatens to bring exegesis back to where it foundered twice before, on a false optimism of a theology of progress and on the distortion of salvation history in a secular form in Nazi eschatology. In either view of justification, historical and ideological presuppositions influenced the exegesis.

Käsemann does not explicitly indicate where his own presuppositions lie, although we have some indications in statements which we will consider later regarding Paul's theology of sarx.[57] We can, however, notice that he is basically formulating a hermeneutic circle similar to Segundo's.

Käsemann is also more thorough in his interpretation of dikaiosyne than is Donohue, although he shows the same influence of social and political presuppositions. When Donohue speaks of Paul's righteousness he describes it as justice. Donohue himself may not be mistaken in his own meaning, but his presentation runs the risk of making Paul's term a human activity. He does not adequately distinguish dikē from dikaiosyne. Paul does not use the former word which has the sense of human virtue or human justice. Paul deliberately uses dikaiosyne precisely to stress that the work of making just is God's activity and not humanity's. This is the same danger that Segundo's social analysis runs into, i.e., of diminishing divine initiative in order to enhance human freedom. It overstates the case.

Käsemann, on the other hand, gives strong emphasis to dikaiosyne as divine power. In fact, his major contribution to the exegesis of this word has been the reconciling of the two major opposing views. Righteousness is not just God's activity, nor just the quality of humanity as redeemed by God. Rather, it is the combination of both. "We take the decisive step along the road to the proper understanding of Paul when and only when we grasp the indissoluble connection of power and gift within the conception of the divine righteousness."[58] With this insight we remain clearly within God's sovereignty, and we see righteousness as a transcendent and eschatological reality.

Nevertheless, within this context, and respecting the transcendent nature of the revelation, there seems a dialectic in which social analysis can focus insights into the nature of God's work in the present reality. Käsemann seems influenced by such social concerns, so that he also emphasizes that aspect of righteousness. He says that the future eschatology is in dialectic with the present, although the present should not be taken out of its context of future eschatology. "The Pauline dialectic of present and future eschatology encroaches on Christian existence as it is actually lived out."[59]

Moreover, the present effects of righteousness are not to be conceived individually but socially. "The righteousness of God does not, in Paul's understanding, refer primarily to the individual. . . . The individual human being is to be seen here in immediate relation to the divine will for salvation, now directed towards the whole earth."[60] In ultimately deciding whether righteousness is to be seen in the optic of existentialism and individualism or through a social perspective, Käsemann returns again to the concept of salvation history. He is concerned not to make righteousness a development arising out of the historical possibilities themselves; this must always be God's work and gift. Still, it has its effects within this history as well as in future reality.

In Paul the historical and eschatological dimensions do not yawn apart in the sense that they are essentially and ab initio different. The eschatological breaks in upon earth in a very real sense. . . . The eschatological is

212

neither supra-history nor the inner aspect of a historicity; it is power which changes the old world into a new one and which becomes incarnate in the earthly sphere.[61]

Finally, Käsemann shows how his social concerns seem to bring him close to many of the concerns of Segundo for the poor and oppressed, and this leads him to find these emphases also in Paul's concept of righteousness. God's power must show itself in social justice and the conquering of oppression. "It is only from a great distance that we can read salvation history without being aware of its catastrophes. But faith must not fall a victim to docetism, must not separate itself from what is human, must not miss the cry of the dying, the despairing, the people at the end of their tether."[62]

Through what is implicit in the methodology of John Donohue and through Ernst Käsemann's own acknowledgement of presuppositions, the third step of Segundo's hermeneutic circle finds points of contact. Biblical exegesis--albeit in a dialectic--can be challenged to change its presuppositions in the light of what life situation brings to it. What we have seen of righteousness in Paul, as well as what we developed on the meaning of kingdom and this world, provides possibilities that can be deepened by Segundo's hermeneutic circle. His social analysis can challenge exegesis to stress more fully and become more deeply aware of the present ramifications of biblical eschatology.

The Bible and Violence

When we take one more specific step to describe how one might work for the kingdom, we approach the possibility of violence. As Segundo said, a person is not fully involved in the work of the kingdom until he or she is involved in a causal way, and that cause may embrace violence.[63] Segundo himself seems somewhat cautious about the role of violence. It seems to be one of the few places where he questions the Marxist social analysis itself.[64] It is certainly the topic on which he expounds positive arguments for the role of violence, but which he seems reluctant to put into practice.[65] Taking the observations we have been making about the verifiability of the first steps of Segundo's hermeneutic circle and taking what we said about Scripture offering value judgments for social analysis, we may be able to address the issue of violence with even more reserve than Segundo, at least from the biblical point of view.

To begin with, we can analyze the positive arguments that Segundo offers for the role of violence. On the most general level, he would claim that violence is necessary if the Christian is to cause the kingdom in some way, and not simply do work that is an analogy, or outline, or just a symbolic anticipation of the kingdom.[66] To this we might respond that the Christian can still be involved causally with the kingdom without embracing violence, even when it seems necessary. This point becomes even more important when one considers the biblical data about how Christ worked for the kingdom. We will consider that momentarily.

Segundo's main argument about the role of violence seems connected with Marxist social analysis which sees violence as a necessary part of changing social structures and removing oppression. At least Segundo embraces this argument in his theoretic agreement with Assmann about the need to deideologize the traditional view toward violence.[67] The traditional Marxist viewpoint, building out of its materialistic determinism, sees conflict as a necessary element of sociology. The class struggle is inevitable. This seems to underlie Segundo's statement that the refusal to consider violence is another way of maintaining the status quo.

214

Once again, on this particular issue, Segundo's hermeneutic circle can be challenged on the first and second steps. One can question the verification of this social analysis and can see it as becoming itself an ideology[n]. It may be true that violence is a part of the human situation, and may even be unavoidable in some instances, but it cannot be taken as the only solution to oppression. Segundo himself has refused to take the aspect of determinism from Marxist social analysis.

What we indicated about trading one form of massification (under the oppressor) for another (under the revolutionary) can be applied more immediately to violence. The nature of a violent revolution is such that one cannot draw its limits. As Paul Lehmann puts it, revolutions end up "devouring their own children."[68] Both revolutions and any other humanization processes start off with the promise of transforming history to make room for what it takes to make and to keep human life human. Revolutions, however, are more ambiguous, since power seeks to absolutize itself. Most revolutions begin to diverge from genuine humanization when promise must turn to fulfillment. The violence then becomes self-consuming, with power oppressing the people in order to remain in power.

Jacques Ellul makes similar points that confirm this observation. He posits three "laws" of violence that give one pause about its use:

1) The first law of violence is continuity: it is almost impossible to stop once it starts.

2) The second law of violence is reciprocity: all who use the sword will perish by the sword. Revolt tends to bring police brutality, so that violence only leads to another form of violence.

3) The third law of violence is sameness: it becomes almost impossible to distinguish good from bad, just from unjust. One cannot say "so far and no farther," because the lines are blurred. Each one tries to justify one's own actions.[69]

Segundo himself seems to recognize these difficulties with violence, since he voices some of the same objections.[70] However, we would make two observations about his approach. First of all, in agreeing with Assmann about the need to deideologize violence, Segundo seems to give the benefit of the doubt to violent revolution. Our critique would take the opposite opinion. Granted that non-violence can maintain the status quo, and granted that some situations may require violent change, the general assumption must be that violence will only beget violence and that it will not change the status quo either. (Or it will set up its own status quo.)

Secondly, Segundo seems to demand that Christianity involve itself with particular revolutions, and <u>internal</u> to these, recognize their relativity in the face of Christian teaching. Our own observations on the ambiguity of violence would suggest that <u>even before</u> a Christian involves himself or herself in a violent revolution, the possibility must be maintained that the entire enterprise is already an ideology[n].

We have challenged Segundo's viewpoint on violence by questioning the verifiability of the first and second steps of his hermeneutic circle. We may also offer some critique on the level of the fourth step, the Scriptural exegesis, by putting it into dialectic with the social analysis. The Bible can challenge the Marxist sociology as well as be influenced by it. We can now apply this fact to the question of violence itself. If we enter our hermeneutic circle on the level of Scripture we find that it offers values that challenge the very presuppositions of violence as part of the process of the kingdom.

Before we begin looking at biblical texts, a brief observation on Segundo's biblical examples will highlight our point. Much is already proven by what Segundo does not consider as by what he does offer by way of Bible texts. In his considerations of violence, he does not focus on any of the texts that are usually considered central to the discussion. The examples that he does offer seem related mostly to interpersonal relationships, the love of person for person.[71] In that context love and violence seem compatible, because violence can be equated with egotism, and all human love can be said to have some egotism.

The problem with this line of argumentation is whether it really speaks to the issue of social violence at all. First of all, the example of violence that he draws from the egotism, the violence of having to choose concrete neighbors and therefore having to let others go by, seems fairly innocuous compared to the prospect of killing hundreds or thousands in order to gain a government. Moreover, is it legitimate to transfer the egotism of an individual to the violence of a group? While it may be legitimate sometimes to use principles of individual ethics for social ethics, the transfer does not always work. It seems to be the case here, where the effects of individual egotism are not comparable to social violence.

If we now look at some texts that Segundo does not consider, we find Scripture putting a strong emphasis on non-violence as the Christian approach to the kingdom. It may be the challenge that the Bible puts to the presuppositions of Marxist social analysis in this regard.

Since we are considering violence in the context of establishing the kingdom, it seems appropriate to concentrate our exegesis on Jesus himself and his own attitudes toward the kingdom. We have already seen that Jesus proclaimed a kingdom that did have its effect in this world, that called for the end of hunger, sickness and oppression.[72] Our question now is how Jesus saw the establishment of that kingdom. It seems that the future dimensions of the kingdom would in some way affect the present dimensions of the kingdom. This qualification would show itself in the non-violent approach of Jesus to the kingdom. The reign of God would be God's work. It would challenge even the structures of this world. But it would come through suffering and death, not through violence.

Consideration of the biblical data on these issues leads us to the disputed question of whether Jesus was a Zealot or not, or at least whether his teaching was sympathetic and parallel to the Zealot movement of Judaism in his day. Clearly the one who most comprehensively reestablished the issue in recent times is S. G. F. Brandon, who maintained that Jesus was, in fact, sympathetic to the Zealots of his day, so that "the profession of Zealot principles and aims was not incompatible with intimate participation in the mission of Jesus."[73] This would mean in effect that Jesus advocated the violent overthrow of the Roman authorities in anticipation of the establishment of God's kingdom in his own day.

Brandon has not been convincing in his claims, and we will examine a number of texts which refute him. Before doing this, however, let us cite a criticism by W. Wink of Brandon's methodological presuppositions. The criticism can apply equally well to Segundo and his hermeneutic circle, and corroborates the point we have been making:

Brandon's Jesus . . . is scarcely distinguishable from a Zealot. And Zealots are scarcely distinguishable from today's revolutionaries. By this series of equations Jesus is made our contemporary. He is the Jesus which Social Christianity needs in order to justify involvement in revolution.

218

        To his credit, Brandon achieves a
remarkable detachment in the course of his
work, but he makes no attempt to hide his
admiration for guerrilla warfare and armed
resistance to imperialist powers. . . .
Since Brandon has been quick to point up the
"pacifist" biases of earlier interpreters of
Jesus, would it be unfair to ask precisely
what significance should be attacked to his
. . . disposition to regard military engage-
ment as a viable means for achieving political
ends.
        In short, for Brandon the Zealots are the
norm, and Jesus becomes intelligible only to
the degree that he can be placed within their
orbit.[74]

        The texts that are usually offered to show
Jesus as a Zealot sympathizer are mostly from the
end of his career, with a few other texts to
complement these. Matt. 10:34 ("I have not come
to bring peace, but a sword"); 22:15-22 and
parallels ("Render to Caesar") are important, as
well as the names of some of the Twelve, which
seem to show possible translation as Zealot names
(Iscariot can mean "dagger-bearer," Barjona can
mean "rebel," James and John are "sons of
thunder," Simon is called "the Zealot"). Then,
the palm entrance of Jesus and his cleansing of
the temple seem to show Zealot tendencies, as
well as the fact that he was put to death on
the charges of sedition.

        Now none of the above texts is decisive,
especially when put into the context of other
texts that show Christ rejecting the Zealot position. We will look at texts more apparently
anti-Zealot and after that we will come back to
consider other possibilities regarding the above
texts.

        To begin with, the temptation account in
the Synoptics seems clearly to indicate that
Jesus resisted the Zealot tendencies in his own
preaching of the kingdom. Each of the temptations

can be seen as a suggestion for Jesus to bring
in the messianic kingdom in a way alien to God's
plan, to bring in the kingdom by force, by human
design and activity. Jesus rejects these proposals.[75] The more direct connection of these
temptations with the use of violence is seen by
the repetition of this type of temptation in
Peter's view of the Messiah (Mark 8:27-33 and
par.). Christ insists that he will be an instrument of the kingdom through suffering, not
through violence. He will not force the kingdom.
The entire messianic secret in Mark seems to
support this same kind of attitude. Jesus keeps
a secret precisely because, among other things,
he does not want to be misunderstood as a
Zealot. John 6:15 (Jesus refuses kingship from
the crowd) and 7:6 (he refuses to go to Jerusalem
for the feast) echo similar themes.[76]

Another passage seems readily acknowledged
by most scholars to be authentic to Jesus, and
here it indicates non-violence on the part of
Christ. Matt. 11:12 (cf. Luke 16:16) speaks of
violence associated with the kingdom. The text
is controverted, since biazetai can be used in
the passive voice with the meaning of "to suffer
violence," or in the middle voice with the meaning of "to use force." We do not have to resolve
the meaning in either direction, since in either
case it would seem to support the view of
political non-violence.

In the positive or praiseworthy sense of
the statement, Jesus is putting the stress on
God's decisive inbreaking into history. It is
an apocalyptic statement in that sense, although
it also has a present reality as its context.[77]
Jesus is saying, "Now the kingdom of God makes
its way with triumphant force." The violence
would be of a figurative sense, not political
revolt. In that case, political violence is
ruled out, since the kingdom is God's work, and
humanity cannot force it in. In that case also,
the second part of Matt. 11:12 would have the
sense, "Men of violence (men able to accept a

reversal of values in their lives) take it by force (by repentance)."

If we take the meaning of Matt. 11:12 in a negative or derogatory sense, it could, like the positive sense, have a spiritual intent of the kingdom suffering violence by those who refuse repentance and who try thus to force their way into the kingdom. In that case, it still would not support a Zealot meaning. However, it is also possible that the text has immediate anti-Zealot overtones. It could mean: "The kingdom of God suffers violently by Zealots who act as violent men seeking to force the kingdom against the Romans." From this foregoing analysis, then, we see that the text is either indirectly or directly non-violent as the manner in which Jesus wishes to bring in the kingdom.[78]

Other texts which seem to indicate non-violence on the part of Jesus are Luke 9:52-56, where he rebukes the disciples for wanting to rain fire and brimstone on the hostile towns; Matt. 5:21ff., which shows Jesus giving his new commandment as one which condemns even anger as well as murder; and Matt. 5:43-47, which counsels prayer for persecutors and love for enemies. Other statements of Jesus on forgiveness could also lend themselves to a non-violent inter-pretation.

With the context of these passages that seem more surely non-violent, we can examine the texts often proposed as advocating the Zealot position. Even these texts admit of another interpretation which seems more likely in the overall context of the gospels. In Matt. 10:34, for example, when Jesus tells of bringing a sword and not peace, we have another apocalyptic saying, telling of God's radical intervention, resulting in a new order and a reversal of values. It leads to division between those who accept the challenge of the kingdom and those who don't. In any case, the "sword" in the passage does not signify the sword which Jesus wields in a crusade

against his persecutors but the sword which the
persecutors use against him and his disciples.
It is not related to the war of the Zealots.[79]

Matt. 22:21 ("Render to Caesar") has often
been seen as opposed to the State, with the "and"
being interpreted as indicating opposition. This
need not be interpreted in support of the Zealot
movement. It fits well with the apocalyptic
teaching of Jesus. The sense would be that
Caesar can be paid tribute, but that the issue is
unimportant in view of the approaching kingdom.
What belongs to God is all that really matters.[80]
The approach would once again be non-violent. A
similar stance of non-violence would seem the
case if the saying was interpreted as positing
two realms, that of the State and that of God,
with both having their demands and responsibilities.[81]

When we approach the last days of Jesus,
we find material again that is best explained,
not as a thwarted Zealot movement, but rather as
a final statement of non-violence. Both the palm
procession and the cleansing of the temple were
envisioned by Jesus as prophetic actions. The
palm procession in its present form shows a great
deal of embellishment by the evangelists. It
could have been, perhaps, a small spontaneous
outburst of enthusiasm by the disciples of Jesus,[82]
or was, perhaps, a prophetic gesture on the part
of Christ to stress the impending approach of the
kingdom and his role in it. It would seem, in
any case, that the stress in the event was on the
humility of Jesus (his coming on an ass), and his
role of suffering and service.[83] Likewise, the
temple cleansing was not an attempt at revolt,
but a symbolic gesture calling for conversion
from the externalism and hypocrisy that would in
effect destroy the temple and require God's in-
breaking into history with the kingdom.[84]

Seeing the charges brought against Jesus
and the title over the cross, we can conjecture
that Jesus was condemned as a Zealot. It was

either out of misunderstanding by the Romans on the basis of the charges of the Jewish leaders, or out of deliberate distortion of the facts by the Romans in collusion with the Jewish leaders who wanted Jesus removed for religious reasons. Once the question of charges and title over the cross is addressed, the main evidence concerning Jesus' Zealot leanings is dismissed. The picture remains consistent. Jesus preached non-violence as the way of the coming of the kingdom of God. It was to be God's work, and would come through Jesus' own suffering and death.[85]

We return to Segundo after this somewhat lengthy, if sketchy biblical excursus. Once again we have qualified his hermeneutic circle while not rejecting it altogether. After having made the point that violence seems not the biblical approach, we can ask ourselves: "Then what can we gain for biblical interpretation from social analysis that recognizes the violence of oppressive social structures?" Walter Wink offers some suggestions regarding Brandon, but some which apply to Segundo as well:

Brandon has not succeeded, in my opinion, in establishing the likelihood that Jesus was sympathetic toward or in collaboration with the Zealot movement. But he has succeeded in reminding us of what we are always so eager to forget: that on any reading of the evidence, Jesus turned the world upside down. His life has engendered the closest thing to a permanent revolution which the world has ever known.[86]

Social analysis forces us to find aspects of Jesus which we would overlook. It helps us see that Jesus himself experienced the fact that violence already exists through the existing oppressive social structures. However, when the social analysis compels us to search how Jesus responded to the violence, it was, we shall find, not by a return of violence, but by suffering and death. This attitude will have to become the prevailing Christian approach and challenges us to deal in different ways with the violence of oppressive structures.

At minimum it may mean involvement with violence ourselves, only because of our sinful situation in which the ideal message of Christ cannot yet be carried out fully. Those occasions, however, must be in a context where the violence is truly the lesser of the evils, something which will be extremely rare. Moreover, "one at least begins with a non-violent bearing as the normal and normative one for the Christian. That is, the use of lethal violence is not on the same level of choice with non-violence, or even non-lethal violence. Its use, if allowed at all, requires a special justification. Further, that special justification itself would also need biblical warrants."[87]

There is also the possibility of using biblical material to move a step beyond the options of either violence or non-violence, to move to a situation that is truly revolutionary and that criticizes either the passive resistance to oppression or the thwarting of genuine revolution by self-defeating violence. Paul Lehmann moves in this direction, a direction that Segundo's hermeneutic circle could push toward, even though Lehmann and Segundo might have different social analysis. Lehmann, like Segundo, says explicitly that the plight of the poor can serve as a catalyst that develops a new (biblical) story which bursts the bounds of unfreedom and serves revolutionary purposes. The Bible may not be violent, but it can be revolutionary. In fact, the power of weakness challenges the weakness of power. Non-violence itself can become a force for change and challenges the structures themselves. "There is a difference between the seizure of power by force [violence] in order to establish a new order [political messianism] and the unyielding pressure upon established power [non-violent revolution], already under judgment for its default of order, in response to the power already ordering all things in a new and humanizing way [messianic politics]."[88]

In a more modest approach along the same lines, R. Cassidy distinguishes a person of non-resistance from one of non-violence. The former refrains from directly confronting evil, while the latter does not, even though both refrain from physical attack.[89] With this distinction, Cassidy does a detailed analysis of all of Luke's gospel to show that Jesus, even in his non-violence, attacked social structures and was in the long run dangerous to Roman society, because he advocated new social and political patterns that would embrace the poor and the oppressed. Cassidy is not just making up the biblical teaching because he is concerned for the poor. Yet he is discovering biblical content not stressed before. It would seem that Segundo's hermeneutic circle and optic of commitment to the poor is verified and, with some modification, is useful to the enterprise of Bible and Christian ethics.

CHAPTER V

NOTES

[1]Robert McAfee Brown, Theology in a New Key (Philadelphia: Westminster Press, 1978), pp. 106-13.

[2]For an overview of Segundo, see Alfred Hennelly, S.J., Theologies in Conflict (Maryknoll, N.Y.: Orbis Books, 1979). For an overview of liberation theology, see Brown's book in the preceding note.

[3]Karl Rahner, A Rahner Reader, ed. Gerald A. McCool (New York: Seabury, 1975), p. 66.

[4]Ibid., p. 67.

[5]Juan Luis Segundo, Our Idea of God (Maryknoll, N.Y.: Orbis Books, 1974), p. 5.

[6]Ibid., p. 114.

[7]Ibid., p. 86.

[8]Juan Luis Segundo, The Liberation of Theology (Maryknoll, N.Y.: Orbis Books, 1976), p. 13.

[9]Rahner, p. 340.

[10]Segundo, Idea of God, p. 178.

[11]Ibid., p. 49.

[12]Cf. Juan Gutierrez Gonzalez, The New Libertarian Gospel, pp. 63-66; and Edward J. Berbusse, S.J., "Gustavo Gutierrez: Utopian Theologian of Liberation," Faith and Reason (1975): 67-96.

[13]Brown, p. 65.

[14]Segundo, Liberation, p. 35, n. 10.

[15]Cf. pp. 65-67.

226

[16] Juan Luis Segundo, "Capitalism-Socialism: A Theological Crux," Concilium 96 (1974): 123.

[17] Cf. page 62 and Segundo, "Capitalism-Socialism," p. 105.

[18] Cf. p. 136 and Juan Luis Segundo, "The Church: A New Direction in Latin America," Catholic Mind 65 (1967): 45.

[19] As we have not been concerned with evaluating the Marxism as such, so we abstract here from evaluating Lenin's concept of massification as such or Lenin's interpretation of Marx. We are interested only in Segundo's interpretation of Lenin.

[20] Pierre Bigo, S.J., The Church and the Third World Revolution (Maryknoll, N.Y.: Orbis Books, 1977), p. 163.

[21] Ibid., p. 175.

[22] Cf. pp. 83-84 and Juan Luis Segundo, The Hidden Motives of Pastoral Action (Maryknoll, N.Y.: Orbis Books, 1978), pp. 37-44.

[23] We showed how Segundo builds the ecclesiastical formulation on Marxist social analysis on pp. 78-86. We showed the relationship of Marx to Teilhard according to Segundo on pp. 130-31, n. 42. The biblical response was seen on pp. 146-65. Our critique here would conclude that Segundo has valid and valuable insight in each of these sections, but seems to overstate his case and runs the danger of elitism.

[24] Segundo, Liberation, p. 236.

[25] Cf. pp. 78-86, and especially p. 85 of this study.

[26] Segundo, Liberation, p. 205.

[27] Cf. pp. 99-106.

[28] Amos Wilder, Eschatology and Ethics in the Teaching of Jesus (New York: Harper, 1950).

[29] Norman Perrin, The Kingdom of God in the Teaching of Jesus (Philadelphia: Westminster, 1963), p. 157.

[30] Ibid., pp. 164-68.

[31] Charles Dodd, The Parables of the Kingdom (London: Nisbet, 1935), p. 54.

[32] Charles Dodd, The Coming of Christ (London: Nisbet, 1951), p. 13.

[33] Joachim Jeremias, New Testament Theology (New York: Charles Scribner's Sons, 1971), pp. 264-68.

[34] Werner G. Kümmel, Promise and Fulfillment (London: SCM Press, 1961), pp. 49-50.

[35] Joachim Jeremias, The Parables of Jesus (New York: Charles Scribner's Sons, 1972), pp. 146-69.

[36] Perrin, pp. 168-85.

[37] Kümmel, p. 92.

[38] Perrin, p. 183.

[39] Jeremias, Parables, pp. 221-27.

[40] Ibid., pp. 198-201.

[41] Perrin, pp. 177-78.

[42] Juan Luis Segundo, "Reconciliación y conflicto," Perspectivas de Diálogo 9 (1974): 172.

[43] Cf. pp. 110-11; 113-20.

[44] Henry Shires, The Eschatology of Paul (Philadelphia: Westminster, 1966), p. 126. Cf. Joseph Fitzmyer, S.J., "Pauline Theology," in Jerome Biblical Commentary, ed. Raymond Brown, et al. (London: Geoffrey Chapman, 1968), no. 79: 41-51. He offers a threefold division of Paul's view, but is not really opposed to Shires, who spells out Fitzmyer's last division.

[45] Shires, p. 138.

[46] Cf. pp. 155-56.

[47] Victor P. Furnish, Theology and Ethics in Paul (Nashville: Abingdon, 1968), p. 118.

[48] Fitzmyer, no. 79:46.

[49] Ibid.

[50] Furnish, p. 133.

[51] Ibid., p. 125.

[52] Cf. pp. 148-50 and 153-55.

[53] John Donohue, "Biblical Perspectives on Justice," in The Faith That Does Justice, ed. John C. Haughey, S.J. (New York: Paulist Press, 1977), p. 88.

[54] Ibid., pp. 89-92.

[55] Ibid., p. 91.

[56] Ernst Käsemann, Perspectives on Paul (Philadelphia: Fortress, 1971), p. 62.

[57] Cf. p. 238.

[58] Ernst Käsemann, New Testament Questions of Today (Philadelphia: Fortress, 1969), p. 174.

[59] Ibid., p. 181.

[60] Ibid., pp. 180-81.

[61] Käsemann, Perspectives, p. 68.

[62] Ibid., p. 69.

[63] Cf. pp. 121-22.

[64] Cf. p. 122.

[65] Cf. pp. 125-27.

[66] Cf. p. 117.

[67] Cf. pp. 121-22.

[68] Paul Lehmann, The Transfiguration of Politics (New York: Harper and Row, 1975), p. 7.

[69] Jacques Ellul, Violence (London: SCM Press, 1970), pp. 93-100.

[70] Cf. pp. 122-23 and 125-27.

[71]Cf. pp. 124-25.

[72]Cf. pp. 195-203.

[73]S. G. F. Brandon, Jesus and the Zealots (New York: Scribner's Sons, 1968), p. 355.

[74]Walter Wink, "Jesus and Revolution. Reflections on S. G. F. Brandon's Jesus and the Zealots," Union Seminary Quarterly Review 25 (1969): 57-58.

[75]John Howard Yoder, The Politics of Jesus (Grand Rapids: Eerdmans, 1972), pp. 30-34.

[76]A. Feuillet, "Le Récit Lucanien de la Tentation," Biblica 40 (1959): 613-31.

[77]Gunther Bornkamm, Jesus of Nazareth (New York: Harper and Row, 1960), p. 51.

[78]P. de Surgy, "L'Evangile et la violence," Lumière et Vie 18 (1969): 94-95.

[79]Martin Hengel, Was Jesus a Revolutionist? (Philadelphia: Fortress, 1971), p. 23.

[80]Ibid., pp. 33-34.

[81]But cf. John McKenzie, "The Gospel According to Matthew," in Jerome Biblical Commentary, ed. R. Brown, et al. (London: Geoffrey Chapman, 1968), 43:150.

[82]D. E. Nineham, Saint Mark (Baltimore: Penguin Book, 1969), pp. 293-94.

[83]Bruce Vawter, The Four Gospels (Dublin: Gill and Son, 1967), p. 302.

[84]Cf. previous remarks about the temple regarding the kingdom and apocalyptic imagery. Cf. also Hengel, pp. 15-18.

[85]Alan Richardson, The Political Christ (Philadelphia: Westminster, 1973) sums up the last week of Jesus on page 51 as follows: "A careful examination of the early Christian tradition concerning the last week of the life of Jesus reveals a convincing and coherent

narrative of the sequence of events which led
to this death. There is no other evidence, and
therefore the alternative to the acceptance of
it is complete scepticism. What the evidence
forbids is the reconstruction of the story with
the object of showing that Jesus was a revolutionary nationalist who countenanced the use of
violence against the Roman occupying forces."

[86]Wink, p. 59.

[87]B. Birch and L. Rasmussen, Bible and
Ethics in the Christian Life (Minneapolis:
Augsburg Publishing House, 1976), p. 117.

[88]Lehmann, p. 91.

[89]Richard Cassidy, Jesus, Politics, and
Society (Maryknoll, N.Y.: Orbis Books, 1978),
p. 40.

CHAPTER VI

SEGUNDO IN THE ECUMENICAL DIALOGUE

Our critique of Segundo's hermeneutic
circle has modified his methodology in the first
three steps. This critique has already brought
us into some biblical exegesis as it entered into
dialectic with the sociological presuppositions
of the initial hermeneutic stages. All in all,
Segundo's observations have remained basically
sound and insightful, especially regarding his
concept of massification, although it seems to
us overstated or too exclusive.

It remains for us now to dialogue with
what he has done on the fourth step of his
circle. We have already offered some critique
of this step and will continue to offer qualifications. However, our main concern now is to take
what we see as valid in Segundo's insights, to
include the refinements that we have already made,
and to bring the refinements into dialogue with
biblical exegesis.

Segundo and First-World Exegetes

We are concerned with showing the openings
that already exist for an exegetical interchange
with the first world biblical community around
much of what Segundo has said. For our purposes
we will take the example of _flesh_ to see how
massification helps interpret it, remembering the
qualifying observations that we have made in this
regard.

We have already noted that Segundo's statement about _flesh_ is somewhat overdrawn in the
contrast he makes between the Old Testament and
Paul. There is a definite difference between what
Paul says about the flesh and what the Old Testament does, but Segundo seems to underestimate the

Old Testament. First of all, is it fair to analyze the texts in the categories of modern
philosophy, in terms of person and nature? Since
the Old Testament had a holistic approach to
humanity, it is hard to conceive of it even being
able to categorize a human being as person or
nature. We may have here in Segundo an attempt
to make his case to such an extent that he brings
an ideology[n] to the text.[1]

In any event, even keeping Segundo's categories, the text must speak to the ideology, and
it seems not to support such a dichotomy between
Old Testament and New Testament. The Old Testament view of humanity in the flesh would be far
more than an impersonal, external relationship
between God and creature, dictated by equally
impersonal laws of nature. Segundo rightly
describes flesh as creatureliness or human sensitivity in reference to the Creator.[2] However,
there is a lot more entailed in creatureliness
than Segundo would posit.

First of all, as we mentioned, a human
being is conceived holistically, so that his or
her entire being enters into the sensitivity and
relationship with others. "The OT never views
man as an abstraction. He is always set in a
specific situation. Hence the interest is more
in the individual man than in human nature in
general."[3] Man and woman are certainly seen as
creatures, but they enter into interpersonal
relationships with other creatures like themselves or with God. Flesh stands for the whole
person. Sometimes it stands for the personal
pronoun "I" in very concrete human situations.[4]
It represents the intimate personal relationships
of consanguinity. It is sometimes synonymous
with heart or the practically untranslatable
Hebrew nefesh, both of which terms reflect man and
woman in their inmost reality (Ezech. 36:26).[5]

In terms of relationship to the Creator,
flesh came to represent a special intimacy with

Yahweh through covenant and law. It was the word
signifying circumcision (covenant in the flesh)
which presupposed a very inward and personal
attitude of trust and obedience. "All flesh"
(Isa. 40:5-6) was a term recognizing humanity's
fragility, but it also saw humanity's call to
experience the very glory of God.

In view of these passages it would be hard
to maintain Segundo's view that the Old Testament
concept of flesh was external and impersonal.
This does not, however, eradicate his insight into
massification and the leads he offers into the
social aspects of flesh. In the New Testament
Paul does have a further insight into flesh. His
insight does not come from the discovery of what
is missing from the Old Testament so much as from
what is found in the New. Paul discovers Christ
and his Spirit, and in that hindsight sees the
inadequacy of the law and the former covenant to
accomplish all that it was intended to do. Paul
gains the insight into sin, not as a series of
actions, but as the de facto human condition itself. With that discovery, in the backdrop of
the death and resurrection of Jesus, Paul can see
flesh then as something negative. It is reliance
on creatureliness rather than on the Spirit of
Christ in order to achieve the full interpersonal relationship with God intended for
humanity. Paul's use of flesh in a negative
sense was facilitated by its meaning within the
dualistic Iranian culture.

The contribution of Segundo's hermeneutic
circle in this context is to help us to become
more conscious of presuppositions and to see if
the sociological concept of massification can
help us gain insight into Paul's text. I
believe that several lines of exegetical research
can join Segundo here, and that they can derive
as part of the meaning of flesh the attitude of
the masses to take the path of least resistance,
the pragmatic and the most direct way of operation in society.

235

No doubt, one of the key texts elaborating the meaning of sarx (flesh) is the dialectical passage of Gal. 5:13-25. If we examine the vice-list given there we have witness that at least one of the elements of sarx is its embracing of traits that foster massification and alienation in society. The list in verses 19-21 may roughly be divided into four parts: sins of sensuality in its narrow sense, vices associated with heathen religion, vices dealing with community conflicts, intemperance and its consequences. Our interest is in some of the vices of the third category. Echthrai (enmity) denotes outbreaks of hatred, and in one of the two other places where it appears in the entire New Testament (Eph. 2:14, 16), it denotes enmity between Jew and Gentile. While the word may here in Galatians be simply a general category to contrast with agape (love) on the list of fruit, it does also have the overtones of racial prejudice and bitterness common to massification so often.

Eris (strife) depicts the life activity that follows on the attitude of echthra. While it certainly has its personal or individual aspects, it is significant that four out of the six times that Paul uses it, he speaks of quarrels within the Church. "The members and leaders of the Church think more about people and parties and about slogans and about personal issues than they do about Jesus Christ."[6] It is the problem of massification within the Church itself. The same may be said of eritheia (selfishness), which is used three out of four times in Paul for the competing parties within the Church. The following words dichostasia (dissension) and hairesis (party split) seem to share in the same sense of divisions and separations that can result from massification within the Church and without.

If we take a quick glance at the list of the fruit of the Spirit in Gal. 5:22, we find at least one that seems to point in the direction

236

of social ethics specifically, and that indicates by contrast what Segundo saw as massification in sarx. It is common knowledge that eirene takes over the Hebrew concept of shalom, and means more than simply lack of war. It entails the right ordering of all relationships, including the social and corporate dimensions of human life. It is the conquering, through the Spirit, of the alienation and rejection of mass-man that would be a trait of life in the sarx. Two authors take this as a major biblical theme that must influence the attitude and perception of the prosperous toward the poor.[7] They are representative of the growing number of first world exegetes who give central attention to new aspects of old texts under the challenge of third world exegesis.

Of course, what we have seen thus far may show that sarx can give background for considerations that include social analysis, but the explicit elaboration of massification may be seen by many as theologizing after exegesis. There are, however, some further considerations that may link sarx more immediately with Segundo's social analysis. These would be considerations of sarx as living under the law in a corporate sense. We must now look at this view in more detail, even if briefly.

Robert Jewett has shown that sarx as a theological concept in Paul grew out of the Galatian polemic. His view can readily verify that flesh relates to conflict situations in history and that it describes massification of people by having them maintain the status quo of institutions.

Jewett sees three stages in the development of sarx out of the Galatian polemic. The first stage grew before the writing of Galatians, but is evident in 6:11-18, where sarx characterizes that in which the circumcisers had placed their trust. There is not yet in this a full dialectic, and the flesh is not yet seen as acting independently as a power. The second stage is in the allegory of 4:21-41, where Paul brings the term into dialectic with the spirit, and also elaborates that circumcision is representative of the entire structure of law. Sarx becomes a form of self-righteousness by trust in the law. Finally, in 5:13ff., Paul makes the third step from arguments against nomists to arguments against the anti-nomians as well. Sarx then becomes a cosmic power as well as anthropological, though it would take on specific characteristics in different polemical situations in history.[8]

In applying the concept of sarx to both nomists and anti-nomians, Jewett has the merit of showing that sarx is a multifaceted and flexible term. It means the creatures' self-reliance ("boasting in self"), whether trust is put in circumcision, the law, or some other structure of creaturely existence. The point is that it grew out of conflict situations and deals with social categories and institutions. While this is not explicitly Marxist social analysis, it is easy enough (Segundo's "learning-to-learn") to see it as paralleling massification as a sociological phenomenon.

Ernst Käsemann advances our insights with a telling statement that brings him into almost direct dialogue with Segundo on the notion of sarx: "Contemporary theology is still having to pay for the fact that it is still a victim of the heritage or curse of idealism to a greater degree than it cares to admit. It could have learned as much from Marxism as it did from Kierkegaard and would then have been unable to go on assigning the absolutely decisive role to the individual."[9] According to Käsemann, Pauline anthropology must be seen in terms of humanity's relationship to the rest of creation, and not so much in terms of its self-understanding.

There is a paradox in the Pauline anthropology in that the Christian is unique as a person and at the same time cannot live in isolation. Paul challenged the gnostic viewpoint that levelled off all distinctions in earthly humanity, and saw life in the spirit as transcending it all. He rather maintained the diversity of gifts which operated in this world, transcending sameness and stereotypes. Does this interpretation of Paul not move close to Segundo's view of Pauline anthropology? Consider the following quotations from Käsemann:

> In the shadow of the cross of Christ he [the believer] breaks through already existing, fixed systems and camps, grasping the Gospel as promissio, no longer measuring life and death by what is to hand. . . . For salvation does not simply mean a state; it is an endless path which has been thrown open to us.
>
> The individual is the representative, not of an idea or an organization, but of the crucified Lord whose unmistakable characteristics can never be appropriated by ideologies or organizations without friction or anomaly.[10]

By the same token, Käsemann, coming close again to Segundo's view of Pauline anthropology, says that a person's uniqueness is not geared to individuation or isolation, but operates in worldly relationships. It is of importance that both body and flesh in Paul's writings are linked with corporeality or material existence in a number of passages. (See Gal. 2:20; 4:13-15. In 1 Cor. 6:12ff., body has to be understood sometimes as seat of sexual life, sometimes as a physical organism, sometimes as the whole person. It seems that the apostle wants to understand human being in the light of his corporeality and his material relationships.) This means that a human being, as Paul understands him or her, is among other things a political being, and must be analyzed with reference to society, part of the world around him or her. Consider another quotation from Käsemann, again quite close to Segundo:

239

We stand bodily in a sphere which can by no means be summed up under the individual aspect. . . . It [the realm of nature] is related, not to existence in isolation, but to the world in which forces and persons and things clash violently--a world of love and hate, blessing and curse, service and destruction, in which man is largely determined by sexuality and death and where nobody, fundamentally speaking, belongs to himself alone.[11]

In the light of these considerations by Käsemann, soma and sarx can receive from him their definitions. Soma is seen in Paul as humanity's corporeality, i.e., its "need to participate in creatureliness and in [its] capacity for communication in the widest sense, that is to say, in [its] relationship to a world with which [it] is confronted on each several occasion."[12]

Sarx stands as synonymous with soma at the start, since it is also humanity in its corporeality. However, sarx is the yielding by humanity to sameness or stereotype in its corporate life. It yields to its relationships and is determined by them. "Existence is always fundamentally conceived from the angle of the world to which one belongs. Existence is 'flesh' in so far as it has given itself over to the world of the flesh, serves that world and allows itself to be determined by it."[13]

Can this not be what Segundo sees as massification, at least as we have generalized it? It would be but a short step to see in the text at least some modified version of social analysis which describes mass-man, again derived by a process of learning-to-learn from the biblical text. From these examples that we have developed which treat of Paul's concept of the flesh, we can see possible contributions of third world hermeneutics to the first world for exegesis.

Segundo and First-World Ethicists

To this point in our study we have been considering the ways in which Segundo sees theology and the Bible speaking to Christian ethics. With qualifications we have stressed the ways in which sociological presuppositions, especially Marxist insight into massification, affects biblical insight, and consequently, also influences the moral teaching ultimately derived. We have also seen how that methodology of Segundo, as we have refined it, can dialogue with first world exegesis. It remains now to concentrate specifically on the ethical issues and to see how they can dialogue with the first world ethicists. In order to do this, we return to the three models for ethics that we discussed in chapter one. We address the two questions we posed in terms of the three models, namely, what is the relationship of the Bible to human experience as a source of moral teaching, and what is the eschatological stance of the Bible as this affects morality?

With regard to the first question, the link of the Bible to human experience, Segundo would seem to come closest to the viewpoints of Rauschenbusch, i.e., that the Bible and human experience speak of the same things. This is already a fascinating ecumenical possibility, for it now allows the possibility for Roman Catholicism to move in paths that were up to now the confines mostly of liberal Protestantism. Rauschenbusch and Segundo converge on a number of points. For instance, when Rauschenbusch says that we need a combination between faith in Jesus, as expressed in the biblical concept of the kingdom, and modern science, which understands human development and social order, we are at Segundo's point that biblical faith must also express itself in ideologyp.[14]

Both Rauschenbusch and Segundo are also quite specific in how they relate Bible and human experience, and both see the medium of

relationship to be that of transformation of the
social order. Segundo follows quite closely in
the steps of Rauschenbusch on the three themes
that we developed under Rauschenbusch in chapter
one.[15] Both stress that the kingdom of God is
a social reality to be concerned with the poor,
the suffering, the oppressed. Rauschenbusch saw
the kingdom as more than a utopia, but said it
was to be realized in concrete action. Segundo
says the same with his claim that the kingdom is
to be caused and not just symbolized.

There are interesting parallels in the
two ethicists regarding the theme of a practical
conception of God from the gospels. They both
show that God is on the side of the poor, and
that the only real image of God in the Scriptures
is of a God of action. They both use Matthew 25:
31-46, the scene of the judgment, as a Scriptural
witness to God's concrete concern for the poor.
Rauschenbusch developed the concept of the Head-
ship of Christ as more than religious piety or
ethereal abstraction. It had social consequences.
Segundo makes interesting observations about the
image of God being ultimately tied to the image
of man and woman, and saw the need to describe
man and woman from the perspective of their
social relations and social obligations in justice:

When we contemplate a force, a profundity,
a being that transcends everything else, it
is quite possible that we are not contemplat-
ing the Christian God at all. On the other
hand, when we or other people dedicate our
effort and our lives to the work of fostering
mutual respect and love and unity among men,
the end product of all the justice, love,
and solidarity created by our world relates us
infallibly to the Christian God whether we are
aware of it or not.[16]

This description of God by Segundo leads
to statements about the meaning of love which
parallel in many ways the thoughts of Rauschenbusch.

242

Both recognize that, by definition, God is love. Both translate that into social terms. We have seen how Rauschenbusch linked the love commandment to the kingdom of God and saw both as a progressive movement toward social justice and a renewed social order.[17] Segundo, in a similar manner, relates love to neighbor-need both in terms of the source and the object of love.

In terms of the source of love, the Bible tells us how God's very essence as love stands behind human loving. John's writings tell us, not that God's love is different from man or woman's, not that human love is analogous to the love of God which is alone absolute, but that human love as such bespeaks God. It does not mean a reciprocal love of neighbor, but rather a total gift of self for the neighbor. Man and woman have not only an exterior knowledge of God's love, but an experience of the very interior of God, who gave us his Son even unto death. It creates a new possibility for humanity so that it can work away from selfishness and establish a new social order upon the needs of the other. "Man does not give himself naturally. Naturally he is only a being who needs everything and seeks what he lacks in every order of his existence. On the other hand, because he has the divine life in him, this man is capable of taking what he has, of forgetting what he lacks, and of giving what he has to others."[18] This is what it means to "love as I have loved you."

In terms of the object of love, Segundo observes that there is only one object, and John even omits the juxtaposition of God and neighbor as double object. There is simply neighbor. Segundo says that the measure of love is not by its object, but by its reality. Real love must be in action and not just words, and that means the visible neighbor. If one seeks one's own powers and turns to self, one is not loving at all, and seeking the love of God as object runs that risk. For God is

243

invisible. Thus to have neighbor as object of love is not to leave a second place for love of God, but is simply to be real in one's love.[19] Thus, both the source and object of love is God in his very essence as love, but in both the source and object of love, the reality moves totally toward social justice, the needs of neighbor, the creation of a new social order.

Robert McAfee Brown has summed up some of the ways in which both Rauschenbusch and Segundo have found the Bible speaking directly to human experience, all in terms of social issues: "Affinities between the two include the social or communal stress as a safeguard against individualistic Christianity, the stress on praxis, a methodology arising out of the human situation rather than being imposed upon it, a passionate commitment to the dispossessed, and a recognition of the systemic nature of evil."[20]

These points that we have been discussing seem to be the lasting contribution of Segundo, continuing the insights made prior to him. In addition to these points of similarity to Rauschenbusch, Segundo also offers clarifications which advance the insights. Whereas Rauschen-busch confined his treatment of ideology to making application of the biblical material, Segundo also makes it clear that ideology is a necessary presupposition to be reckoned with even before looking at the biblical material. Whereas Rauschenbusch was somewhat benign and optimistic in his socialism, Segundo makes it clear that conflict is often the necessary ingredient of social justice and a new social order. This is perhaps a central insight which we owe to Segundo. It would be more accurately perceived because Segundo speaks from the con-text of the third-world poor, whereas Rauschen-busch spoke from a first-world context. The insight would remain valid, even with our revisions of Segundo's hermeneutic, provided we adequately distinguished violence from force or resistance, or provided that we saw non-violence as the "prejudiced" position of the Scriptures even if violence was unavoidable on some occasions.

Segundo also moves with more nuance through the Scriptures, undoubtedly because of the increased sophistication which has developed in exegesis since the time of Rauschenbusch. Segundo is not as direct in his application of biblical material, while still nevertheless finding the Bible quite specific regarding social ethics. The solution comes from what we developed as Segundo's process of "learning to learn" from the Bible.[21] He does not find a complete ideologyP in the text, and would not say that Scripture offers Marxist social analysis. However, as we saw in his treatment of flesh, he would learn from the biblical statements about massification and that would lead him to learn about Marxist social analysis. Thus, there is a specific contribution of Scripture to social ethics, while not being direct.

Segundo's continuation and extension of Rauschenbusch offers fruitful insight to what is a fairly common approach to ethics in first-world Roman Catholic theology. This is represented by the model of Charles Curran, to whom Segundo can offer some challenges. It is interesting to note at the start that Curran scarcely fits into the picture of Catholic moralists that Segundo paints, with their insistence on moral absolutes. No doubt his picture is drawn from the Latin American scene. Nevertheless, while Curran is closer to Segundo in terms of a more dynamic morality, he differs in a number of perspectives. Curran's model puts a great deal of stress on human reasoning and experience, and denies that the Bible can offer specific moral teaching. His main reason seems to be his contention that the Bible itself is read with presuppositions and, therefore, cannot be reliable for moral norms in any universal way. One does better relying on rational moral discourse.[22]

Segundo has shown that Scripture is indeed
conditioned, but his hermeneutic circle helps to
expose the presuppositions which condition the
text and influence our reading of it. It may
help us derive more out of the text than Curran
is willing to find. Besides that, Curran himself acknowledges that even the use of reason,
the analysis of natural law, is conditioned and
is approached with presuppositions of time and
place. Segundo clarifies that many of the presuppositions are socio-economic, and enables us
to deal more adequately with natural law in
terms of contemporary life situations. Might it
not be possible that with the unveiling of the
same presuppositions behind moral reasoning and
the reading of the Scriptures, that Scripture
might speak more directly and say more explicitly
the same thing as human experience?

Two examples may serve to illustrate our
point. In the first example there may be use
for the concept of massification as Segundo
develops it out of the Marxist sociology. It
may provide helpful insight even into questions
of sexuality, which are currently being over-
looked. Curran, for instance, stresses the need
to see natural law as conditioned by time and
place, and says that the current treatment in
the area of sexuality up until recently has been
too much concerned with the physical act as
such.[23] It has not incorporated enough consideration for the personal dimensions which give
ultimate definition to the act of human sexuality.

While Curran has been helpful in bringing
needed human dimensions to sexuality, he can
perhaps be pushed even farther by Segundo's sociological considerations. It seems that even the
area of human sexuality can feel the effects of
socio-economic massification. Has not the issue
of birth control, for instance, been largely
first-world concern, or at least a suggestion
from the first world to the third world? Does it
not receive much of its evaluation in terms of
values that are linked to first-world or at least

246

to dominating cultural life styles and abundance? In a country which lacks social security and medical facilities and a host of other conveniences, a large family is seen in a much more positive perspective. It may almost be seen as a necessity for survival. In comparing the views of first world to third world in this area of sexuality we may actually be witnessing, therefore, another subtle form of massification which uses birth control as a convenient way to solve the problem of the poor without having to alter one's own role of domination. The same may be said of the area of abortion.

Curran has already opened the door to considerations of this kind, when he says that natural law developed out of a static society which was hierarchically arranged and which was predicated on order and harmony. This would seem to imply that changing socio-economic conditions would affect the analysis of natural law in our own day. Nevertheless, Curran does not pursue this line of thought. Segundo seems to make another significant contribution in carrying out the implications of Curran's thought. In fact, Segundo's suggestions would seem to apply to all areas of natural law morality. Now, if we take this approach to human experience and read it in the light of social analysis, then Scripture may be saying something along the same lines, since it reveals the same insights once the presuppositions are unveiled.

A second example may illustrate how Scripture can make explicit what comes from moral experience as well. This example comes not immediately from Segundo's social analysis, but from an extension that we would make from it. His concept of massification seems too narrow, we said, in its confinement only to socio-economic areas. If we extend it into other areas, we may again derive some helpful insights into determining moral principles. We could, for instance, take what the Scriptures say about massification and apply it in terms of sexual massification.

By sexual massification we mean the imposition of stereotypes in the area of human sexuality which forces people to conform to certain roles, and which in the long run compels some people to live by the standards established by others. Moral principles that would derive from role determinations, from pre-established ideas about male and female ways of acting, would be influenced by such sexual massification. We could apply it to the discussion of homosexuality, for instance, where perhaps the nature of homosexuality becomes a threat to heterosexuality and where moral judgments are passed in order to remove a threat rather than to establish the genuine nature of things. Thus, Segundo's hermeneutic circle may again expose the presuppositions behind moral reasoning, and in exposing these same presuppositions behind the reading of Scripture, may enable the Scriptures to dialogue with human experience on the same topics. The Scriptures would be saying the same thing as human experience, though not directly.

Approaches such as we have been suggesting would be a challenge to Curran and to other first-world ethicists, especially those who come out of a similar model, one that embraces many in the Roman Catholic tradition. It may bring them to a closer look at Scripture as well as reason. Still, models like Rauschenbusch and Curran both have reliance on human experience and consider it central to ethical positions, even if they vary on the degree in which the Scriptures can speak also. Perhaps Segundo's insights can bring them closer together. What Segundo may challenge more is an approach such as Ramsey's which does not consider human experience as central and which purports to find moral teaching mostly from the Scriptures.

Ramsey serves as a good example for this approach to the Bible because he has already shown in his own methodology how unworkable it is to rely totally on Scripture without any recourse to human experience or reasoning. He would still derive teaching from Scripture which he would not derive from human reason, but as we saw, he would at least use reason as a secondary source.[24] Segundo would push Ramsey even farther. His hermeneutic circle would claim that human experience and reason has to be on the scene from the very start to finish, although Scripture also plays a vital part. The fact is that the two sources of moral enlightenment must engage in dialogue all along the way.

Segundo, for instance, can certainly point out to Ramsey how presuppositions from life experience influence all of our biblical texts and our reading of them. How deontological can Ramsey be, if Segundo is convincing that there is no pure, objective reading of revelation? It seems that Ramsey would ultimately distinguish too widely the divine and the human roles in revelation. Segundo helps us keep them joined. In his methodology it is, in the long run, a question of balancing presuppositions, rather than of "being objective" as if presuppositions did not exist.

Ramsey himself already moves on occasion in the direction of Segundo. He says, for instance, that the ideals a scientist sets for humanity are usually based upon the preconceived notions that a scientist has about himself and the world, not upon any objective view of the world as such.[25] Segundo would corroborate that, especially as his methodology is extended to other forms of massification, as we suggested.

Moreover, Segundo's concepts of massification from a socio-economic viewpoint may also show presuppositions behind Ramsey's statements about morality which he derives from the Bible. Does Ramsey not fall into maintaining the status quo when he shifts so dramatically from advocating human freedom to preserving social order?[26]

249

He seems strong on the unique biblical foundation for non-preferential love, but ends up preserving that for an individual ethics only. He misses the implications for social justice and freedom, ends up building on human experience anyway, and then interprets that human experience as requiring absolute rules of love in such a way that the existing social order holds sway. Segundo's insights may provide a healthy corrective.

On the other hand, Ramsey's insistence on the role of Scripture may serve to caution Segundo against making his social analysis an ideology[n] in itself. Scripture cannot just precede or just follow the life situation, but it can also balance the interpretations of that life situation. We have already seen how the biblical material on the kingdom and on violence may enter into dialectic with social analysis and may challenge the presuppositions. Ramsey's method of doing ethics would allow for that more than Segundo's, although Segundo's must qualify Ramsey's by stressing the importance of the presuppositions. In other words, Scripture and human experience must be in dialogue all the way along.

What we have been saying to this point about the dialogue of Segundo with first-world ethics may seem to cool the fervor over social justice that is the hallmark of genuine liberation theology. That may be the inevitable result of trying to analyze the methodology of Segundo more than his content on social issues specifically. In any case, the centrality of social justice and the need to change structures come to the fore with the consideration of the eschatological teaching to be compared with first-world ethical models. When placed side by side with any of the three ethicists whom we are considering, Segundo surpasses them all in offering an interpretation of the Bible that stresses a this-worldly eschatology and that insists on the urgency of causing the kingdom that will alleviate the suffering of the poor and oppressed.

It is a debatable point as to whether
Segundo reads only a present, this-worldly
eschatology from Scripture or also an other-
worldly future eschatology. It may be that
Segundo agrees in theory with Curran on a continuous and discontinuous eschatology, but in
practice operates with Rauschenbusch on a continuous eschatological model. It seems that he
is so caught up with the urgency of the plight
of the poor that he treats only of realizing the
kingdom in this world and does not give enough
attention to the kingdom yet to come.

Ambiguity in Segundo can be seen in the
way he treats of temporal progress and in the
way he treats the theology of kingdom compared
to other biblical themes. In his biblical
exegesis of the vocabulary of grace Segundo
seems to advocate a Christ-transforming-culture
model of ethics, since it is this life being
transformed, but the transformation requires
more than this life situation.[27] Nevertheless,
when he treats the theme of kingdom of God he
sees it as sharing the same finality as temporal
progress.[28] This seems to be the ethical model
of Christ-of-culture, or, since Segundo acknowledges culmination in eternity, a Christ-above-
culture model. In either case, this view toward
temporal progress sees the eschatology as continuous with this world reality and seems to
contradict the first view we described of Christ-
transforming-culture, and its discontinuous
eschatology as well.[29]

The ambiguity is extended in the way
Segundo treats a number of biblical themes,
such as we saw under the heading of salvation
in chapter four, and the way in which he treats
the theme of kingdom, such as we saw in chapter
three. Various biblical themes in chapter four
stress that the eschaton is already, but not yet.
On the other hand, the theme of kingdom, while it
may theoretically have some aspects of not-yet,
is treated by Segundo almost always from its
aspect of being the eschaton already to be

achieved. Humanity is to cause the kingdom now; no one wants to place _this_ life in jeopardy just for the sake of gaining _another_ life; no one wants to give his or her all simply for the symbol or anticipation of a kingdom, but only to achieve it in reality. As we mentioned, Segundo seems so intent on stressing the realized and realizable dimensions of kingdom that he passes over the discontinuous aspects of the eschaton for all practical purposes.

In the end, Segundo seems to be closest to Rauschenbusch in his eschatology, and should probably be corrected by a more balanced eschatology such as Curran's. Rauschenbusch has often been criticized as being too optimistic in terms of what humanity can achieve, and history did as a matter of fact dampen his optimism. It seems that Segundo is in danger of falling into the same trap. We have mentioned that he acknowledges even more than Rauschenbusch the conflictive nature of the social reality, and is more aware of the actual suffering of the poor and oppressed. However, it seems that this realistic evaluation of life becomes a hidden form of liberal theology's theory of progress, for Segundo's eschatology ends up looking only at continuity with this world and seems to imply that socialism can eventually eliminate oppression in this world.

Segundo cites Vatican II to support his view of continuous eschatology. Curran points out that Vatican II itself is overly optimistic in its description and that there has to be more of a sense of sin and more discontinuity in the eschatology.[30] As a matter of fact, Paul VI did move toward a greater stress on the sinfulness of this-world reality and a discontinuity with the eschaton. He did this in _Progressio Populorum_. In making these observations on the Church documents, Curran is making the same observations on Segundo, and may therefore be a healthy check on this aspect of liberation theology.

252

A model of Christ-transforming-culture would ultimately encompass more of the human reality and would embrace even a number of the poor passed over by Segundo. We would not want to minimize the healthy concern for the poor and the prospects for improving their condition. Nevertheless, there is in fact a whole group of poor, and it seems there always will be an entire group of poor who will not leave their condition during their lifetime. Segundo no doubt would claim that poverty can be eradicated and the condition of the poor does not always have to exist. It seems to me that the burden of the proof is on him, since the history of humanity to this point has shown otherwise. Moreover, there is still the question of the many who would die over the next years while we worked to eradicate poverty. Unless we have an eschatology that can speak to them, we make them simply instruments for someone else's improved condition and say nothing to their own lives personally. As Segundo put it himself, no one wants to sacrifice his or her life for the sake of another life. But what about those whose life will take on transformed significance only in another life?

To advocate only an eschatology of continuity is to eventually bring despair to an entire group of people who will never experience the continuity, even if this be a group destined to disappear from human history. It is one strong reason why Christianity has also a view to discontinuity in eschatology. It offers hope in the most hopeless of situations. It need not lead to passive resignation; it can move to action; but most of all it offers meaning even when there is no success as a matter of fact in history.

A point we made about entering the hermeneutic circle on various levels can be applied to this aspect of eschatology. As Segundo forms his circle, praxis always precedes theory. We have tried to show that praxis itself includes value judgments that ultimately are a part of theory. As Carl Braaten puts it, theory can be pre-practical as well as post-practical: "Theory as explanatory is post-practical; it presupposes the existence of facts and actions which call for explanation. Theory as vision, however, is pre-practical; it is prior to every human decision or action."[31]

If what we said about the hermeneutic circle is true, and if what we said about the hopelessly oppressed is true, then eschatology can serve an invaluable purpose as pre-practical theory. It offers the hope that makes any praxis viable. It is only after there is this hope that praxis makes sense and that then there can be post-practical theory to explain the social analysis and to make it effectual. Eschatology cannot be just the consequence of social analysis, but a value system which speaks to social analysis. In that case, it is a discontinuous eschatology as well as a continuous one.

It goes without saying that Ramsey's view of eschatology would be a help in showing the relativity of this world's ethical obligations and achievements. He would stress the discontinuity with this-world reality, though his eschatology would be inadequate for treating any continuity. Ramsey says something to Segundo, but Segundo ultimately challenges the one-sidedness of Ramsey's eschatology.

Ramsey's insight into the other-worldly character of the eschaton is brought home by another field of study, that of the social world of early Christianity. Oddly enough, a social analysis of the early Christians by scholars such as Gager and Theissen comes to the opposite opinion from Segundo's as to what eschatology develops when devised from the perspective of commitment to the poor.[32] These biblical students claim that the poverty of the early Christians led them to naturally expound an other-worldly eschatology. Gager, for example, says that the early Christians were alienated from Roman political society and were also without wealth. The millenarian movement was the first to develop. The gospel was simply a reversal of outsider-insider distinction, so that those who were alienated could see themselves as those who were accepted. For those who were poor, poverty came to be seen as the true wealth which would be rewarded in a life to come.

These insights show that theology from the perspective of the commitment to the poor needs an other-worldly eschatology, a point we have been stressing here. Nevertheless, it remains true that a totally discontinuous eschatology will maintain only the status quo in this life. Segundo's social analysis also holds weight. In view of this, we are led again to see that theology needs to develop an eschatology that is both continuous and discontinuous.

Concluding Remarks

This study has been a fruitful undertaking, at least for the author; he hopes that it was also for the reader. The benefits have come mostly from the interdisciplinary nature of the enterprise, the need to explore various areas of interest, which in turn have yielded insights that penetrate to many facets of human life. It may also be the weakness of the study that it requires, for the deepest analysis of the question, that one be a sociologist, a political scientist, an exegete, an ethician and--perhaps most importantly--a socially committed Christian. That is beyond the capacity of this author, but he does hope that at least he has pointed in worthwhile directions and that experts in each area will build on what has been presented.

The conclusions of this study have already been given in this chapter, and there is no need to repeat them now. We have expounded at length on how Segundo answers the two questions we have asked about the relationship of the Bible to Christian ethics. We have seen how he views the relation between Bible and human experience as sources of ethics, and how he interprets the eschatology of the Bible for ethics. We have also shown how he would address the first world biblicists and ethicists as they engage in the analysis of these same questions.

As we draw to a close it seems fitting simply to mention the salient facets of human life that have been uncovered for this student of Segundo and to show the directions that have been opened up for further exploration.

First of all, Segundo has fostered a greater awareness of the need for and the benefits of social analysis. The world is becoming a smaller and smaller place to live in and we are assuming more and more responsibility for each other's welfare. Segundo has confronted us with a reality that we are often ignorant of and that most often we would not want to face in any case: the poverty of the third world. Even more than the simple fact of the poverty is our own involvement in causing and perpetuating it. We have challenged Segundo as overstating his case, but we miss the whole point of his valid message if we do not sense the need for commitment to the poor and do not accept his challenge to assume our responsibilities to change the structures.

For someone especially within the Roman Catholic tradition--but for many others as well-- Segundo has also opened possibilities for dialogue with Marxism. He is certainly not the first, but he is part of a movement that may facilitate a concerted and effective attempt to learn from and to teach to a way of life that has already affected the entire population of the globe in modern times. We have challenged Segundo here,

too, with overstatement, but we have also gained
from him a "demythologized" appreciation of
Marxism that removes it from the category of
total evil and makes it a human theory with its
strengths and weaknesses.

Finally, in terms of social analysis,
Segundo's presentation of the concept of massification seems invaluable, especially if enlarged
beyond--without coopting--the socio-economic
sphere. It reminds us of the need to assume
responsibility for our actions and points out to
us how we mostly let inertia and routine take
over most of our human existence. This appears
most poignantly in our social sins, but is a
fact in just about every area of life.

A second major area of interest that
Segundo has addressed well for this author is
that of biblical interpretation. We have found
it necessary to challenge and modify Segundo here
also, but he has offered insights that are at the
heart of biblical hermeneutics these days. It
seems fairly clear that current exegetes are
wrestling with how to make the Bible relevant in
today's world, while still respecting the biblical world. They are also wrestling with the
problem of maintaining objectivity in biblical
interpretation while also acknowledging the
subject who does the interpreting. It is a
thorny problem without immediate solution.
Neither Segundo nor our own modifications of
Segundo pretend to give the full answer.

Nevertheless, Segundo has forced us to
confront the question directly and has offered
some insights into the answer. He frankly
acknowledges that we bring presuppositions to
the biblical text and wants to work with that.
He also tries to maintain distance between the
text and our own history while still keeping the
Bible as norm. We have modified his circle to
get more of a dialectic, but we respect his
sensitivity to the delicate balance between

objectivity and subjectivity and the need to work toward the balance. Segundo has given insights into both the interpretation of the text and the application to our own times.

Especially insightful has been his awareness of the social dimensions to both our presuppositions and our applications. It is a significant complement to the individual existentialist perspectives of first world philosophy in its theories on revelation and biblical hermeneutics. We have not always agreed with his applications of his theories, but we have learned from his insistence that social analysis must be a key ingredient in biblical studies.

Finally, Segundo promotes reflection in the major area of ethics. Besides the obvious insight into the social obligations that Segundo points out to the Christian, we also have insight into how to do ethics itself. We have directed the entire study toward conclusions for ethics. In addition to points related to the two questions we have probed, we also find confirmation of what has been developing more generally in ethics in modern times. Segundo encourages our view that Christian ethics cannot be static, definitive, and concerned only with absolutes. We are dealing rather with a science that must be creative, that must evolve with new circumstances and insights into human existence. More than anything else, Segundo highlights that Christian ethics must be social in nature, both for deriving principles and for applying them.

This study ends with the hope that it has synthesized well a method for addressing the Bible to Christian ethics, that it has offered further insights that will contribute further to that methodology, and that it has begun the dialogue that will enable this method and other models to enrich each other in the future.

CHAPTER VI

NOTES

[1]Cf. pp. 148-49.

[2]Cf. p. 147.

[3]*Theological Dictionary of the New Testament*, s.v. "psyche," by Edmond Jacob, p. 631.

[4]Alexander Sand, *Der Begriff "Fleisch" in den paulinischen Hauptbriefen* (Regensburg: Verlag Friedrich Pustet, 1967), p. 224. Cf. Ps. 63:2.

[5]Ibid., pp. 227-31.

[6]William Barclay, *Flesh and Spirit* (Nashville: Abingdon, 1962), p. 44.

[7]Bruce Birch and Larry Rasmussen, *The Predicament of the Prosperous* (Philadelphia: Westminster, 1978), chap. 7.

[8]Robert Jewett, *Paul's Anthropological Terms* (Leiden: E. J. Brill, 1971), pp. 112-15.

[9]Ernst Käsemann, *Perspectives on Paul* (Philadelphia: Fortress, 1971), p. 11.

[10]Ibid., p. 5 and p. 4.

[11]Ibid., p. 21.

[12]Ibid.

[13]Ibid., p. 26.

[14]Cf. pp. 21 and 99.

[15]Cf. pp. 22-24.

[16]Juan Luis Segundo, *Our Idea of God* (Maryknoll, N.Y.: Orbis Books, 1974), p. 57.

[17]Cf. p. 24.

[18]Juan Luis Segundo, "La Función de la Iglesia," *Diálogo* 2 (1966): 8.

[19] Juan Luis Segundo, La Cristiandad ¿Una Utopia?, vol. 2: Los Principios (Montevideo: Mimeografica "Luz," 1964), pp. 72-74.

[20] Robert McAfee Brown, Theology in a New Key (Philadelphia: Westminster, 1978), p. 141.

[21] Cf. pp. 143-45.

[22] Cf. pp. 12-13.

[23] Cf. p. 8.

[24] Cf. pp. 28-30 and 35-36.

[25] Cf. p. 32.

[26] Cf. p. 34.

[27] Cf. p. 169.

[28] Cf. p. 114.

[29] Cf. p. 14.

[30] Charles Curran, Catholic Moral Theology in Dialogue (Notre Dame: Fides, 1972), pp. 130-35.

[31] Carl E. Braaten, Eschatology and Ethics (Minneapolis: Augsburg Publishing House, 1974), p. 142.

[32] John Gager, Kingdom and Community (Englewood Cliffs: Prentice-Hall, 1975), pp. 22-28; Gerd Theissen, Sociology of Early Palestinian Christianity (Philadelphia: Fortress, 1978), pp. 15-16.

BIBLIOGRAPHY

Books by Juan Luis Segundo

Función de la Iglesia en la Realidad Rioplatense.
    Montevideo: Barreiro y Ramos, 1962.
Etapas Precristianas de la Fe: Evolución de la
    Idea de Dios en el Antiguo Testamento.
    Montevideo: Cursos de Complementación
    Cristiana, 1962.
Berdiaeff: Une Réflexion Chrétienne sur la
    Personne. Paris: Editions Montaigne,
    1963.
Concepción Cristiana del Hombre. Montevideo:
    Mimeografica "Luz," 1964.
La Cristiandad ¿Una Utopia? Vol. 1: Los Hechos.
    Montevideo: Mimeografica "Luz," 1964.
La Cristiandad ¿Una Utopia? Vol. 2: Los
    Principios. Montevideo: Mimeografica
    "Luz," 1964.
De la Sociedad a la Teología. Buenos Aires:
    Ediciones Carlos Lohle, 1970.
Masas y Minorias en la Dialéctica Divina de la
    Liberación. Buenos Aires: Editorial
    La Aurora, 1973.
Grace and the Human Condition. Maryknoll, N.Y.:
    Orbis Books, 1973.
The Community Called Church. Maryknoll, N.Y.:
    Orbis Books, 1973.
Our Idea of God. Maryknoll, N.Y.: Orbis Books,
    1974.
The Sacraments Today. Maryknoll, N.Y.: Orbis
    Books, 1974.
Evolution and Guilt. Maryknoll, N.Y.: Orbis
    Books, 1974.
The Liberation of Theology. Maryknoll, N.Y.:
    Orbis Books, 1976.
The Hidden Motives of Pastoral Action. Mary-
    knoll, N.Y.: Orbis Books, 1978.

Articles by Juan Luis Segundo

"Problemas teológicas de Latinoamerica." Paper delivered to an international conference of Latin America during Vatican II, Brazil, 1964.

"La Función de la Iglesia." Diálogo 1 (1965): 4-7.

"La Función de la Iglesia." Diálogo 1 (1966): 5-10.

"El Diálogo, Iglesia-Mundo, Reflexión." Diálogo 1 (1966): 3-7.

"El Diálogo, Iglesia-Mundo." Diálogo 1 (1966): 5-12.

"Lo Que el Concilio Dice." Diálogo 1 (1966): 3-13.

"Que Nombre Dar a la Existencia Cristiana?" Perspectivas de Diálogo 2 (1967): 3-9.

"La Condición Humana." Perspectivas de Diálogo 2 (1967): 30-35.

"La Condición Humana." Perspectivas de Diálogo 2 (1967): 55-61.

"La Vida Eterna." Perspectivas de Diálogo 2 (1967): 83-89.

"La Vida Eterna." Perspectivas de Diálogo 2 (1967): 109-10.

"Intellecto y Salvación." In Salvación y Construcción del Mundo, pp. 77-86. Barcelona: Editorial Nova Terra, 1967.

"Universidad Latinoamericana y Consciencia Social." Paper delivered at international conference of Catholic educators, Buga, Colombia, February 1967.

"The Church: A New Direction in Latin America." Catholic Mind 65 (March 1967): 43-47.

"Camilo Torres, Sacerdocio y Violencia." Vispera 1 (May 1967): 71-75.

"Un nuevo comienzo." Vispera 1 (August 1967): 39-43.

"América Hoy." Vispera 1 (October 1967): 53-57.

"Hacia un exégesis dinámica." Vispera 1 (November 1967): 77-84.

"Profundidad de la Gracia." Perspectivas de Diálogo 2 (1967): 235-40.

"Profundidad de la Gracia." Perspectivas de
      Diálogo 2 (1967): 249-55.
"Christianity and Violence in Latin America."
      Christianity and Crisis, March 4, 1968,
      pp. 31-34.
"Social Justice and Revolution." America 118
      (April 27, 1968): 574-77.
"¿Dios Nos Interesa o No?" Perspectivas de
      Diálogo 3 (1968): 13-16.
"Del Ateísmo a la Fe." Perspectivas de Diálogo
      3 (1968): 44-47.
"Padre, Hijo, Espíritu: Una Historia." Perspec-
      tivas de Diálogo 3 (1968): 71-76.
"Padre, Hijo, Espíritu: Una Sociedad." Perspec-
      tivas de Diálogo 3 (1968): 103-9.
"El Poder del Habito." Perspectivas de Diálogo
      3 (1968): 90-92.
"Padre, Hijo, Espíritu: Una Libertad I."
      Perspectivas de Diálogo 3 (1968): 142-48.
"Padre, Hijo, Espíritu: Una Libertad II."
      Perspectivas de Diálogo 3 (1968): 183-86.
"Has Latin America a Choice?" America 120
      (February 22, 1969): 213-16.
"¿Hacia una Iglesia de Izquierda?" Perspectivas
      de Diálogo 4 (1969): 35-39.
"Riqueza y Pobreza Como Obstáculos al Desarrollo."
      Perspectivas de Diálogo 4 (1969): 54-56.
"Ritmos de Cambio y Pastoral de Conjunto."
      Perspectivas de Diálogo 4 (1969): 131-37.
"¿Autoridad o Qué?" Perspectivas de Diálogo 4
      (1969): 270-72.
Introduction to Iglesia Latinoamericana ¿Protesta
      o Profecia?, pp. 8-17. Buenos Aires:
      Ediciones Busqueda, 1969.
"Evangelización y Humanización: ¿Progreso del
      Reino y Progreso Temporal?" Perspectivas
      de Diálogo 5 (1970): 9-17.
"Desarrollo y Subdesarrollo: Polos Teológicos."
      Perspectivas de Diálogo 5 (1970): 76-80.
"La Ideología de un Diario Católico." Perspec-
      tivas de Diálogo 5 (1970): 136-44.
"El Posible Aporte de la Teología Protestante
      para el Cristianismo Latinoamericano en el
      Futuro." Cristianismo y Sociedad 8
      (1970): 41-49.

"Wealth and Poverty as Obstacles to Develop-
ment." In Human Rights and the
Liberation of Man in the Americas,
pp. 23-31. Edited by Louis Colonnesse.
Notre Dame: Notre Dame Press, 1971.
"La Iglesia Chilena ante el Socialismo I."
Marcha (1971).
"La Iglesia Chilena ante el Socialismo II."
Marcha (1971).
"La Iglesia Chilena ante el Socialismo III."
Marcha (1971).
"Education, Communication and Liberation: A
Christian Vision." IDOC International--
North American Edition (November 13,
1971): 63-96.
"Las Elitas Latinoamericanas: Problemática
Humana y Cristiana ante el Cambio Social."
In Fe Cristiana y Cambio Social en
América Latina: Encuentro de El Escorial,
1972, pp. 203-12. Salamanca: Sigueme,
1973.
"Teología y Ciencias Sociales." In Fe Cristiana
y Cambio Social en América Latina:
Encuentro de El Escorial, 1972, pp. 285-
95. Salamanca: Sigueme, 1973.
"On a Missionary Awareness of One's Own Culture."
Jesuit Missions Newsletter (May 1974):
1-6.
"Reconciliación y Conflicto." Perspectivas de
Diálogo 9 (1974): 172-78.
"Fe e Ideología." Perspectivas de Diálogo 9
(1974): 227-33.
"Theological Response to a Talk on Evangeliza-
tion and Development." Studies in the
International Apostolate of Jesuits
(November 1974): 79-82.
"Teología: Mensaje y Proceso." Perspectivas de
Diálogo 9 (1974): 259-70.
"Capitalism-Socialism: Crux Theologica."
Concilium 96 (1974): 105-23.
"Converso e Reconciliacao na Perspectiva de
Moderna Teologia da Libertacao."
Perspectiva Teologica 7 (1975): 163-78.
"Teilhard de Chardin." Conference, Montevideo,
1975.

"Condicionamientos Actuales de la Reflexión
Teológica en Latinoamerica." Liberación
y Cautiverio: Debates en torno al Metodo
de la Teología en América Latina, pp. 99-
101. Mexico City: Comité Organizador,
1975.
"Statement by Juan Luis Segundo." In Theology
in the Americas, pp. 280-83. Edited by
Sergio Torres and John Eagleson. Maryknoll, N.Y.: Orbis Books, 1976.
"Direitos Humanos, Evangelizacao e Ideología."
Separata da Revista Eclesiastica Brasileira
37 (1977).

Books of the Three Major Ethicists Considered

By Charles Curran

Christian Morality Today. Notre Dame: Fides,
1966.
A New Look at Christian Morality. Notre Dame:
Fides, 1968.
Catholic Morality in Dialogue. Notre Dame:
Fides, 1972.
Politics, Medicine and Christian Ethics.
Philadelphia: Fortress, 1973.
New Perspectives in Moral Theology. Notre Dame:
Fides, 1974.
Ongoing Revision. Notre Dame: Fides, 1975.
Themes in Fundamental Moral Theology. Notre Dame:
University of Notre Dame Press, 1977.
Transition and Tradition in Moral Theology.
Notre Dame: University of Notre Dame
Press, 1979.
Absolutes in Moral Theology? Edited by Charles
Curran. Washington: Corpus Books, 1968.

By Paul Ramsey

Basic Christian Ethics. New York: Charles
Scribner's Sons, 1950.
Nine Modern Moralists. Englewood Cliffs:
Prentice-Hall, 1962.

<u>Who Speaks for the Church?</u> Nashville: Abingdon,
        1967.
<u>Deeds and Rules in Christian Ethics</u>. New York:
        Charles Scribner's Sons, 1967.
<u>Fabricated Man</u>. New Haven: Yale Press, 1970.
<u>The Patient as Person</u>. New Haven: Yale Press,
        1972.
<u>Ethics of Fetal Research</u>. New Haven: Yale
        Press, 1975.
<u>Ethics at the Edges of Life</u>. New Haven: Yale
        Press, 1978.

By Walter Rauschenbusch

<u>Dare We Be Christians?</u> Philadelphia: Pilgrim,
        1914.
<u>Christianity and the Social Crisis</u>. New York:
        Macmillan Co., 1920.
<u>Christianizing the Social Order</u>. New York:
        Macmillan Co., 1921.
<u>A Theology for the Social Gospel</u>. New York:
        Abingdon, 1945.

<u>Literature on Liberation Theology</u>

Assmann, Hugo. <u>Theology for a Nomad Church</u>.
        Maryknoll, N.Y.: Orbis Books, 1975.
Berbusse, Edward J. "Gustavo Gutierrez: Utopian
        Theologian of Liberation." <u>Faith and
        Reason</u> (1975): 67-96.
Berryman, Phillip. "Latin American Liberation
        Theology." <u>Theological Studies</u> 34 (1973):
        357-95.
Boff, Leonardo. <u>Jesus Christ Liberator</u>. Mary-
        knoll, N.Y.: Orbis Books, 1978.
Brown, Robert McAfee. <u>Theology in a New Key</u>.
        Philadelphia: Westminster, 1978.
College Theology Society. <u>Liberation, Revolu-
        tion and Freedom</u>. New York: Seabury,
        1975.
Dussel, Enrique. <u>Ethics and the Theology of
        Liberation</u>. Maryknoll, N.Y.: Orbis Books,
        1978.

266

_____. *History and the Theology of Libera-tion*. Maryknoll, N.Y.: Orbis Books, 1976.

Fiorenza, Francis. "Latin America Liberation Theology." *Interpretation* 28 (1974): 441-57.

Geffre, Claude, and Gutierrez, Gustavo, eds. "The Mystical and Political Dimensions of the Christian Faith." *Concilium* 96 (1974).

Gutierrez, Gustavo. *A Theology of Liberation*. Maryknoll, N.Y.: Orbis Books, 1973.

Gutierrez Gonzalez, Juan. *The New Libertarian Gospel*. Chicago: Franciscan Herald Press, 1977.

Hellwig, Monika. "Liberation Theology: An Emerging School." *Scottish Journal of Theology* 30 (1976): 137-51.

Hennelly, Alfred. "Theological Method: The Southern Exposure." *Theological Studies* 37 (1977): 709-35.

_____. *Theologies in Conflict*. Maryknoll, N.Y.: Orbis Books, 1979.

Herzog, Frederick. "Liberation Hermeneutic as Ideology Critique?" *Interpretation* 28 (1974): 387-403.

Kloppenburg, Bonaventure. *Temptations for the Theology of Liberation*. Chicago: Franciscan Herald Press, 1974.

Maldonado, Enrique, ed. *Liberación y Cautiverio: Debates en torno al Metodo de la Teología en América Latina*. Mexico City: Comité Organizador, 1975.

Miguez-Bonino, Jose. *Doing Theology in a Revolutionary Situation*. Philadelphia: Fortress, 1975.

Persha, Gerald. *Juan Luis Segundo: A study concerning the relationship between the particularity of the Church and the universality of her mission*. Maryknoll, N.Y.: Orbis Probe Books, 1979.

Sobrino, Jon. *Christology at the Crossroads*. Maryknoll, N.Y.: Orbis Books, 1976.

Literature on Social Analysis

Berger, Peter. Pyramids of Sacrifice. Garden
     City: Doubleday, 1976.
Bigo, Pierre, S.J. The Church and the Third
     World Revolution. Maryknoll, N.Y.:
     Orbis Books, 1977.
Celestin, George. "A Christian Looks at Revolu-
     tion." In New Theology No. 6, pp. 93-102.
     Edited by Martin Marty and Dean Peerman.
     London: Macmillan Company, 1969.
Daly, Robert, S.J. "The New Testament: Pacifism
     and Non-Violence." American Ecclesias-
     tical Review 168 (1974): 544-62.
Dupré, Louis. "Marx and Religion: An Impossible
     Marriage." In New Theology No. 6,
     pp. 151-64. Edited by Martin Marty and
     Dean Peerman. London: Macmillan Company,
     1969.
Eagleson, John, ed. Christians and Socialism.
     Maryknoll, N.Y.: Orbis Books, 1975.
Ellul, Jacques. Violence. London: SCM Press,
     1970.
Fierro, Alfredo. The Militant Gospel. Mary-
     knoll, N.Y.: Orbis Books, 1977.
Greinacher, N., and Müller, A. "The Poor and
     the Church." Concilium 104 (1977).
Gremillion, Joseph. The Gospel of Peace and
     Justice. Maryknoll, N.Y.: Orbis Books,
     1976.
Hebblethwaite, Peter. The Christian-Marxist
     Dialogue. New York: Paulist Press, 1977.
Jaspers, Jos. "The Power of the Majority."
     Concilium 90 (1973): 19-27.
Laurentin, Réné. Liberation, Development and
     Salvation. Maryknoll, N.Y.: Orbis Books,
     1972.
Metz, J., and Jossua, J. P., eds. "Chris-
     tianity and Socialism." Concilium 105
     (1977).
Müller, A., and Greinacher, N., eds. "Political
     Commitment and Christian Community."
     Concilium 84 (1973).

Petulla, Joseph. Christian Political Theology:
    A Marxian Guide. Maryknoll, N.Y.:
    Orbis Books, 1972.
Shaull, Richard. "Christian Faith as Scandal
    in a Technocratic World." In New
    Theology No. 6, pp. 123-34. Edited by
    Martin Marty and Dean Peerman. London:
    Macmillan Company, 1969.
Shinn, Roger. "Faith, Science, Ideology and the
    Nuclear Decision." Christianity and
    Crisis, February 1979, pp. 3-8.
Smith, Rolland. "A Theology of Rebellion." In
    New Theology No. 6, pp. 135-50. Edited
    by Martin Marty and Dean Peerman. London:
    Macmillan Company, 1969.

            Exegetical Literature

        On the kingdom and this world

Dinkler, E. "Earliest Christianity." In The Idea
    of History in the Ancient Near East.
    Edited by R. Dentan. New Haven: Yale
    University Press, 1955.
Dodd, Charles H. The Coming of Christ. London:
    Nisbet, 1951.
_____. Gospel and Law. Cambridge: University
    Press, 1963.
_____. The Parables of the Kingdom. London:
    Nisbet, 1935.
Donohue, John. "Biblical Perspectives on Jus-
    tice." In The Faith That Does Justice,
    pp. 68-112. Edited by John C. Haughey,
    S.J. New York: Paulist Press, 1977.
Feuillet, André. "The Reign of God and the
    Person of Jesus according to the Synoptic
    Gospels." In Introduction to the New
    Testament, pp. 753-98. Edited by A.
    Robert and A. Feuillet. New York: Desclee,
    1965.
Fitzmyer, Joseph, S.J. "Pauline Theology." In
    Jerome Biblical Commentary, no. 79.
    Edited by Raymond Brown, Joseph Fitzmyer,

and Roland Murphy. London: Geoffrey
    Chapman, 1968.
Furnish, Paul V. Theology and Ethics in Paul.
    Nashville: Abingdon, 1968.
Jeremias, Joachim. New Testament Theology.
    New York: Charles Scribner's Sons, 1971.
    _____. The Parables of Jesus. New York:
    Charles Scribner's Sons, 1972.
Käsemann, Ernst. New Testament Questions of
    Today. Philadelphia: Fortress, 1969.
    _____. Perspectives on Paul. Philadelphia:
    Fortress, 1971.
Knox, John. The Ethic of Jesus in the Teaching
    of the Church. New York: Abingdon, 1961.
Kümmel, Werner G. Promise and Fulfillment.
    London: SCM Press, 1961.
Leon-Dufour, Xavier. Dictionary of Biblical
    Theology. New York: Seabury, 1977.
Lyonnet, Stanislas. "Pauline Soteriology."
    In Introduction to the New Testament,
    pp. 820-65. Edited by A. Robert and A.
    Feuillet. New York: Desclee, 1965.
Miranda, José. Marx and the Bible. Maryknoll,
    N.Y.: Orbis Books, 1974.
Mitton, C. Leslie. Your Kingdom Come. Grand
    Rapids: Eerdmans, 1978.
Morfin, Luis Gonzalez, ed. Enjuiciamos a "Marx
    y la Biblia". Mexico: Buena Prensa, 1975.
Perrin, Norman. Jesus and the Language of the
    Kingdom. Philadelphia: Fortress, 1976.
    _____. The Kingdom of God in the Teaching of
    Jesus. Philadelphia: Westminster, 1963.
Schnackenburg, Rudolf. The Moral Teaching of
    the New Testament. New York: Herder and
    Herder, 1971.
Shires, Henry. The Eschatology of Paul.
    Philadelphia: Westminster, 1966.
Whiteley, D. E. H. The Theology of Paul.
    Philadelphia: Fortress, 1972.
Wilder, Amos. Eschatology and Ethics in the
    Teaching of Jesus. New York: Harper,
    1950.

On Violence

Benoit, Pierre. The Passion and Resurrection of
    Jesus Christ. New York: Herder, 1969.
Bornkamm, Gunther. Jesus of Nazareth. New
    York: Harper and Row, 1960.
Brandon, S. G. F. Jesus and the Zealots. New
    York: Charles Scribner's Sons, 1968.
Cassidy, Richard. Jesus, Politics, and Society.
    Maryknoll, N.Y.: Orbis Books, 1978.
Cullmann, Oscar. Jesus and the Revolutionaries.
    New York: Harper and Row, 1970.
_____. The State in the New Testament. New
    York: Scribner's, 1956.
Hengel, Martin. Was Jesus a Revolutionist?
    Philadelphia: Fortress, 1971.
_____. Victory over Violence. Philadelphia:
    Fortress, 1973.
Lehmann, Paul. The Transfiguration of Politics.
    New York: Harper and Row, 1975.
Richardson, Alan. The Political Christ.
    Philadelphia: Westminster, 1973.
De Surgy, P. "L'Evangile et la Violence."
    Lumière et Vie 18 (1969): 87-110.
Vawter, Bruce. The Four Gospels. Dublin: Gill
    and Son, 1967.
Wink, Walter. "Jesus and Revolution. Reflec-
    tions on S. G. F. Brandon's Jesus and
    the Zealots." Union Seminary Quarterly
    Review 25 (1969): 37-59.
Yoder, John H. The Politics of Jesus. Grand
    Rapids: Eerdmans, 1972.

On flesh

Barclay, William. Flesh and Spirit. Nashville:
    Abingdon, 1962.
Burton, Ernest. The Epistle to the Galatians.
    Edinburgh: T. & T. Clark, 1971.
Cooper, E. J. "Sarx and Sin in Pauline Theology."
    Laval Review of Theology and Philosophy 29
    (1973): 243-55.
Jewett, Robert. Paul's Anthropological Terms.
    Leiden: E. J. Brill, 1971.

Karris, Robert. "Flesh, Spirit and Body in
      Paul." The Bible Today 70 (1974): 1451-
      56.
Käsemann, Ernst. "On Paul's Anthropology." In
      Perspectives on Paul. Philadelphia:
      Fortress, 1971.
Kümmel, Werner G. Man in the New Testament.
      London: Epworth Press, 1963.
Ladd, George E. A Theology of the New Testament.
      Grand Rapids: Eerdmans, 1974.
Sand, Alexander. Der Begriff "Fleisch" in den
      paulinischen Hauptbriefen. Regensberg:
      Verlag Friedrich Pustet, 1967.
Stacey, W. David. The Pauline View of Man.
      London: Macmillan Company, 1956.
Theological Dictionary of the New Testament.
      S.v. "pneuma," by H. Kleinknecht et al.
      _____. S.v. "sarx," by E. Schweizer et al.
      _____. S.v. "psyche," by E. Jacob et al.

Literature on the Bible and Ethics

Aquinas, Thomas. Summa Theologica. I-II.
Barr, James. "The Authority of the Bible: A
      Study Outline." Ecumenical Review 21
      (1969): 135-50.
Birch, Bruce, and Rasmussen, Larry. Bible and
      Ethics in the Christian Life. Minneapolis:
      Augsburg Publishing House, 1976.
      _____. The Predicament of the Prosperous.
      Philadelphia: Westminster, 1978.
Böckle, Franz. Law and Conscience. Translated
      by M. James Donnelly. New York: Sheed
      and Ward, 1966.
Braaten, Carl. Eschatology and Ethics.
      Minneapolis: Augsburg Publishing House,
      1974.
Davis, Henry, S.J. Moral and Pastoral Theology.
      4 vols. 6th ed. New York: Sheed and
      Ward, 1949.
Everding, H. Edward, and Wilbanks, Dana W.
      Decision Making and the Bible. Valley
      Forge: Judson Press, 1975.

Fuchs, Josef, S.J. Natural Law: A Theological
    Investigation. Translated by Helmut
    Reckter, S.J. and John A. Dowling.
    New York: Sheed and Ward, 1965.
Gager, John G. Kingdom and Community. Engle-
    wood: Prentice-Hall, 1975.
Gilson, Etienne H. The Christian Philosophy of
    St. Thomas Aquinas. Translated by L. K.
    Shook, C.S.B. New York: Random House,
    1956.
Gustafson, James M. Can Ethics Be Christian?
    Chicago: University of Chicago Press,
    1975.
_____. Christ and the Moral Life. New York:
    Harper and Row, 1968.
_____. The Church as Moral Decision-Maker.
    Philadelphia: Pilgrim, 1970.
_____. Theology and Christian Ethics.
    Philadelphia: Pilgrim, 1974.
_____. Protestant and Roman Catholic
    Ethics. Chicago: University of Chicago
    Press, 1978.
Hamel, Edouard. "L'usage de l'Ecriture Sainte
    en théologie morale." Gregorianum 47
    (1966): 53-85.
_____. "La théologie morale entre l'Ecriture
    et la raison." Gregorianum 56 (1975):
    273-319.
Herzog, Frederick. Liberation Theology: Libera-
    tion in the Light of the Fourth Gospel.
    New York: Seabury, 1972.
Hiers, Richard H. Jesus and Ethics. Phila-
    delphia: Westminster, 1968.
Hordern, William, gen. ed. New Directions in
    Theology Today. 7 vols. Vol. 2: History
    and Hermeneutics, by Carl E. Braaten.
    Philadelphia: Westminster, 1966.
Kaufman, Gordon. "What Shall We Do with the
    Bible?" Interpretation 25 (1971): 95-112.
Kelsey, David H. The Uses of the Scripture in
    Recent Theology. Philadelphia: Fortress,
    1975.
Ladd, George. "The Search for Perspective."
    Interpretation 25 (1971): 41-62.

Long, Edward LeRoy, Jr. A Survey of Christian
    Ethics. New York: Oxford University
    Press, 1967.
Mehl, Roger. Catholic Ethics and Protestant
    Ethics. Translated by James H. Farley.
    Philadelphia: Westminster, 1971.
Murphy, Roland, and Peter, Carl. "The Role of
    the Bible in Roman Catholic Theology."
    Interpretation 25 (1971): 78-94.
Niebuhr, H. Richard. Christ and Culture. New
    York: Harper and Row, Harper Torchbooks,
    1951.
Outka, Gene, and Ramsey, Paul, eds. Norm and
    Context in Christian Ethics. New York:
    Charles Scribner's Sons, 1968.
Rahner, Karl. A Rahner Reader. Edited by
    Gerald McCool. New York: Seabury, 1975.
Richardson, Alan, and Schweitzer, Wolfgang, eds.
    Biblical Authority for Today. London:
    SCM Press, 1951.
Robinson, James M. "The Dismantling and Re-
    assembling of the Categories of New
    Testament Scholarship." Interpretation
    25 (1971): 63-77.
Rommen, Heinrick A. The Natural Law: A Study
    in Legal and Social History and
    Philosophy. Translated by Thomas R.
    Hanley. St. Louis: B. Herder Book
    Company, 1947.
Sanders, James A. "Reopening Old Questions
    about Scripture." Interpretation 28
    (1974): 321-30.
Sleeper, C. Freeman. "Ethics as a Context for
    Biblical Interpretation." Interpreta-
    tion 22 (1968): 443-60.
Smart, James D. The Interpretation of Scripture.
    Philadelphia: Westminster, 1971.
Smith, Jonathan Z. "The Social Description of
    Early Christianity." Religious Studies
    Review 1 (1975): 19-25.
Stringfellow, William. An Ethic for Christians
    and Other Aliens in a Strange Land.
    Waco: Word Books, 1973.

Theissen, Gerd. Sociology of Early Palestinian Christianity. Philadelphia: Fortress, 1978.

Tracy, David. Blessed Rage for Order. New York: Seabury, 1975.

Verhey, Allen. "The Use of Scripture in Ethics." Religious Studies Review 4 (1978): 28-39.

Wilder, Amos. Kerygma, Eschatology, and Social Ethics. Philadelphia: Fortress, 1965.

ABOUT THE AUTHOR

Anthony J. Tambasco is currently Assistant Professor of Theology at Georgetown University, Washington, D.C. He has a Ph.D. in Christian Ethics from Union Theological Seminary in New York City, a degree obtained after advanced degrees in Systematic Theology and in Sacred Scripture from Catholic Institute of Paris and Biblical Institute of Rome, respectively. His academic interests have focused especially on the relationship of the Bible to Christian ethics. He has also lectured extensively in workshops and seminars throughout the United States and has made several journeys to Latin America to give theological conferences.